THE WORLD AND ITS PEOPLES

A windmill near the Belgium-Netherlands border.

BELGIUM
THE NETHERLANDS
LUXEMBOURG

GREYSTONE PRESS / NEW YORK

PHOTO CREDITS: S.E.F. / Istituto Geografico de Agostini /
I.G.D.A.-S.E.F. / Cliché C.G.T. / Foto O.B.C.E. / Foto Sabena /
Foto R. Froldi / Foto K.L.M. / Foto Pan American / Foto
A.C.L. / Foto G. Marussi / Foto S. Prato P. / Foto Shell /
Foto Stassen / Foto R.V.D. / *the Chrysler Corporation for the
end papers that keynote "The World and Its Peoples" theme.*

Library of Congress Catalog Number: 64-17349

Cover and Book Designed by Harold Franklin

MANUFACTURED IN THE UNITED STATES OF AMERICA

THE WORLD AND ITS PEOPLES—EDITORS AND CONTRIBUTORS

Table of Contents

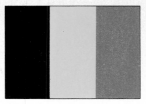

BELGIUM

THE NETHERLANDS

LUXEMBOURG

The Verwesdijk Canal at Bruges (Brugge), in northwestern Belgium.

BELGIUM

LOCATION AND GENERAL FEATURES

A NORTHWESTERN EUROPEAN NATION slightly larger than the state of Maryland, Belgium is one of the Continent's leading countries in degree of industrialization, volume of trade and population density. It has also played an important role in the fields of art, literature, music and science.

To the north of the country lies the Netherlands, to the east the Federal Republic of Germany (West Germany), and to the south and west France. In the southeast, Belgium is separated from West Germany by the Grand Duchy of Luxem-

Left: A view of Brussels, the national capital of Belgium and the provincial capital of centrally-situated Brabant.

bourg, and on the northwest there is a 42-mile coastline along the North Sea. The country extends from 49° 30' to 51°30' north latitude and from 2°35' to 6°25' east longitude and has an area of 11,779 square miles.

Belgium's geographical position has contributed greatly to its importance as a commercial and industrial power. Via its neighbor, France, it has access to the countries around the Mediterranean Sea. It is also a terminus for land routes and waterways from Germany and central Europe to the North Sea, and it is through Belgium that the main lines of communication run between Scandinavia and southern Europe. This strategic position, however, has not been without its disadvantages, for time and

again down through the centuries Belgian territory has been invaded or has served as a battlefield for more powerful neighbors.

Belgium's present frontiers are essentially those established by the Treaty of London in 1839, although certain minor adjustments were made after the two world wars. Political considerations were more important than geographical or ethnic factors in determining these frontiers. In the north the coastal area of Flanders has the same geographical characteristics as the adjoining Netherlands' province of Zeeland, and this similarity continues along the entire Belgium-Netherlands border. There is little observable difference between the people living on either side of this frontier.

The same rivers, plains and land-

scape prevail on both sides of the border with France; so arbitrarily was the line drawn that a number of towns lie partly in France and partly in Belgium. However, the frontier with West Germany, though it is not marked by an abrupt change in landscape, corresponds roughly to the line where the Belgian French spoken by the Walloons gives way to German.

Belgium has been one of the Benelux countries since 1947. In 1922 it ratified an economic union with Luxembourg, and 25 years later Belgium and Luxembourg entered into a customs union with the Netherlands. All three countries, along with France, West Germany and Italy, are full members of the European Economic Community, or Common Market.

A quiet pastoral scene in East Flanders, one of the nine provinces of Belgium.

BELGIUM, NETHERLANDS, AND LUXEMBOURG

Statute Miles 5 0 5 10 20 30 40 50

Kilometers 5 0 5 10 20 30 40 50 60

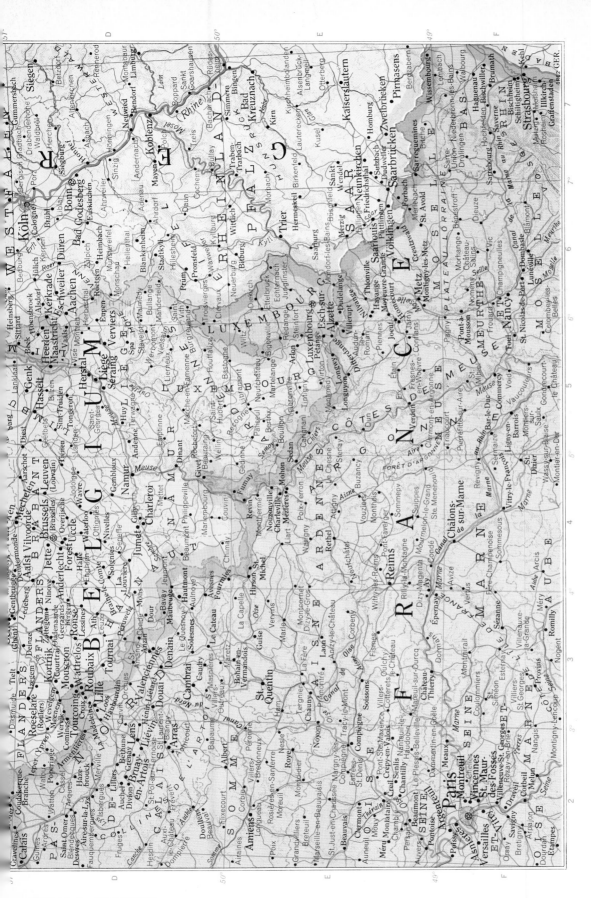

Lambert Conformal Conic Projection
SCALE 1 : 2,000,000 1 Inch = 32 Statute Miles

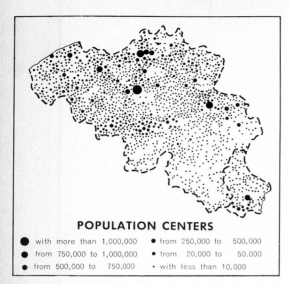

Distribution of population

POPULATION CENTERS

- ● with more than 1,000,000
- ● from 250,000 to 500,000
- ● from 750,000 to 1,000,000
- ● from 20,000 to 50,000
- ● from 500,000 to 750,000
- · with less than 10,000

ORGANIZATION OF THE STATE

Administrative Divisions

ADMINISTRATIVELY, BELGIUM IS DI-vided into nine provinces: Antwerp, Brabant, East Flanders, Hainaut, Liège, Limburg, Luxembourg (a province bearing the same name as the neighboring country), Namur and West Flanders. Each province has a governor, appointed by the king, and a popularly elected legislative body, the provincial council. Provinces are subdivided into districts, cantons and, finally, communes. There are 2663 communes in the entire country, each governed by a burgomaster (mayor) and a board of aldermen.

The National Government

Belgium declared its independence from the Netherlands in 1830, and the following year its new status was recognized by the major European powers. Its constitution, adopted in 1831, was revised in 1893 and 1920-21.

The Belgian constitution provides for the separation of the executive, legislative and judicial branches of government. The titular head of state is a king, who summons and dismisses Parliament, may propose legislative acts, serves as commander-in-chief of the armed forces and appoints cabinet ministers and provincial governors. The royal family is the house of Saxe-Coburg, and only male members of the family may ascend to the throne. The sovereign since 1951 has been Baudouin I.

In practice, the authority of the Belgian monarch is limited, for any action he wishes to take in the political sphere must be sanctioned by the appropriate cabinet minister. Belgian cabinets vary in size, but since World War I have always included a prime minister charged with coordinating government policy. A cabinet may remain in office only so long as its programs win majority support in Parliament. When this support is lacking, the ministers resign; then either a new cabinet is formed which can command a majority vote in Parliament, or, if this proves impossible, Parliament is dissolved and general elections are held.

PARLIAMENT

The Belgian Parliament consists of two houses, with equal powers. Members are elected for four-year terms, and voting in Parliamentary elections is compulsory for all Belgians aged 21 and over.

Elected members of the Senate must be citizens over the age of 40. They are chosen by a complicated process: some senators are elected directly, some indirectly by the provincial councils, still others by vote of the senators who have been chosen by the first two methods. In addition to the elected senators, the king's sons, or, if there are none, the princes of the royal family, are entitled to sit in this house after their 18th year. They cannot vote, however,

The city of Namur, situated at the confluence of the Sambre and Meuse rivers, has been the scene of numerous historic conflicts since it was founded in the Middle Ages (on the site of an older settlement of Roman times). The promontory shown here, forming the fork between the Sambre and the Meuse, is crowned by a citadel that once controlled commercial traffic on both of the rivers.

The Meuse, one of Belgium's most picturesque rivers, enters the country from France, to the south, and flows north and northwest until it crosses into the Netherlands (where it is known as the Maas). Flowing through Belgium for a total of about 130 miles, the Meuse has long served as a transportation artery.

until they reach the age of 25.

The Chamber of Representatives is composed of citizens aged 25 and over. The deputies are elected by direct, secret ballot. Their number is in proportion to the size of the population—the present ratio is one deputy to about 40,000 inhabitants.

The Legal System

Justice is administered by a Court of Cassation or Supreme Court, sitting at Brussels; three courts of appeal at Brussels, Ghent, and Liège; 26 Courts of first instance, and some 229 justices of the peace. There is an assize court in each province, and there are some commercial and industrial tribunals. Belgium has trial by jury. Although capital punishment is provided for by law, the death penalty is seldom invoked.

Religion

Belgians enjoy complete freedom of worship. The great majority of the population is Roman Catholic, but there are considerable numbers of Protestants and Jews.

Belgium constitutes a single province within the Church and is divided into seven dioceses. Mechelen, the metropolitan see and archbishopric, Bruges, Ghent, Liège, Namur, Antwerp and Tournai are the dioceses.

Education

Education is free and compulsory between the ages of 6 and 14, and illiteracy is virtually unknown in Belgium. There are more than 9000 primary schools, and it is mandatory that there be at least one such school in each commune. The responsibility for education is shared almost equally by the state and the Roman Catholic Church, and the Catholic schools receive generous

The charming mountain village of Bohan is nestled along one of the sinuous curves of the Semois River in the Ardennes region of southeastern Belgium. The Semois, which rises in the Ardennes plateau, winds its way west and north for some 110 miles before passing into France. The numerous picturesque towns of the Semois valley are among Belgium's most popular tourist attractions.

state subsidies.

Belgium has about 330 secondary schools. Higher education is provided by many institutions. The State University of Ghent (1817) gives instruction in Flemish and that of Liège (1817) in French. The Free University at Brussels (1834) and the Catholic University of Louvain (1426) instruct in both languages. In addition to these four state universities, there are agricultural schools, commercial colleges and a polytechnical institute, and Brussels, Liège, Antwerp, Ghent and Mons have royal academies of art.

Money and Measures

The basic monetary unit of the country is the Belgian Franc, issued by the National Bank and valued at about 2 United States cents. The metric system is used for measurements of length, area, weight and volume.

Status of the Colonial Empire

Until recently, Belgium held the vast territory of the Belgian Congo in Western Africa as a colony (so designated in 1908) and a mandate over Ruanda-Urundi in East Africa (after 1919). In the early 1960s the Belgian Congo became independent as the Republic of the Congo and Ruanda-Urundi broke up into the two independent states of the Republic of Rwanda and the Republic of Burundi.

PHYSICAL GEOGRAPHY

Geology and Topography

EXCEPT FOR THE ARDENNES PLATEAU in the southeast, Belgium's terrain is generally low-lying and rather flat. The geology of the country is varied and complex, but soils deposited dur-ing the Tertiary and Cretaceous eras have had the greatest influence on the present topography.

Belgium may be divided into three broad geographical regions: Flanders and the Campine in the north; the central plateaus; and the Ardennes area.

FLANDERS AND THE CAMPINE

Flanders is a lowland area, underlaid by a deep substratum of rock and covered by a thick layer of sedimentation, sand and clay. The coastal region, which extends from five to ten miles inland, has broad sandy beaches and lines of sand dunes. This region is mostly man-made. As early as the 8th century men began to drain marshes and build dikes to protect the reclaimed areas from flooding, thus creating fertile fields, known as polders, lying below sea level.

The coastline is straight, with Ostend the only port of importance situated directly on the North Sea. The other seaside settlements are either small fishing villages or holiday resorts. Antwerp, Belgium's principal port, is about 23 miles inland on the estuary of the Scheldt River.

Inland, Flanders is almost completely flat. The land is crisscrossed by drainage channels and about half of it is under permanent pasturage. This area has long been one of the most heavily settled parts of Europe.

The Campine region, sometimes called the Kempenland plateau, crosses the Belgian provinces of Antwerp and Limburg and continues in the Netherlands province of North Brabant. Heaths, dunes and pinewoods cover its surface, while some coal deposits lie below. Characteristically arid and infertile, some of this land is being made suitable for agriculture through intensive fertilization and irrigation.

THE CENTRAL REGION

Central Belgium (roughly, the provinces of Brabant and Hainaut) is an undulating plateau area, rising to a height of about 700 feet in the south. The surface is covered with a relatively thin but extremely fertile layer of sand, clay and *limon* (fine windborne dust). The southern extremity of this region is marked by a deep valley running in a southwest-northeast direction along the lines of the Sambre and Meuse rivers. This valley, about 100 miles in length but only from 3 to 10 miles wide, is of considerable economic importance, for it forms a line of communication from the Seine to the Rhine and contains rich coal deposits. The valley is also of topographical significance, since it divides the southeastern part of Belgium from the rest of the country.

THE ARDENNES REGION

Below the point where it is joined by the Sambre to form the Sambre-Meuse valley, the Meuse River cuts in a north-south direction through Namur province, dividing it almost exactly in two. The area on the west of the river is known as Entre Sambre-et-Meuse, while the eastern part

is called the Condroz, or Low Ardennes. Farther southeast the elevation of the land increases and limestone formations provide a varying topography. There are both flat and steep-sided river valleys, and in places the limestone has been eroded to form craters, gorges and caves. Some of the caves, such as the grottoes of Han on the Lesse River, are famous for their size and the beauty of the limestone formation.

Southeast of this limestone region is the Belgian section of the Ardennes plateau. Still quite extensively wooded, this plateau, other parts of which lie in France, Luxembourg and West Germany, is of comparatively low elevation. The maximum altitude, on the gently rounded summit of Botrange near the German frontier, is only 2283 feet.

The plateau represents what is left of the high Hercynian mountain

Liège, the capital of the province of the same name, is situated at the junction of the Meuse and Ourthe rivers in eastern Belgium. An old and historic city, Liège is a major industrial center as well as the prime commercial hub for trade with Germany. It is also one of the chief cultural centers of Wallonia (a collective term for the French-speaking provinces of Belgium).

range, which was thrown up at the end of the Paleozoic period and subsequently eroded and smoothed down. It has gentle, only slightly undulating contours, except where the rivers flowing across it have cut deeply to create picturesque valleys.

The inland slopes of the Ardennes along the border with France and Luxembourg form a small, self-contained area. Protected by the plateau itself from westerly winds, this region has a mild climate and has been given the name of *Bon Pays* (good country) by Belgians and neighboring Luxembourgers alike.

In comparison with the nearby plateau the contours of the *Bon Pays* area are rather rugged. The soil in some parts is made up of easily crumbled marl, while in others it is sandstone or limestone more resistant to erosion, and therefore the landscape is characterized by alternating series of depressions and hilltops. These hills run down gently to the south, but their northern slopes are somewhat steeper. Small plateaus, nearly always wooded, may be seen from one hilltop to the next.

Rivers

Belgium is crossed by a number of rivers, all of which have an extremely abundant flow thanks to consistent rainfall and the impermeable subsoil. None of the principal rivers belongs entirely to Belgium, however.

Although it rises in France, and most of its estuaries are in the Netherlands, the Scheldt is one of Belgium's two most important rivers. Its length in Belgium is about 150 miles. With its tributaries, the principal ones being the Dender, the Lys, the Rivpel and the Senne, the Scheldt drains almost half the whole area of central Belgium. It is a typical river of the plains, regular in flow and with a very gradual fall. The tide runs a long way inland from the estuaries, both up the Scheldt itself and up its tributaries, reaching as far as Ghent.

The Meuse, the second important river, flows across Belgium for about 130 miles. It enters the country from the French sector of the Ardennes plateau, later to take over and follow the valley of the Sambre, its only important tributary from the left. Several rivers join the Meuse from the right, however. Among them are the Lesse, which flows underground for parts of its course, and the Ourthe, which receives the waters of the Ambieve before meeting the Meuse. After the Meuse crosses the border with the Netherlands it is known as the Maas.

Since its valley is deep, the Meuse is already at a low altitude when it enters Belgium and its gradient is less steep than those of its tributaries that originate in the Ardennes. The latter swell considerably at times of heavy rainfall, causing the Meuse itself to rise and necessitating the construction of dikes and retaining walls.

Both the Scheldt and the Meuse are navigable and therefore represent important lines of communication in the economic life of the country.

The principal river in the northeast is the Yser, which flows from France into Flanders and on to the sea after a course of some 30 miles through Belgium. The Yser is not given to undue variations in size, is easy to canalize and is navigable.

Climate

Belgium lies within the zone of Europe which is subject mainly to a maritime climate. Seasonal temperature variations are therefore comparatively slight, rainfall is heavy, the sky is normally overcast and winds and storms are frequent. Altitude and distance from the sea are the main factors in climatic variation.

Winter temperatures are highest near the coast, and even in the interior the average January temper-

An elderly Flemish woman in Bruges (Brugge) works at her craft, lacemaking, for which the city, capital of the province of West Flanders, has long been famous.

ature is usually above freezing. Summers in the interior are warmer than along the coast. To the south and southeast in the Ardennes plateau region, continental climate influences are felt and temperatures are a little more extreme. Averages for the whole country, however, show the temperature rarely much below freezing in the winter and rarely above 75°F. in the summer.

Rainfall is evenly distributed throughout the year over most of Belgium. There is a slight difference between the coastal area, where the proximity of the sea makes for precipitation throughout the year, with a peak in the autumn, and the interior, where rainfall is heaviest in summer. Although there are many rainy days, the actual amount of rain per year is comparatively low: approximately 24 inches in the central region and along the coast, and 36 or slightly more in the Ardennes.

The Atlantic Ocean exerts the main influence on wind direction, which is predominantly westerly in summer and southwesterly in winter. These winds coming off the sea throughout the year bring with them the prevailing humidity and rainfall. East winds do occur occasionally, however, especially in the spring, and they bring to the uplands unexpectedly cold days and bright, clear skies.

WILDLIFE

There are a few large mammals in the Ardennes area, including wildcats, pine martens, and roe and red deer. Throughout most of the country, however, where the land is flat and intensively cultivated, there are only the small animals found everywhere in Europe, such as badgers, otters, weasels, shrews, mice and squirrels. The birds are typical of those found elsewhere in western Europe. Belgian waters have neither great quantities nor wide varieties of fish.

HUMAN GEOGRAPHY

The relics found in some of the limestone caves indicate that man lived in the region of present-day Belgium during Paleolithic (early Stone Age) times. After the glaciers of the Great Ice Age had retreated, in about 8000 B.C., primitive tribes moved into the area from the south.

Two beguines stroll along a path leading from the beguinage of Bruges (Brugge). The beguinage, of which there are several in Belgium, is a religious community of women who, though not bound by holy vows, have voluntarily subjected themselves to a strict code of discipline and a spiritually-oriented communal life. The first beguinage was established at Anderlecht in the year 1200. According to a much-told story, one of the beguines at Anderlecht had herself walled into a tiny, cell-like chapel and remained there for 40 years, her only contact with the outside world being through a small opening in the wall.

There are traces of a more advanced culture in Neolithic times (c.6000 to 3000 B.C.), when settled agriculture, animal husbandry and the use of polished stone implements appear to have replaced the earlier food-gathering way of life.

Several waves of migrating peoples came during the Bronze and Iron ages. When the Roman legions arrived in 55 B.C. they found the southern area inhabited by Celtic-speaking tribes (the Belgae described by Julius Caesar) and the northern area by Germanic peoples.

THE PEOPLE TODAY

Since the Roman occupation, there have been no significant ethnic ad-

POPULATION: BELGIUM		
PROVINCE	AREA	POPULATION
	(Sq. miles)	(1962)
Antwerp	1,104	1,455,644
Brabant	1,268	2,011,842
East Flanders	1,150	1,276,803
West Flanders	1,249	1,075,949
Hainaut	1,438	1,249,536
Liège	1,521	1,007,516
Limburg	930	586,279
Luxembourg	1,706	216,975
Namur	1,413	370,870
TOTAL	11,779	9,251,414

The historic Grote Markt, the main square of Antwerp. Antwerp, situated on the right bank of the Scheldt River in northern Belgium, is one of the busiest ports in Europe. The city is the hub of a network of rivers and navigable canals that connect the Belgian hinterland with the North Sea.

ditions to the population, although Belgian soil has been overrun periodically by warring neighbors and other conquerors. Belgium today is still divided linguistically along a line that has changed little over the centuries. It runs from the Meuse a little downstream from Liège, south of Brussels, to the French frontier on the upper reaches of the Lys River. North of this a Germanic language, Flemish, which is officially called Netherlandsch, is spoken, while to the south the language is Walloon, which bears more resemblance to the French tongue. Both languages are official in the Belgian state. German is spoken in the Eupen-Malmedy region along the border of West Germany.

Intermarriage was inevitable between peoples living in proximity for hundreds of years, but certain racial as well as linguistic differences are still evident. The Flemings are tall and fair-haired and have light complexions. The Walloons are shorter, and have dark hair and swarthy skin, in keeping with their Mediterranean ancestry.

GROWTH AND COMPOSITION OF THE POPULATION

Since Belgium achieved independent statehood its population has increased from 3,785,000 to 9,251,414 (1962). Of the countries of Europe, only the Netherlands has a higher population density. The average in Belgium is about 786 persons per square mile. In industrial urban areas the figure is higher.

The rate of increase in Belgium's population was greatest during the 19th century. There were 4,500,000 people by 1856, and 7,500,000 by the outbreak of World War I in 1914. Both the war itself and a continuing decline in the birth rate combined to slow down population growth. Flemings make up about 55 per cent of the population and Walloons 45 per cent.

IMMIGRATION AND EMIGRATION

During the 19th century and the first decades of the 20th century, emigration and immigration were on a small scale; there were slightly more Belgians leaving the country than there were foreigners entering. After World War I, however, immigration began to predominate. Many workers came in from neighboring countries and from as far away as Italy, attracted by Belgium's booming industries.

Many foreigners, particularly Italians, left the country after the outbreak of World War II, but during

Modern automobiles and 15th-century buildings contrast oddly on the famed Grand-Place in Brussels, capital of Belgium. The Grand-Place is the site of the original settlement of Brussels, which was founded in the 10th century.

the immediate postwar period immigration rose again. By 1947, there were 268,000 foreigners in Belgium, 81,000 of them Italians. By the end of 1954, there were an estimated 161,000 Italians in the country; the figure has continued to increase, but not as precipitously.

Belgians who emigrate go principally to France as industrial or seasonal agricultural workers. The seasonal pattern, however, was more common in the past than it is today. Before World War II there were more than 260,000 Belgians resident in France; the figure has not increased appreciably since then. There are some Belgians living in other European countries, but relatively few have emigrated overseas. Many of those who settled in the Belgian Congo left when the independent Republic of the Congo was established.

POPULATION DISTRIBUTION

About two-thirds of the people live in or near urban areas. The most thickly populated province is Brabant, followed by Antwerp, East Flanders, Hainaut and West Flanders.

Right: *A rural landscape in the Condroz, a fertile district in south-central Belgium where vast fields alternate with the remnants of one-time forests.*

These all have population densities considerably above the national average of 786 persons per square mile.

Considered by region, rather than by provinces, the industrial areas stretching between Mons, Charleroi and Liège, along the wide valley that crosses the country, have a particularly high population density. Other thickly populated areas include the valley of the Scheldt, the Ghent and Antwerp districts and a wide area around Brussels.

RURAL SETTLEMENTS

Although industry dominates the country's economy and urban life in Belgium has a long tradition, one-third of the people still live in small towns and villages. The extremely efficient transportation network enables industrial workers to travel daily to the larger centers from their homes in the country.

A typical feature of many Belgian villages is that their centers are composed of farm buildings constructed around interior courtyards; the homes of commuting industrial workers tend to be located as single dwelling units on the outskirts.

Throughout the farming areas of West Flanders and parts of East Flanders, relatively isolated farm units predominate, though, because of the division and subdivision of property and the high population density, they are still quite close to each other. Near the coast and on the reclaimed land transformed into polders, large farms are the rule. In much of the hill country, the Sambre-Meuse valley and the Campine and Antwerp areas, single homesteads are often strung out in a line along the roads or canals, with towns and villages taking shape here and there.

Towns and Cities

There are many cities in Belgium, each with its special character and history. The provincial capitals and a few other important cities are de-

Left: *The center of the town of La Roche is situated on a neck of land formed by the sinuous course of the Ourthe River. The surrounding countryside of the Ardennes region is one of undulating hills thickly wooded with broad-leaved trees.*

scribed briefly below, in alphabetical order.

ANTWERP (Flemish, Antwerpen; French, Anvers; *pop. 253,295*)

The capital of the province of the same name, Antwerp lies on the right bank of the Scheldt River. The city received municipal rights in 1291, but it is believed to have been settled in 660. It developed into a flourishing textile center and port, as well as a commercial and financial center, in the 15th century. Antwerp's growth suffered a serious setback at the hands of Spanish troops who sacked it in 1576, but its importance as a cultural center continued to increase.

The closing off of the Scheldt to navigation in 1648 seriously hampered the city's growth. It began to revive after 1803, when Napoleon

improved its harbor, and its status as a leading port was regained in 1863 when the Scheldt was reopened to free navigation. Despite setbacks during World Wars I and II, when it was held by the Germans, Antwerp is today one of modern Europe's busiest ports. It is linked with its hinterland by a network of navigable canals, and its trade traffic has expanded considerably in recent years.

In medieval times Antwerp was a well-fortified city, and vestiges of ancient walls remain, some restored or converted to wide boulevards, as do parts of an old castle now known as the Steen. There is a 14th- and 15th-century Gothic cathedral which houses several paintings by the artist Rubens, who lived and worked here. Still other paintings of his are in the 17th-century Church of St. James, which also contains his tomb.

Antwerp's town hall dates from the 16th century, and its Stock Exchange *(Bourse)*, founded in 1460, is the oldest in Europe, although its buildings were reconstructed in 1868-72. Old guild houses line the market place, there is a museum of fine arts and the botanical and zoological gardens are beautifully maintained.

In addition to its importance as an import and export center, Antwerp is the site of many flourishing industries, among them textile factories and shipyards. Diamond cutting and exporting has gone on here since the 15th century. There are also oil refineries, auto assembly plants, distilleries, breweries, and sugar refining and tobacco processing plants.

ARLON *(Pop. 46,629)*

Arlon is the capital of the province of Luxembourg. A Roman settlement (it has an interesting museum of Roman antiquities), it was fortified in the 4th century A.D., but the French tore down the fortifications in 1670. It was designated the provisional capital of Luxembourg province in 1830.

Many of Arlon's people work in steel plants nearby, not only in Belgium but also in France and Luxembourg. The city's own industries, which are mainly light, include wool processing, pottery-making and the manufacture of briar pipes and cigars. Arlon also serves as a marketing center for cattle and grain.

BRUGES
(Flemish, Brugge; *Pop. 52,220)*

The capital of West Flanders, Bruges was founded in the 9th century. In medieval times it became a thriving textile and trading center. It also developed as a cultural center, noted particularly for the work of such artists as Jan van Eyck and Hans Memling.

The tapestry and weaving industries of Bruges reached their height in the 15th century. At the end of this century, the town's importance began to decline due to the silting up of the Zwyn, its outlet to the sea. It was not until the 19th century and the coming of the Industrial Revolution that Bruges was able to revive its industries and trade. Once more with access to the North Sea, due to a canal connecting the city with the port of Zeebrugge and another leading to Ostend, Bruges' exports mounted. Still another canal

connects the city with Ghent.

The many old buildings which have been preserved give modern Bruges a somewhat medieval appearance. Numerous bridges cross the canals and waterways. There is a famous Gothic town hall, dating from the 14th century, which has a 47-bell carillon. Its antiquity has drawn many visitors to Bruges, and tourism ranks high among its industries today. Delicate lace, for which Belgium is famous, is made here. Varieties of orchids and laurel are grown on the city's outskirts.

BRUSSELS (Flemish, Brussel; French, Bruxelles; *Pop. 1,439,536)*

Brussels is a provincial capital (Brabant) and also the national capital. Founded in the 10th century, it grew from a village on an island in the Senne River to a medieval market town serving one of the main trade routes between Cologne and Flanders. The dukes of Louvain, and later the dukes of Brabant, chose Brussels as their residence and built protective walls around the settlement. The present town plan still shows traces of the pentagon-shaped medieval center, though many of the narrow streets which survived into the 19th century have given way to wide boulevards.

Brussels has had a stormy history, having been ruled by the Habsburgs, bombarded during the wars of the French King Louis XIV and conquered by the Kingdom of the Netherlands. The Belgian movement for independence was organized here. Although the city itself was not extensively damaged when the Germans occupied it during both world wars, its citizens suffered many hardships.

Brussels is a lively, animated city, well-endowed with fine old buildings and handsome new ones. In the Grand-Place, the site of the original 10th-century settlement, are several guild halls, and a 14th- and 15th-century town hall *(hôtel de ville)*. The city's oldest house of worship is the ancient church of Ste-Gudule, which was rebuilt in the 13th century, after having burnt down in the 11th. Also of interest is the Cathedral of Notre-Dame-du-Sablon which dates from the 15th and 16th centuries.

Among Brussels' other attractions are its Palace of Fine Arts, many museums, botanical gardens, Royal Palace, and Parliament buildings. It is the headquarters for the European

Economic Community or the Common Market. A World's Fair was held in the city in 1958 and the *Atomium*, its central symbol, still stands on the fairgrounds, commanding a magnificent view of the city.

The list of Brussels' manufactured products is a long one and includes textiles (among them, lace), clothing, leather goods, chemicals, pharmaceuticals, machinery, foodstuffs and beer. Served by highways, railroads and canals which link it with the North Sea and inland coalfields, Brussels is also a flourishing trading center.

CHARLEROI *(Pop. 26,175)*

Situated on the Sambre River in Hainaut province, Charleroi was founded in 1666, although its site had been settled many years earlier. France took the city in 1667 and fortified it, and subsequently it came under the domination of Spain, France, Austria and Holland. Charleroi was the scene of a World War I battle which was won by the Germans, and was occupied by the Germans again in World War II.

The city has a conservatory of music and a modern city hall. There is also an archaeological museum containing relics of prehistoric times, as well as exhibits dating from the Frankish and Roman eras.

Located in the center of Belgium's principal coal field, Charleroi is an important rail and canal junction. Its industries process metals, chemicals and glass, as well as turning out railroad and electrical equipment.

GHENT (Flemish, Gent; French, Gand; *Pop. 157,811)*

The capital of East Flanders and the province's largest city, Ghent is situated at the confluence of the Lys and Scheldt rivers. The Ghent-Terneuzen canal is navigable, giving the city access to the sea at Terneuzen on the western Scheldt estuary in the Netherlands.

Ghent began as a monastery built on an island in the 7th century, and was soon fortified and expanded. It developed into a leading inland port during the early Middle Ages, and also into a center for the production

Right: *View of a quaint street in Ghent, capital and largest city of the province of East Flanders. Unlike most large Belgian cities, Ghent was virtually unharmed during the two world wars and thus has retained much of its medieval aspect, as seen here.*

of fine textiles, with the most powerful guild of weavers in Flanders. In the 13th century, it won its independence and held it almost continuously until the Spanish arrived in the late 15th century. It was here that the Pacification of Ghent, uniting the provinces against Spain, was signed in 1576.

Ghent is largely a city of islands which are separated by canals and lesser waterways and connected by numerous bridges. It was virtually unharmed during the two world wars, and many sections of the city retain their medieval appearance. There are guild halls, the Castle of the Counts of Flanders, and other ancient buildings. Remnants of the Abbey of St. Bavon date from the 7th century, the Church of St. James from the 12th, the Church of St. Nicholas from the 13th. The Gothic Cathedral of St. Bavon was completed in 1531. Ghent's university was built in 1816.

The prosperity of Ghent comes largely from the activity of its port and the output of its many industries. Cotton, linen and jute textiles are made here, as well as heavy electrical equipment, and there are flour mills and breweries. Ghent is also a flower-marketing center, and flower seeds and bulbs are grown in the environs. Decorative and exotic blooms are cultivated in extensive hothouses, while the fields are made brilliant by begonias in the summertime.

HASSELT (Pop. 36,618)

Hasselt, the capital of Limburg province, is located on the Demer River and near the Albert Canal. In 1831 the Belgian forces lost an important battle here in their war for independence from the Netherlands. The town is most noted for the fact that every seven years it is the gathering place for thousands of pilgrims,

who come celebrate the Feast of the Assumption. Hasselt has distilleries and also produces gelatin and tobacco products.

LIÈGE
(Flemish, Luik; *Pop. 153,240*)

The capital of the province of the same name, Liège is situated at the confluence of the Ourthe and Meuse rivers and has gradually extended along their banks. It lies at the southern end of the Albert Canal.

The area around Liège was inhabited before the coming of the Romans. The city had its official beginning as a bishopric in the 8th century, received its charter as a commune in 1066, and was a famous center of culture during the Middle Ages. Napoleon made it a part of France in 1794, and this status was maintained until 1815, when the city became part of the Kingdom of the Netherlands. Its citizens participated vigorously in the 1830 revolution. The city was taken and held by the Germans in both world wars.

Liège is the site of the Cathedral of St. Paul, dating from the 10th century, and of the Church of St. Denis, also of the 10th century. The state university at Liège was founded in 1817.

The location of Liège at the junction of highways, railroads, rivers and canals makes it a leading center of trade and traffic with Germany. Highly industrialized, the city produces armaments; aluminium, zinc, and rubber products; machinery and machine tools; and leather goods. It also has paper and flour mills and breweries, as well as automobile assembly plants.

LOUVAIN
(Flemish, Leuven; *Pop. 33,088*)

Famous mainly as a cultural center, Louvain is situated in the province of Brabant about 14 miles east of Brussels on the left bank of the Dyle River. According to legend it was the site of a camp established by Julius Caesar, but it did not gain importance as a town until the 11th century, when it developed into a cloth-producing center. It gained renown for educational and cultural leadership after the founding by John IV of Brabant of its university (1426).

Louvain suffered considerable damage when it was burned by the Ger-

mans at the outset of World War I. Among its industrial activities are the brewing of beer, distilling of liquors, shoe manufacturing and the processing of chemicals.

MECHELEN
(also known as Malines; *Pop. 64,701*)

Located near the southern border of Antwerp province, Mechelen was a fief of the Bishop of Liège as early as 754. It has been the seat of the Belgian archbishopric since 1559.

Mineral resources and related industries

Coal

Iron

Iron works

Oil refineries

Gent (Ghent)

Antwerpen (Antwerp)

Campine (Kempen)

Clabecq

La Louvière

Charleroi

Liège

Differdange, Esch-sur-Alzette Belval

Athus

Belgian agriculture is highly specialized. Horticulture under glass is conducted on a large scale, as shown here, making possible consistently high yields despite the coolness and dampness of the climate.

During the religious wars of the 16th century, the city was sacked repeatedly, and in the 17th and 18th centuries it was taken and retaken by the French, the Dutch and the British. The French tore down its fortifications in 1804. Heavy damage was inflicted during World Wars I and II.

Despite having been the scene of so much conflict, Mechelen still has many ancient buildings, among them the 13th-century Church of St. Rim-

baut. There is a palace constructed during the time of Charles V of Spain (early 16th century), and there are two 16th-century churches, the Church of Our Lady and the Church of St. John, both containing paintings by Rubens.

Mechelen is best known for its lace, though this industry is not nearly as important today as it used to be.

The town also produces woolen and linen textiles, tapestries, needles and furniture.

MONS
(Flemish, Bergen; *Pop. 26,136*)

The capital of Hainaut province, Mons is situated at the junction of the Conde-Mons Canal and the Canal du Centre. This site was first settled

View of docking facilities on the Scheldt River at Antwerp. Antwerp's crowded docks stretch for more than 30 miles along the Scheldt. Visitors from other European countries and from the U. S. often enter Belgium by way of Antwerp.

in the 7th century. Although it was overrun by the Dutch, the Spanish and the French in the 16th, 17th and 18th centuries and was the site of two World War I battles between the Germans and the British, Mons still boasts some ancient buildings. There is a 12th-century chapel, and the Gothic Cathedral of St. Waudru and the town hall date from the 15th century.

Mons was a prosperous trading town and cloth market as early as the 14th century. Its prosperity today stems from its position as a canal and railroad junction, in the midst of the Borinage coal-mining area. It is a coal and sugar marketing center and has numerous industries, among them leather tanning.

NAMUR *(Pop. 32,511)*

Namur, capital of the province of the same name, is located at the junction of the Sambre and Meuse rivers. The city was ruled by the counts of Namur from 908 to 1421,

when it was seized by the counts of Burgundy. It was the scene of many historic conflicts, being taken by Louis XIV of France in 1692 and retaken three years later by William of Orange. It was once heavily fortified, but its protecting walls were demolished by German artillery in World War I, and further damage was suffered in World War II.

Cutlery, machinery, and leather goods are among the products made in Namur. There are also flour mills, and commerce thrives due to the city's strategic location.

OSTEND (Flemish, Oostende; French, Ostende; *Pop. 56,747*)

Ostend, on the North Sea coast in West Flanders, is one of Belgium's principal ports. It is the point of convergence for the country's principal railways and canals. Ostend was a fishing village in the 9th century and had grown into an important shipping center by the 16th, when it was fortified. In the early

17th century, it was besieged by the Spaniards and almost completely destroyed. The city was rebuilt and survived German occupation in World War I when it was used as a submarine base, and again in World War II when it was severely bombed.

Ostend is popular as a summer resort, and one of its outstanding features, in addition to many interesting old buildings, is its sea wall, which is 30 feet high and 100 feet wide and extends for a distance of about 9 miles.

In addition to its port activities, the city has many industries connected with its proximity to the sea, such as fisheries, shipbuilding and rope and net making. Fine lace is also produced.

ECONOMIC GEOGRAPHY

EXCEPT FOR SETBACKS SUFFERED DURing periods of political or religious upheaval, Belgium has enjoyed a generally thriving economy since the early medieval period, due in large part to its strategic location. It was particularly in the low-lying plains and along the Flanders coast that industry and trade flourished. Flax and wool production, and the yarns and cloth made therefrom, were the basis for the lively commerce that developed, with Bruges the main port of entry and exit for many years.

The metal industry developed farther inland, using wood from the forests of the plateau for fuel. As early as the 13th century, coal was mined near Charleroi. After the bulk of maritime trade passed from Bruges to Antwerp, the latter increased in importance as a trading center until the Kingdom of the Netherlands gained its independence. Then Antwerp, standing on an estuary controlled by the Dutch, began to decline. The economy as a whole suffered from the religious conflicts of the 16th century and the political wars of the 17th.

Under the Austrians in the 18th century, the Belgian economy revived somewhat until the Netherlands, fearing growing Belgian competition, closed the Scheldt to navigation. But Belgian agriculture continued to improve and expand, while the metal and metal-working industries of the interior held their own, particularly at Liège. The industry that prospered most was the manufacture of arms.

When the Industrial Revolution came along in the 19th century, Belgium already had a long tradition of manufacturing and was ready to take advantage of new textile and other machinery, and of new agricultural methods. Metallurgy, coal and textile production and agriculture flourished; the Scheldt was reopened and Antwerp resumed its position as a leading trade center. For about 20 years after independence, the Belgian economy again went into a decline, due to the loss of Dutch markets, the inexperience of the new government and a setback in agriculture caused by the potato blight and by generally poor harvests of other crops.

But as Belgium's government became stabilized, further rapid industrialization ensued, and the country regained its economic leadership, helped in no small measure by the completion of its railroad network by 1875. Agriculture improved, coal production increased, and new metal and chemical industries were established.

The German occupation in World War I again brought severe setbacks to the Belgian economy, but wealth from the Congo, which had become a colony in 1908, and the economic union with Luxembourg (B.L.E.U.), established in 1921, helped to stimulate recovery. Progress soon came to a halt, however, as Belgium suffered along with the rest of the world through the Great Depression of the 1930s.

Then came World War II, and though Belgium and Luxembourg weathered the period better than the Netherlands, the damage done to their economies by the war was serious. In 1947, B.L.E.U. formed a customs union with the Netherlands, and the term Benelux, meaning this three-country customs union, came into being. The Belgian economy today is based mainly on the processing of imported raw materials and re-exporting the finished products.

Agriculture

Belgian agriculture, though employing only about 10 per cent of the country's working force and generally pursued on relatively small farms, is highly developed and responsible for 6 to 7 per cent of the gross national product. The most modern and efficient techniques are used to insure high yields of a great variety of crops. Nevertheless, though self-sufficient in most meat and dairy products, Belgium must import many grains, as well as fodder, corn, beets and hay.

In addition to the reclaimed land, or polders, even the infertile regions of the Campine and the Ardennes are progressively being given over to cultivation. Where this is not possible, large-scale afforestation is being undertaken.

Of Belgium's 4,047,756 acres of farmland, about half (2,007,784 acres) is devoted to pasturage. Grains account for 1,252,544 acres; industrial raw material crops, 228,507 acres; tuber and root crops, 152,179 acres; fruit orchards, 79,450. The balance is used for seed and forage production, vegetable gardens and nurseries.

Wheat is the most extensively grown cereal crop, followed by oats, barley and rye. The major wheat-producing areas are Hainaut, Brabant, the Hesbaye region and the Flemish polders. Production is far from sufficient for domestic needs, and as much as 80 per cent of the wheat used in the country must still be imported. Oats and barley are cultivated mainly in the inland areas, and rye in Flanders and the Campine, but quantities of these cereal grains must also be imported.

Fodder is grown in rotation with cereal crops. Most natural meadows and pastureland are found in the Ardennes area. Sugar-beet production is of great importance, and Flanders has long been known for its flax; in fact, Belgium is one of the world's largest producers of this crop.

The Atomium, giant symbol of the achievements of 20th-century science, was built for the 1958 Brussels World's Fair, which attracted millions of visitors.

The growing of fruit is largely concentrated in the moist Hesbaye and Herve regions. Flowers and fruit are also grown around Brussels, Louvain and Mechelen. Commercial production of flowers is a specialty highly developed on the outskirts of Ghent.

LIVESTOCK

Livestock-rearing is Belgium's most important agricultural pursuit. In 1962, there were some 2,832,000 head of cattle in Belgium, and dairy production is considerable, though not as highly developed as it is in the Netherlands. Cattle-raising is carried on mainly in the Ardennes and other areas of southern Belgium. Pigs and hogs are also raised and number about 2,000,000. The number of horses stood at 145,175 in 1962, representing a considerable decrease in the last decade, due to the increased use of mechanized equipment on farms. However, the sturdy, heavy, draft horse bred in Belgium is still world-famous. Sheep and goats were also more numerous a decade or so ago; today they number about 84,350 and 5830 respectively.

Fishing and Forestry

The Belgian fishing industry is of minor importance, and the country must import considerable quantities of fish. The industry is based in Ostend, and most of the catch is taken in ocean waters. The 1962 catch amounted to 53,375 tons, at least a quarter of which was herring.

Forests cover about 1,484,500 acres of Belgian territory, roughly 20 per cent of the country's area. About 27,000 cubic feet of timber are cut annually.

Industry

Belgium's industrial activities account for 31.5 per cent of the country's gross national product, and industry employs 40 per cent of the working population. Belgium has long been rich in coal, which is located conveniently near iron ore deposits. Coal is still mined extensively, even though some of the veins are giving out or are expensive to work.

There are two principal coal fields. One is in the south in the Sambre-Meuse valley, centered around Liège, Namur, Mons and Charleroi. The second, the Campine coal field in the north, is of particular importance because it yields significant quantities of coking coal. Total coal production runs about 24,000,000 tons per year.

Belgium lacks petroleum, but has large refineries at Antwerp and Ghent which process imported oil. The country's major rivers have generally flat courses, which means that very few hydroelectric stations can be built. There is not enough hydroelectric power and coal to meet the country's energy requirements; this deficit is made up by imports.

IRON AND STEEL

The iron-ore deposits in the southern part of the country are practically exhausted, and Belgium's steel production depends on imports from France, Luxembourg and Sweden. Annual output of steel is now over 8,000,000 tons, 70 per cent of which is exported. In addition, lead, zinc and copper are processed, the last particularly in the Liège area.

The steel that is not exported is used in Belgium's own metal-working industries to produce machine tools and structural parts for bridges, buildings and ships. Armaments and electrical and railway equipment are also made. There are locomotive works at Seraing, La Louvière and Tubize:

TEXTILES

The textile industry, one of Belgium's oldest, is still flourishing. It is mainly concentrated in the west, particularly in Flanders and the cities of Ghent, Courtrai, Tournai, Antwerp and Mechelen, but there are also several inland textile centers. Cotton yarn and fabric production has surpassed that of linen, but Flanders remains a leading flax-producing center.

Textile production in the early 1960s averaged 111,531 tons of cotton yarn, 53,242 tons of woolen and worsted yarns, 14,337 tons of linen yarns, and 62,138 tons of jute yarns per year.

The manufacture of clothing is centered in Brussels and other leading cities, and the lace for which Belgium has been famous for centuries is made in many towns, but mainly at Bruges.

OTHER INDUSTRIES

The making of glass and crystal ware are important industries in the southern coal-field area. Belgium is one of the world's leading producers of glass panes, and most of the glass industry's products are exported. The highly developed diamond-cutting industry, centered at Antwerp since the 15th century, exports most of its products and is a valuable source of revenue.

The country's chemical industry,

Brugge (Bruges)
Eekloo
Gent (Ghent)
Antwerpen (Antwerp)
Villebroek
Mechelen
Izegem
Aalst
Leuven (Louvain)
Mouscron, Kortrijk (Courtrai)
Ronse
Brussels (Bruxelles)
Liège
Tubize
Tournai
Braine-le-Comte
Verviers
La Louvière
Auvelais
Mons
Charleroi
Namur
Luxembourg

Major industrial centers
Engineering industries
Chemical industries
Electrical engineering
Textile regions
Textile centers
Paper
Glass
Ceramics

Major industries

Interior of a Belgian steel-rolling mill. The expansion of the Belgian metallurgical industry has been assisted by Belgium's own rich coal deposits and also by the ease with which iron ore from France, Germany and Sweden can be obtained.

much of it concentrated on the production of fertilizers, accounts for some 7 per cent of the total manufacturing output. Heavy chemicals, pharmaceuticals, plastics and paints are also produced. Although most chemicals are made in the area between Ghent and Antwerp, and along the Albert Canal to Liège, some are produced in Brussels, Mons, Charleroi and Namur.

The foodstuffs industry is highly developed. In addition to meat and dairy products, Belgium has sugar-beet processing factories centered at Tirlemont in Brabant, and imported cane sugar refineries at Ghent and Antwerp.

TOURISM

The tourist industry has long been important in Belgium's economy. Accessibility of the country to all forms of modern transportation, easy transit within the country, numerous hotels to choose from and restaurants famous for the excellence of their cuisine combine to make Belgium attractive to visitors. Even more im-

portant are the well-trimmed beauty of the countryside and the abundance of ancient buildings and towns, each with its special history.

Transportation

Belgium's dense network of roads, railways and canals can carry an immense amount of traffic. There are more than 7100 miles of major highways, of which more than 6317 miles are government roads. In addition, there are about 30,000 miles of secondary roads. Belgium's railways cover 2837 miles, and connect with those leading to all major cities in Europe.

The inland waterways extend for a total of 984 miles. It is estimated that about half the goods carried within the country travel by water. The Albert Canal, which runs 80.5 miles from Liège to Antwerp, thus linking the coal fields with the sea, is the best known of Belgium's man-made water routes.

Belgium's merchant marine is surprisingly small. In 1963 there were 93 ships: 4 steamers, 76 cargo vessels and 13 tankers. The majority of the ships calling at Belgian ports are foreign-owned. Antwerp accounts for 90 per cent of all cargo tonnage.

Foreign Trade

Belgium's foreign trade must be considered in the context of its customs union with Luxembourg, then of the Benelux customs union, and, finally, of the country's membership in the Common Market. In the past decade, Belgian-Luxembourg (B.L.E.U.) trade has shown a general upward trend, except for 1958, and exports exceeded imports in 1962. The Netherlands is B.L.E.U.'s largest customer, but with the creation of the Common Market, trade with the other member countries (Italy, France and West Germany) rose sharply. Trade with the United States is also high.

Old Gothic houses line a canal in the Flemish city of Ghent, which consists of a maze of nearly a hundred islands connected by some two hundred bridges.

NATIONAL CHARACTERISTICS

ONE WOULD EXPECT A NATION AS small as Belgium—barely one-fourth the size of Pennsylvania—to have a fairly homogeneous population. Yet such is not the case. Two linguistically distinct peoples inhabit this little nation, which has been aptly described as "the courtyard of Europe" —a courtyard overlooked by three large "buildings": France, Germany and England.

Flemings and Walloons

These two peoples—the Flemings and the Walloons—speak wholly different languages and live, for the most part, on opposite sides of a linguistic frontier that extends along an imaginary east-west line through the center of the "courtyard."

The Flemings, comprising about 55 per cent of the population, inhabit chiefly the northern half of Belgium, including the provinces of West and East Flanders, Antwerp and Limburg. This region as a whole is commonly called Flanders. The language of the Flemings is Flemish, officially called Netherlandsch, a tongue nearly identical to Dutch.

The Walloons, comprising about 45 per cent of the population, live in the southern half of the country, including the provinces of Hainaut, Namur, Liège and Luxembourg. These provinces are collectively called Wallonia. The Walloons speak a dialect of French.

Sandwiched between the regions of Flanders and Wallonia, in the middle of the "courtyard", is the province of Brabant, which contains the national capital, Brussels. Most people of Brabant speak both Netherlandsch

and French and serve as a mediating and unifying influence on their less cosmopolitan countrymen to north and south. It has been said, with some justice, that the inhabitants of Brabant, and of Brussels in particular, are "the truest Belgians", meaning that their sense of national consciousness is not weakened by any divided loyalty based on language or ethnic descent.

Much, perhaps too much, has been made of the ethnic, as opposed to the linguistic, differences between the Flemings and the Walloons.

Theoretically, the "typical" Fleming is a tall, sturdily built, blue-eyed fellow with a broad face and blond or reddish hair—a true heir of his Germanic heritage. He is positive, often to the point of stubbornness,

simple in his tastes, pious and friendly, but rather too easily aroused to anger. His intense religiousness makes him a devout and passionate supporter of Catholicism. It was in Flanders that the religious struggle of the Reformation raged so bitterly and for so long, and it was in Flanders, too, that the Counter Reformation was felt so harshly.

The "typical" Walloon, on the other hand, is supposed to have a smaller and more delicate frame and darker coloring than the Fleming. Physically, he looks more like an Irishman or a Welshman, both of whom share with him a common, though distant, Celtic heritage (significantly, the Flemish word for Walloon is *Waelsch*). The Walloon tends to be gayer and more lighthearted

Old buildings overlooking the Meuse River in the Wallonian city of Namur. Namur has been called the "gateway to the Ardennes." It is picturesquely situated on a group of low hills rising above the Meuse at its junction with the Sambre.

than his countryman to the north. He speaks French and has adopted many French ways. His attitude to religious matters is more good-natured, conciliatory and devoid of zealotry. Although a good Catholic, he shies away from even the mildest sort of fanaticism.

But such traditional differences between Fleming and Walloon must be taken with a grain of salt. Intermarriage over the centuries has blurred ethnic and cultural differences until, today, language remains the only concrete characteristic whereby one can be distinguished unmistakably from the other.

A Crowded Country

Belgium, despite its small size, is often called "the country of a hundred cities." Standing on a hillside overlooking a broad valley, one can often count out the pointed church steeples of a dozen little towns, each town appearing much like the other yet each a distinct, self-governing municipal unit with its own proud citizenry.

Internal distances in Belgium are 200 to 300 miles at the most (the journey by train from Ostend to Arlon, the two towns furthest apart, takes about five hours). The country's population density is high, averaging about 786 persons to the square mile.

Among this densely packed population, one finds the whole range of living standards and occupations: the fisherman and sailor of West Flanders and the highly skilled worker of the large industrial centers; the peasant and small property owner of the Flemish polders and the hardy Campine farmsteaders; the canal miners from the Black Country of the Borinage and the diamond cutters who hand down their rare and difficult skill from generation to generation.

Tradition and Patriotism

Today, in spite of having given its citizens one of the highest living standards in industrially-oriented Europe, Belgium still preserves a deep attachment to local tradition. Playing their part in this tradition are religious ideals, a stubborn love of liberty, a propensity for the pleasures life has to offer, a passion for sociability and a love of the colorful pageantry offered by public ceremonies, festivals, processions and marches.

Sociability is an especially characteristic trait of the Belgians, whether Flemings or Walloons. This small country had, at recent count, 848 choral societies, 2090 brass bands, 1017 orchestras, not to mention innumerable guilds, "serments,"

Weirdly costumed haguettes *parade through the town of Malmédy during the annual Carnival celebration. The* haguettes *brandish pincers called* racoquillons, *with which they frighten and even seize persons (especially children) who come too near.*

The giant effigy of St. Nicolas Waas moves along in a procession through the town of Aalst in East Flanders. Most Belgian towns have their own "giants," which are important features in local celebrations. Many "giants" are centuries old.

Detail from The Country Dance, *a painting by Pieter Brueghel the Elder (c. 1520–69), whose charming, if sometimes brutal, renditions of 16th-century Flemish life in rural Belgium rank among the masterpieces of European art.*

confraternities, cooperatives and clubs, private and public.

The vast majority of Belgians, both Walloons and Flemings, are Roman Catholic. This fact is the main common denominator of the people and a cohesive element. It explains why the people of Flanders, in particular, so close in many ways to the provinces of the Netherlands, were able, during the revolution of 1830 which marked Belgium's break with the Kingdom of the Netherlands, to take their stand with the declaration: "I am not Dutch, and do not wish to be!"

CHILDREN

BY TRADITION, THE KING OF THE BELgians is godfather to the seventh consecutive son born into a family. Fifty years ago, there were about twenty such baptisms each year. Today, however, the King is not called upon so often—a sign of changing times and customs. But the large number of well-fed and well-clothed children, whether in the polder-lands of the northwest or the Ardennes

region of the southeast, is still striking.

In the industrial and mining areas in the large towns, where the working classes have to a great extend adopted European middle-class standards, the birth rate has fallen considerably in recent decades. However, it is still among the highest in Europe in rural areas such as East and West Flanders, Limburg, and Ardennes and the Campine.

FESTIVALS FOR CHILDREN

There is no other country in Europe where St. Nicholas' Day (Dec. 6) is celebrated with such pomp; on this day a unique succession of games, ceremonies and public distribution of presents is carried on. Belgian children thus have not only Christmas but also St. Nicholas' Day to anticipate and to enjoy each year.

In various parts of the Ardennes, the local Walloons still keep up a tradition that was once widespread throughout the country. On Dec. 21, St. Thomas' Day, the school children light small paper cockerels at their school gates, a survival, according to some students, of prehistoric pagan

sacrifices of Belgian folklore. This would seem to be borne out by the fact that, as late as the turn of the century, the school teachers, as a traditional gesture, used to give their pupils live cockerels to decapitate.

On Holy Innocents' Day, Dec. 28, children are allowed, much to their delight, to dress up in adults' old clothes and parade around in them. Then, with the grudging permission of their parents, they let loose temporary havoc in the home and get into all kinds of mischief throughout the neighborhood. The custom dates back to a medieval tradition the significance of which remains obscure.

RELIGIOUS EDUCATION

Belgian children are brought up within a framework of traditional beliefs, kept alive throughout the country through centuries-old customs. Nevertheless, many young Belgians, when they reach the age of sixteen or seventeen, profess uncertainty over their religious beliefs, sometimes declaring themselves agnostics or even atheists. This, in spite of the fact that 60 per cent attend Catholic schools where 80 per cent of the teachers are lay priests and the other 20 per cent Jesuits. In their schools, many remarkably free-spirited arguments about religion take place between students and teachers —a manifestation of the Belgian habit of testing a belief, however fundamental, on its merits and, should it be found wanting, to alter or even abandon it.

UNIVERSITY LIFE

THE BELGIAN ATTITUDE TOWARD education, as seen above in specific regard to religious tradition, is extremely broad-minded and liberal. The Free University of Brussels, one of four universities in Belgium, is proud of its title "Free" and is, ostensibly at least, at the opposite pole from the Catholic University of Louvain. The other two universities, those at Ghent and Liège, are officially "agnostic" in their attitude toward religion, and both professors and students are given complete freedom of choice and opinion. Yet, the "free" and "agnostic" Universities often produce men of deeply felt Catholic faith, and Louvain University always has its share of "freethinkers." Thus, traditions—both orthodox and liberal—are continually challenged throughout the course of the academic career. Whether or not one chooses to conform, the choice is entirely one's own and is based upon personal investigation.

The name Louvain as a center of higher education belongs to the fine central tradition of European culture along with Bologna, Leiden, Salamanca, Upsala, and Heidelberg. At Louvain the time-honored traditions, often based on historical events, are jealously guarded. It was here that Erasmus of Rotterdam founded his famous "College of Three Tongues" in 1518.

Each year the solemn opening of the academic course is preceded by a Mass in honor of the Holy Ghost held in the collegiate church of St. Peter. After Mass, the new professors publicly take an oath of loyalty. On this occasion, as during all important University ceremonies, the University authorities and the academic body don their fine gowns and walk in colorful procession through the streets.

DOMESTIC IDEALS

IN GENERAL, BELGIAN YOUTH SHARES the same easy, self-possessed attitude toward love and courtship common to most Europeans of this day and age. The conservative, middle-class majority of the Belgian people are equally dedicated to an ideal of hard work and the attainment of domestic security. Their aim is usually the possession of a piece of land. In fact, the number of landowners comes to almost one-third of the total population.

The material ambition of the average Belgian, therefore, is his own house, standing on his own land. Beyond this quite reasonable aim lies the greater dream of the rich man, which often appears to be the possession of a castle as a symbol of power and success. (There are at least three thousand castles in Belgium, most of them in private hands.)

The urge of ownership, wealth and profit is deeply rooted in the Belgians, whose resourcefulness in every field of activity dates back to the golden age of the Middle Ages and Renaissance, the time of the great commercial power and mercantile supremacy of Belgium's cities.

"Brother, remember that you must die... rich!" runs a modification of the grave warning given each other by the Trappists in their monasteries. This was said by a foreigner observing the Belgians' attitude to the good things of life which their undoubted religious sincerity does nothing to abate.

The Belgian ideal of marriage is solidly linked to this attitude. A new family is, first if not foremost, an economic unit to be founded on a

Detail from another of Brueghel's paintings, this one depicting a group of Flemish children, each of whom is playing with a handmade toy characteristic of the time.

sound financial base and guarded against that greatest of all evils... poverty. To an extent greater than that of the citizens of most countries of the world, today's Belgian has achieved this domestic ideal.

ASSOCIATIONS AND SPORTS

THE BELGIAN URGE TO SOCIABILITY, keenly felt by both Flemings and Walloons, dates back for centuries and is embodied in the many venerable confraternities and associations which still survive, though somewhat changed in form. Nowadays, indeed, they are very little more than an excuse and an opportunity for meeting, eating in good company, enjoying the gregarious life and singing and carousing together. All this is in contrast, it should be said, with the Belgians' usual indifference to cohesion in political matters (in spite of the national motto: "United We Stand").

In the more restricted circle of the town, or the parish, the Belgian loves to take part in one of the innumerable associations. The old craft guilds built their halls on the main squares of the towns and cities: the sailors', boatmen's, coopers', cabinet-makers', bakers', brewers', cutters', painters' companies are but a few of the many surviving examples. Today, most of these halls have been made into museums, though many associations still carry on from different headquarters.

THE HISTORY OF THE MANY MADONNAS

Such guilds and associations have given rise to numerous local customs and oddities. There is, for instance, the strange history of the three hundred and more hand-sculptured Madonnas which astonish the visitor by their profusion and beauty as he wanders through the old parts of Antwerp, such as the *Schiperskwartier,* which for centuries has been a haunt of sailors.

These Madonnas are to be found at second-floor level, at crossroads, or under the roof eaves, almost always with a lamp constantly burning. Many of them are works of great beauty, sometimes two or three centuries old. The Guild of St. Luke, which grouped all artists together, used to demand a work from each of its members, and this almost always took the form of a Virgin, the

This man is a costumed participant in the May Day parade at Rutten, near Tongres, in the province of Limburg. In addition to his collar of shells, he wears a black pilgrim's costume and carries a long wooden staff. The symbolism of the costume relates to an historical event, the massacre of St. Evermeire in the year 699.

The Ommegang, held at Brussels, is one of the most famous and colorful Belgian festivals. Shown here is the famed "giant" horse, Bayard, bearing the four sons of Aymon, the legendary enemy of Charlemagne. "Giants" from many cities throughout Belgium are displayed at the Ommegang.

patron of Antwerp. After being judged by the elders of the guild, each statue was offered by its sculptor to his own part of town. It was then set up in a good position, adorned with a canopy and a lamp and provided with light in perpetuity, which members of the guild still supply.

The 'Serments'

Guild is the Flemish name for these corporations, which the Walloons know as *serments* (derived from a word meaning "oaths", because members were called on to swear an oath of allegiance to the town and its institutions). In addition to the craft *serments*, there were also associations that provided a voluntary militia and gave special training in weapons that were more difficult than usual to handle. There were thus crossbowmen's, archers', arquebusiers' and swordsmen's *serments*.

Competitions were organized to stimulate enthusiasm and group pride. The *serments* also enjoyed the privilege of taking part in the *ommegangs,* or parades, which wended their way around the church and then around the town itself during fairs and on other special occasions.

These associations, which date in some cases from the 13th and 14th centuries, no longer retain their military significance. The age-old pride, rivalry and traditions, however, have all remained much as they were.

'KINGS' AND 'EMPERORS'

The headquarters of the *serments*, often housed in old inns, are often shrines filled with historic souvenirs and records and can still be visited. Their walls are lined with portraits of the "kings", often done by first-class draftsmen; these "kings" are the winners of the annual competition, the *Tir du Roi*. If a king gains three wins in a row, he earns the title of "Emperor." The famous Kessels, "imperial" marksman extraordinary, received a sash from the Brussels municipality which he was permitted to wear on all public occasions.

The portraits bear the words "le roi est mort, vive le roi!" (The king is dead, long live the king) as a reminder of the short duration of these reigns. Nor is this the only reminder; the whole picture is punctured with holes, for the effigy of the reigning "king" is used each year as the target for the current competition.

Popular Sports

The annual games are the high point of the associations' activities, although their members' evening and weekend meetings also play an important part in Belgian life. Members meet, drink beer, chat, practice archery with both long and cross bows, play darts—often in the tiny gardens beside the inns, or indoors depending on the game—while others sit around watching, arguing and predicting the result.

ARCHERY

The archers have special practice grounds set aside for them nearby which they can use as soon as the season begins. Both long and cross bows demand a special technique. One can shoot *au berceau* (horizontally) or *à la perche*, (with the target hoisted atop a long vertical pole). This latter method is especially in vogue from mid-April to mid-October, while the *au berceau* variety continues throughout the year.

Naturally, the type of arrow and bow—or cross-bow, which because of

This elderly couple from a small town near Brussels have dressed up in traditional stylized Carnival costumes sewn together with hundreds of colorful patches.

its added weight requires greater physical strength and stamina—varies with a person's style. Some inns have collections of all types and ages hanging on their walls as splendid trophies.

Other Sports

Stuifspel, vogelpik, jeu des quilles and pigeon fancying, as well as the less exotic sports of hunting and fishing, are all popular pastimes.

The strangest huntsmen's club ever to exist in Belgium was probably the one that hunted only cockchafers, (large beetles). According to one straight-faced writer, at the end of the 19th century: "Their outings are conducted on military lines on fixed dates; they carry wooden guns under their arms, and they are booted and generally equipped like infantrymen on a campaign."

'STUIFSPEL,' 'VOGELPIK' AND 'JEU DES QUILLES'

Stuifspel is one of the most popular games. It is very inexpensive to play as it requires only a small rubber ring *(palet)*, flat on one side and round on the other. The players line up along the base line and try to throw the *palet* onto a target set inside a wooden box (which also serves to deflect the shots of over-impetuous players).

Vogelpik, which means "the peck of a bird", is the name given to darts. It is extremely popular in places of entertainment; a visitor may, if he is not careful, nearly have his hair parted by one of the small multicolored darts that has gone astray from its target.

Jeu des quilles, or ninepins, is another popular pastime which the Belgians take extremely seriously.

None of these games, incidentally, is an improvisation to be indulged in, in an idle moment. There is always an appropriate club, with regular meetings and the usual triumvirate of chairman, secretary and treasurer, while the players themselves are models of technique and virtuousity. The whole cult is centered at the *estaminet,* part tavern and part club, which has been described as "a quiet sanctuary." Noise is extremely rare inside the *estaminet,* and any disturber of the peace is soon hushed into silence by the players.

PIGEON FANCYING

Kijker is the name given to a breeder of homing pigeons, and *kijkers* are numerous in the towns and suburbs of Belgium, where pigeon fancying is extremely popular.

The *kijker* is easy to recognize in the street by his wicker or reed basket, which he carries with such loving care; it holds the beloved birds on whom he lavishes untold affection and painstaking training, talking to them all the while with nicknames and diminutives full of tender passion, such as *chouque,* or *tatche.*

One can often witness the scene that takes place when the *kijker,* half tender, half angry, uses all his force of persuasion, followed by threats, followed again by renewed blandishments, to entice the pigeon back into its basket from a nearby rooftop or balcony.

The number of Belgian pigeon fanciers runs into the tens of thousands. They have a special radio program broadcast to them every Sunday by the national radio service, and they use a jargon that, in its fantastic technicality, is totally incomprehensible to the outsider.

FOLK CUSTOMS AND FESTIVALS

Musical Societies

THERE ARE AN INCREDIBLE NUMBER of choral societies and orchestras— *Orpheons, Grandes Harmonies,* and so on—throughout the country, which also tends to illustrate the Belgian's sociability in musical matters. In Hainaut, choral music is essentially popular in origin, while Liège, which is famous for its violonists, boasts two renowned choral societies, the *Legia* and *Les Disciples de Grétry.* Brass bands and orchestras are also in special demand at the many festivals that take place through the year.

According to an old treatise on Belgian folklore: "On certain days in the year and during local festivals, these different musical bodies compete in front of an audience that places the greatest importance on the outcome. The prize consists of a gold medal which is hung from the richly embroidered flag of the winning society after being handed over by the burgomaster in person." It is interesting to note that these bands are still to be found in processions and at pilgrimages and funerals.

Autumn (1913), *a painting by Rik Wouters, gives visual expression to the sense of bourgeois well-being that pervades the typical middle-class Belgian home.*

FUNERAL CUSTOMS

When a member of one of the many associations dies, it is up to the association in question to see that due respect is paid to the deceased. Even the famous Chambers of Rhetoric, which grew up in Flanders in the 15th century and were later to become literary circles and organizers of poetry competitions, originally provided for the funeral arrangements of their members.

The funeral cortège must include a band, with drums, banners and flags—the colors of bygone victories. Thus arrayed, the members of the association of which the deceased was a member gather together for two separate occasions: once for the funeral itself and once, afterwards, for the ceremony of the "placing of the cross," again to the accompaniment of music.

This latter ceremony was described at the end of the 19th century as follows: "Four members carry the inclined cross, and the whole corporation proceeds at funeral pace dressed in their regalia, showing their mourning by carrying arms. You feel in these men the conviction that they assume a corporate significance united under the same banner. The cortège marches solemnly through the streets, spreading out as it crosses the open country and comes to the wide avenues of the cemetery. When the symbol of death has been laid, they return, much more quickly, to drink toasts in the inn".

It might be added that the extremely old custom of finishing a funeral with a banquet and toasts, which is not of course confined to Belgium alone, is in keeping with the Belgians' pronounced gregariousness and love of celebration. Many a banquet begun in mournful silence is ended on a crest of high gaiety.

THE EATING OF 'DEATH BREAD'

Although dying out, there is also the tradition of *zielenbrooje*, or death bread. Now associated with All Souls' Day (Nov. 2), it dates back to the pre-Christian era. To eat these buns, made of extremely fine flour and colored with saffron, was to make symbolic expiation. Each *zielenbrooje* eaten on the eve of Nov. 2 signified the redemption of one soul.

On Nov. 2, particularly in the Ardennes, one may see processions winding along, through mist-shrouded cemeteries, the participants holding lighted candles in their hands. The candles are finally placed on the grave of the last person to die in each family.

Puppets and 'Giants'

Belgian carnivals and processions, when not of the funeral variety, would be incomplete without their finely costumed puppets, "giants" and animal figures portraying legendary beasts and characters. Even when there is no special occasion, religious scenes, playlets and farces are played in the puppet theaters that abound in cities, towns and villages.

Many puppet plays retell traditional local stories, such as those of Geneviève de Brabant, Til Eulenspiegel, the Lion of Flanders, or Aimon's Four Sons. Some puppet plays are versions of popular cloak-and-dagger thrillers, such as *The Three Musketeers* by Dumas the Elder, or the popular *Les Pardaillans*, which contains 72 episodes.

At Liège it is the custom to visit the puppet show at Christmas when a picturesque and quite delightful version of the Nativity story is performed. Liège's most popular puppet is Tchanchet, who tells everyone "what's what" without any beating about the bush, from the Saracen emperor to the hundred other characters, including princes, devils and knights.

At Verviers, not far from Liège, there is another well-known puppet show where scenes of Bethlehem, both before and after the birth of Jesus, are enacted with true grace and delicacy.

THE TOONE THEATER

In Brussels, the popular little theater of Toone has a loyal clientèle both inside and outside the working-class district of Marolle. The audi-

Two children get a special treat—a donkey ride—on a beach along the North Sea coast. The tide runs out to a great distance during the morning and early afternoon, exposing hundreds of yards of clean, white sand that is covered up again with surprising swiftness as evening approaches.

torium of the Toone Theater, a hall with whitewashed walls, adjoins a room which is a museum of puppet history, with scenes, engravings and old playbills on the walls, rare and attractive dolls and dramatically contrived groups of Grand Guignol characters, heroes of the French Revolution, Lucifer, Napoleon and others, all displayed in a dusky, reddish, highly-atmospheric light.

The Toone company consists of almost 200 puppets, which are worked by wires and dressed with amazing detail in the most realistic way: a medieval knight, for instance, wears a suit of armor made up of over 1600 pieces.

The strange language used at these performances is also of some interest, particularly to the student of the language of folklore. It is entirely comprehensible to the local spectators, who are mainly inhabitants of the old poorer districts where the old dialects are still spoken. It is a composite language, a mixture, based chiefly on Flemish, with Walloon and Spanish additions and even with smatterings of a dialect called *burgondsch,* a linguistic relic of Burgundian rule. These inimitable shows end with very pungent farces, called *stukske ba,* meaning "little pieces," or "tidbits." These are bursting with untranslatable terms and apt expressions, proverbs and raileries full of sly local allusions.

THE 'GIANTS'

In addition to the diminutive puppets, Belgian folklore and custom is also rich in giants of all sorts—both the legendary kind and the man-made variety. The latter, huge constructions of wood, cloth and other materials, are estimated to number more than 300 throughout Belgium today. Carnivals and processions are dominated by their strange traditional shapes.

Belgian "giants" are kept carefully in the town halls to be taken out on special days; at their public appearances they observe a code of ceremony which has been laid down rigidly over the years. As they stride along majestically in procession or stop to jump, dance and pirouette, they arouse a delight and an enthusiasm among the onlookers which, in small towns especially, is of an extraordinary intensity and sincerity.

The giants of Namur, which were destroyed in a fire in the town hall at the beginning of the last war and which included the famous Percot,

An impressive spectacle, the Procession of the Penitents, takes place each year in the town of Furnes (Veurne) in West Flanders. A day of somber ceremonies, including the presentation of scenes from the Old and New Testaments, is ended with the procession of hooded figures carrying their crosses through the streets.

were the oldest in all Belgium. Among the oldest in existence today are the giants of Nivelles—Argayon, his wife, and Godet the horse—which date back to 1367; they still take part in various processions and other festivities, particularly at Carnival time.

Carnival Celebrations

The most famous Belgian Carnival is the one held at Binche, a small town in the heart of the Black Country (the Borinage, or rich coal-mining district between Charleroi and Mons). The fantastically costumed *Gilles* of Binche, described below, are famous for miles around. On Shrove Tuesday (the day before the beginning of Lent) crowds of tourists

come to watch the traditional spectacle, though the festivities really begin the previous Sunday.

THE CARNIVAL OF BINCHE

During the days preceding the festivities whole wagon-loads of oranges pour into Binche, for they too have a part to play in the merrymaking. For three days and three nights the town echoes with the endless rhythm of airs and marches that can be played only by local players because they are so highly complicated; the townsfolk sing and whistle them ceaselessly, crowding into the streets and squares, which resound with noisy laughter and shouts.

In the 16th century Binche experienced the luxury of the court of

Mary of Hungary, who had a castle built there (later destroyed by Henry II of France) which "made the seven wonders of the world look pale", as one observer wrote. This was the period that saw the origins of the present-day Carnival, for the first of of these extraordinary celebrations was, in fact, put on by Mary in honor of her brother, Charles V, and his son, the future Philip II of Spain, on an occasion when they visited her.

This was in 1549, at a time when explorers had only recently discovered and publicized the world of the Incas in Peru. In order to be up to date and exotic, the courtiers disguised themselves as Inca princes—or at least as they imagined them to be—wearing on their heads tremendous headdresses of ostrich feathers so high that they "touched the sky," as the Papal legate said in his description of the event.

BECOMING A "GILLE"

The only authentic *Gilles* are at Binche; the other groups which have grown up elsewhere under this same name are only imitations.

A *Gille* is not chosen at random; it would perhaps be an exaggeration to say that a man is "born" one, but at least, if he is to be one at all, he begins to think about it and to plan for it from his childhood, saving his first pocket money for the eventual purchase of the costume.

There is something almost touching in the obstinacy with which the inhabitants of Binche concentrate their energies on attempting to gain the honor of becoming one of the six or seven hundred *Gilles*. Once obtained, the position is retained for life. Theoretically, anyone can be a *Gille*, from the rich middle-class burgher, who has no difficulty in finding the considerable sum necessary to buy the highly complicated costume, to the workman or craftsman, who may have to make any number of sacrifices in order to buy the costume (or who may hire it from one occasion to the next, also at some expense).

The costume consists of a sort of smock bordered with lace and padded out with straw to imitate two humps, one at the front and one at the back, and decorated with black and orange lions and other brilliant designs; a woolen belt hung with heavy bells, and more bells, like those hung on a horse's collar, round the neck and on the chest; big clogs, colored and tasseled; and, the crowning glory—ending in a flurry of ribbons by which it is fastened under the chin—a wonderful snow-white cascade of ostrich feathers, worth a small fortune in themselves.

This is a· *Gille*: he emerges, face painted, on the first Sunday of Carnival, glowing with pride and holding his broom, or *ramon*, which will be replaced in the afternoon by a wicker basket or oranges. •In the meantime the inhabitants will have put up grilles in front of their windows, in readiness for the fierce sweet-smelling bombardment of fruits which will sail above the heads of the crowd, breaking any fragile unprotected target or falling noisily to earth again amid the trampling of the crowd and the clatter of the clogs.

DANCING AND FIREWORKS

The *carola* of the *Gilles* echoes through the streets, which are bright with the red, green and black provincial colors. The *Gilles* dance to the obsessive rhythm of old airs; they pirouette tirelessly, bells clanging and ostrich feathers twirling, waving their brooms and throwing oranges to the onlookers, who are waiting eagerly for nightfall.

At nightfall the drums roll in the main square, thousands of torches are lit and the first fireworks leap upward. The sharp smell of sulphur mingles with that of oranges. Everyone is out on the square, waiting for the *Gilles* to come and lead the way in the great final *farandole*, which is danced to the music of an old *pavane*; the *Gilles* start off dancing in a circle, which widens endlessly as the townspeople join in.

OTHER CARNIVALS

There are at least two other well-known carnivals, those of Eupen and Malmédy. The towns are not far from the German border, and because of this the festivals have a distinctly German flavor. They too are centered around certain characters, who are less famous than the *Gilles*—the weird *haguettes* with their extraordinary costumes and masked faces topped by cocked hats and plumes of feathers.

They go around the town in a procession, brandishing the *racoquillons* or *happe-char*, pincers attached to a large wooden spring, which they hold in their hands and with which they seize any noses or ears, hats or garments within reach. Meanwhile, other masked harlequin figures, armed with big wooden swords, and *sauvages* (savages) with long clubs freely distribute blows and paddlings.

These are followed by a dancing procession of *nutons* (gnomes), *fous* (fools), wizards, cobblers, "long-noses" and "long-arms." The crowd soon gets caught up in their prancing, galloping, twisting and turning, while bold chimney sweeps perform all kinds of absurd and dangerous antics on the houses, climbing out of the chimneys and hanging from the roofs.

HIS MADNESS, PRINCE CARNIVAL

Eupen also has a fancy-dress parade and floats: the main one is the chariot of "His Madness, Prince Carnival," whose day of triumph is the Monday before Shrove Tuesday, known as *Rosenmontag*, a German term meaning Rose Monday, and which, in Eupen, is the high point of festivities. As on other similar occasions, men in various historical uniforms walk beside the carts; these are the *Funkencorps*, the Prince's guard, including innumerable pages and mock ministers.

Each town has its own carnival and its own particular characteristic figure; only some of the most famous have been described here.

In mid-Lent there is a one-day revival of the Carnival celebrated in an unusual manner in two places: at Stavelot, on the banks of the Amblève, and at Fosses. At Stavelot, the *blancs-moussis*, masked figures dressed entirely in white, except for their scarlet noses, invade the town, gamboling around, performing acrobatics, throwing confetti, bursting balloons and so on.

At Fosses, the *chinels* are the heroes of the day. They are weird figures with humps who take part in a mock ballet through the streets to the sound of music which may stop at any moment in the middle of a beat and leave them standing stock still, ready to start off again like clockwork as soon as it takes up where it left off. All the while they glance out of the corner of their eye for unwary watchers so as to knock a pipe or cigarette flying with a jerk of their humps.

Lent

At the end of Carnival, an extremely old festival takes place in Grammont. On the morning of the first

Right: A gaily costumed couple performs the traditional Dance of the Declaration of Love during a colorful festival in the streets of Brussels.

Sunday in Lent services are held as the Catholic liturgy requires. There follows a pilgrimage, which attracts large crowds from the surrounding districts. Singing hymns and prayers, the long procession is led by the town's clergy along the road to the Oudenberg, or "old mountain," where there is a chapel dedicated to the Virgin of the Mountain.

From the top of the Oudenberg there is a beautiful view of the surrounding regions of Brabant, Flanders and Hainaut. Once there, the crowd participates in what is no longer a religious ceremony but a profane rite.

AN ANCIENT CUSTOM

The priests and municipal authorities move into a space in the middle of the crowd. Everything needed for the rite is standing ready on a table: a bottle of red wine, a 15th-century loving cup of embossed silver and a large jar containing small live fish. All around stand baskets of sweets which will serve the same purpose

as the oranges at Binche. A woman fills the cup with wine; the fish are then put into the cup, and this is passed to the deacon and then on to the burgomaster, the magistrates and the town councilors.

With the greatest possible elegance, everyone attempts to take a drink and at the same time swallow one of the fish; their faces are splashed by the wrigglings of the victims, and the crowd starts to laugh and sing an old Flemish song "The Little Fisherman."

After this comes the *krakelingenwerp,* or throwing of the *krakelingen,* the several thousand sweets in the baskets. Pushing and shoving, the crowd tries to catch them in mid-air, then swarms off for a picnic and dancing in the fields.

No one really knows the original meaning of this rite, but it is older than the first definitely established date of its celebration, 1398. However, the last part of the festivities, which takes place in the evening, bears traces of very ancient pagan

cults in honor of the sun and of spring.

The noisy, excited crowd becomes attentive and silent as darkness falls. This is the most mysterious moment of the ceremony, the moment of the *Tonnekenbrand,* when a barrel of pitch and resin is set alight and hoisted on the end of a long pole. It is the symbolic burning of a tree, thought to be connected with preChristian rites celebrating the birth of spring. The burning of the *tonneken* is the signal for the lighting of a whole chain of bonfires, and the darkness is driven back from the surrounding hills by the flames.

THE FESTIVAL OF CATS

The festival of cats at Ypres, on the western borders of Flanders, appears to be older still, dating back as far as 960. To find the original connection with cats, the historian has to go back to the time when the region was beginning to adopt Christianity and was giving up the ancient Celtic cults, in particular the worship of the goddess Freya, Wotan's sister, who followed him into battle on a chariot drawn by cats, according to certain pagan beliefs.

After the pagan gods had been driven out, a pseudo-religious ceremony, called *kattespel,* was inaugur-

One of the most unusual Belgian folk rites, celebrated each year in the East Flanders town of Grammont, takes place at the end of Carnival. The priests and local authorities, each in turn, swallow the contents of a silver loving cup containing red wine and two or three small fish. With the greatest possible elegance, the town dignitaries "take their medicine" while the noisy crowd gathers around laughing and shouting encouragements. The origins of the strange rite, which dates back to the 14th century, are no longer known, but are thought to be derived from the practices of ancient pagan cults.

A larger-than-life-size puppet, similar to the "giants" so popular throughout Belgium, enhances the atmosphere of a café in Bruges (Brugge). During festival time, such cafés fill up with noisy, laughing crowds who dance, sing and carouse until the early morning hours.

ated. The Fool of Ypres would climb to the top of the belfry of the town's main tower and throw screaming cats down on to the crowd below; the rite was celebrated in this way until the end of the 18th century. Nowadays the Fool still plays his part, but the cats that he hurls into the square below are made of cloth. The huge cats which are paraded through the streets on allegorical floats in the procession of cats, are also made of cloth and are followed by two local giants, Golia and Robert le Frison.

FOOLS' MONDAY

The atmosphere of Carnival returns with the *lundi des fous* (Fools' Monday) at Renaix. This is the high point of a period of festivities which begins the Sunday after Epiphany (Jan. 6) with the arrival of the "king of the *bonmes*." The *bonmes* are the "mad heroes" of the carnival of Renaix. There are several thousand of them, wildly and strangely dressed, and they reach the peak of their simulated lunacy on the evening of Fools' Monday. In honor of their king and queen, they dance and shriek.

Sacred and Profane Festivals

It would require volumes to give a complete survey of the variety of Belgian festivals. All that can be done here, in so short a space, is to give the outlines and a few of the details of the subject. It is not always easy to state whether these celebrations are religious or not. One reason for that difficulty is that many such festivities were forbidden and persecuted by various rulers at various times in history. For instance, in the 18th century, when Joseph II of Austria prohibited all religious processions, the Belgians, rather than give up their customs, preferred to alter them and suppress the religious aspects. The ceremonies were made profane, and this element subsequently remained stronger than the religious, even after the prohibitions were withdrawn.

There are, however, numerous quite definitely religious processions; each parish, town and village has at least one. The most widespread is

certainly the *Fête Dieu*, or Corpus Christi procession, which is a most solemn occasion and sometimes—as at Liège and Antwerp—takes place on the water, with long processions of boats of all sorts: a *fête nautique*. The processions of the *Dédicace*, which celebrate the dedication of a church to its saint, are much the same as the festivals that towns in other countries have for their patron saints; and for this reason they have been accompanied for a long time by fairs called *ducasses* in Wallonia and *kermesses* in Flanders.

Processions such as the very famous one of the *Holy Blood* at Bruges (the chief Flemish festival, just as the festival at Binche is the most im-portant Walloon festival) are called *parlants*, or "speakings."

This is because of the custom of interpolating scenes from the Old and New Testaments or the lives of the saints, acted by the Chambers of Rhetoric.

PROCESSIONS COVERING MANY MILES

When a procession loses its specifically religious character and adopts the fashion of wandering for miles over the territory of other communes, the result is known as a *tour* (or *grand tour*, depending on the length of the itinerary which may often be tens of miles and last for from ten to fifteen hours).

Sometimes the priests do not wear

Portrait of an Old Woman, *a painting by the late 15th-century Flemish painter Hans Memling. The woman's headdress, typically and uniquely Flemish, is of the type still worn at many rural festivals and celebrations.*

St. Eloi or St. Guidon. In these *chevauchées*, each individual is acting for himself; he takes part in the procession in order to have his own horse blessed, but in spite of this whole groups are formed. They walk, trot and sometimes gallop around the whole procession in great circles.

At Grez, in Brabant, people who own horses take part in the *Serment de Saint Georges* (Oath of St. George), their patron saint. Every April, local riders on their superb Brabançon thoroughbreds gather together, along with numerous riders from surrounding districts.

An altar is hoisted on to a haycart, and there the priest exposes the Blessed Sacrament; the cart is drawn solemnly through the countryside and the priest gives his blessing as it goes along, reaching even the furthest villages. The horsemen form two lines on either side of the procession, suddenly leaving for wild gallops through the countryside and returning in time for a final blessing.

Carillons

One can have no real idea of the atmosphere of these various festivals without a mention of the sounds that accompany them and give them life. Other peoples are familiar with the chiming of bells on special occasions, but the Belgian carillons are something quite different.

Carillons are heard not only in the rarified atmosphere of Bruges, Mechelen, Ghent or the other towns still preserved, architecturally, more or less as they always have been; the same chiming is heard in towns ringing with the noises of industry, where the townspeople do not usually have time to stop and listen to the "orchestra of strings and the giant harpischord" which seem hidden in the carillon, as a romantic traveler of the last century wrote.

The carillon forms the inevitable musical background of every Belgian festival, together with choirs and fanfares. While the crowds watch the processions, they hum or whistle the ancient *reuzelieds*, or songs of the giants, while the bells echo the tunes from the tops of the singing towers.

The bells also echo the song of the *Gilles*, "The Little Fisherman" and many other old popular songs.

their official vestments; the reliquary, or statue of the saint, is usually carried by whichever guild traditionally has this right. Originally of modest proportions, these *tours* have now become very long; the external form remains, while the religious meaning is lost.

A procession is also an opportunity for a *marche*, and additional honor is given to it by companies of marchers, in traditional old military uni-

forms. This custom is thought to date from the time when pilgrimages and processions might be attacked by brigands and had therefore to be accompanied by armed protectors.

RIDERS IN PROCESSIONS

Finally, there are the *chevauchées*, or groups on horseback, which follow processions or pilgrimages to shrines dedicated to saints who are protectors of horses or of cattle, such as

Before striking the hour the carillon will always play a few bars of some old song, and in this way Belgian children learn these songs.

The carillons are religious in origin. In local legends, bells and carillons often appear side by side with witches, spells, demons and evil influences of all kinds, giving an idea of the hold they have always had over the popular imagination, irrespective of the truth or falsehood of the various tales. By reading the Latin inscriptions engraved on the oldest of these bells, one realizes their importance as spurs to religious enthusiasm.

INSCRIPTIONS ON BELLS

Such inscriptions began to be added to the decorative friezes of the bells during the 15th century. One of the oldest and most impressive reads: "I praise the true God / I call the people together / I summon the clergy / I mourn the dead / I put the plague to flight / I lament at funerals / I avert the lightning flash / I proclaim the Sabbath / I awaken the lazy / I disperse the winds / I soften the hearts of the cruel."

As time passed, it became common to use the vernacular instead of Latin, and the inscriptions became more intimate, closer to the feelings or the people and to their everyday life. The following is written on a *matins* bell: "I ring at six to tell you / when you have to go to work and when to return." On a bell rung as a fire alarm is the inscription: "Oh Lord put out this raging flame / Arise, run, help, put it out!"

Naturally enough, the development of the carillon was a long and laborious process, intimately connected with the perfecting of bell-casting techniques and clock-making. It was a long journey from the single bell to the 52 that make up the carillon at Ghent, the 49 at Mechelen (said to be the most perfect in Belgium) and the 47 at Bruges, Antwerp and Oudenarde.

CONCERTS OF BELLS

As a technique of bell-casting developed, enabling bells to be made which not only had a purer sound

This imposing medieval structure at Mechelen, in the province of Antwerp, is the only remaining section of the walls that surrounded the town in the Middle Ages.

Above: *A lone beguine strolls in silence outside the beguinage at Bruges. Silence and contemplation are the main features of the beguinages, female religious communities sheltered from the bustle of the outside world.*

Right: *This married couple from the town of Stavelot in the Ardennes is dressed in the simple, everyday costumes characteristic of the region. Traditional ways and customs still persist in this remote and idyllic region.*

but also a greater variation of musical tone, and while at the same time clocks became more complex and more perfect, so the idea of the *voorslagh* arose. (*Voorslagh* is an old Flemish word, giving the idea of several bells ringing at the same time). In the 14th century the idea arose of connecting these powerful

musical instruments to the automatic mechanism of the clocks. Clocks were put into almost every tower; their mechanism was arranged, by means of a revolving cylinder, to act automatically on the bells just before they struck the hour on the big bell. The mechanism of the clock put the *voorslagh* of the other big and small

bells into action, and they would play a simple tune, perhaps part of a popular song, before the hour was struck.

The tower and its carillon became the focus of the most intense municipal rivalry. Each town wanted a more elaborate and amazing carillon than its neighbor. Study, research

and ever-increasing skill extended the *voorslagh* to the half hours as well, and then to the quarter hours. The repertoire of tunes also increased, and finally each quarter was marked by embellishments up and down the musical scale, flowing arpeggios and showers of silver notes.

Thus it gradually became possible to have a concert of bells, to "play" on bells by means of a special keyboard composed of innumerable knobs and levers, each one corresponding to a certain sound on a certain bell. Here it is no longer the mechanism of a clock that counts, but the skill of the *carillonneur*, the bell-ringer, who may be a musician of the stature of the famed Jef Denym, *carillonneur* to the cathedral of Mechelen, seat of the Primate of Belgium.

JEF DENYM, THE BELL-RINGER OF MECHELEN

Jef Denym's father had occupied the position before him, but had been forced to retire from his high refuge in the tower of St. Rombaut when his sight failed. Jef had known every corner of the tower and carillon from early childhood, but it was only on Christmas Day, 1887, that he took up his father's position publicly. He had a thorough grounding in engineering and a genuine feeling for music. This quiet, firm man, with an indomitable will, prepared and carried out technical and musical improvements which made him the greatest *carillonneur* in history, and the founder of the only school for those who want to master the difficult art of bell-ringing.

Denym managed to evolve a system by which the clappers of the bells

A quiet corner on one of the canals in the city of Bruges. Many of the smaller canals are no longer used for commercial traffic and have been given over to swans and pleasure-seeking boat enthusiasts.

likely to interest only friends and local enthusiasts, but after a time his fame spread throughout Belgium and beyond, and thousands of people came to Mechelen to listen to his summer recitals.

This music was sometimes no more than a faint tinkling of bells; at other times it roared and beat down from the great cathedral tower like the thundering of the sea. The outlines of the top of the tower were half hidden in evening darkness, so that the music seemed to come from much higher up, to fill the sky and to float out over the roofs of the town.

The Beguinage

On the whole, the Belgians are a people in tune with the progress of the modern world, making their mark in everything from modern music to modern technology. They are also extremely hard-working. But there is one place in Belgium where time seems to have stood still, where the hectic rhythm of humanity seems to have slowed down: this is the beguinage.

The institution called the beguinage dates back to the 13th century, to a time when Europe was being swept by communal forms of religious life which still embodied, in a changing form, the anchorite's mysticism.

The beguinages, which emerged in the mystically-inclined district of Flanders, were female communities, semi-religious in the sense that their members were not bound by holy vows though they were subject to a strict code and discipline of communal life.

Today, as then, they wear dark habits and white wimples. But the beguines are not nuns; they are pious women who have withdrawn from the world, accepted certain rules and live in the beguinage supported by their own incomes or their own work. They are allowed out during the day, but must be back before the evening Angelus, when they are summoned by the bell of their own church and the doors close on the outside world until the following morning.

Nowadays, however, the original spirit is, if not entirely lost, at least considerably enfeebled, though the beguinage is still the last harbor of many desperate souls. The places still have their own special atmosphere.

Even by walking along the long grey or white outer walls one feels the power of the strange quiet world on the other side, separated from the battle of this world by a bridge over a canal or a low arched portico.

Inside those encircling walls are the neatly-trimmed lawns and narrow paths that are so typical of the beguinages, with their identical rows of little houses all the same height (only the church is higher, being the house of God) and with their green shutters and flowering window-boxes. Every beguine has her own house, quite unlike the nun's bare cell. Large beguinages have a bigger building where novices spend their two years of preparation. After this each has her own little house, in which she keeps her own possessions.

When they are not at prayer, or alone in meditation according to the rules of their community, the beguines are engaged in various traditional occupations such as embroidery, lace making or the making of cakes such as the *cramique* (a kind of ring-shaped bun with raisins, homely in both taste and appearance). Others spin and weave, or copy exemplary maxims and pious sayings in a clear and ornate script onto cards which they will have elaborately decorated beforehand. One of these exhortations says: "Let all things be done decently, and in order"— a mild exhortation that could read as the motto of the beguinages.

Every now and again one hears the voices of the beguines raised in song, as they sing the hymns during their services; and, almost as a calculated final touch, the music of the distant carillons combines with their sweet voices.

The Grand Beguinage founded by Joanna of Constantinople at Ghent has over two hundred beguines. Ghent also has a little beguinage, as flower-filled as the fields of azaleas and rhododendrons which surround the town. There are also beguinages at Bruges, Tongeren, Brussels, Lier and elsewhere. Some have become museums, like the one at Anderlecht, which is famous for the curious story of the beguine who was walled up alive.

When, in the year 1200, eight women and a mother superior founded the beguinage of Anderlecht, the rule (and a mild one at that) re-

were constantly under the control of the *carillonneur*, who could thus work with them as he pleased. He made it possible for the clapper to strike the bell rapidly and repeatedly, giving the effect of one continuous note and emphasizing the singing qualities and ever more varied sonorous possibilities of the carillon. Once he had reached the peak of technical achievement (and it proved to be almost impossible to go much higher in this field) Denym turned his attention to harmony.

At first this kind of music seemed

Above: *The resplendent costume worn during Carnival time by the so-called Gilles of the town of Binche consists of a colorfully decorated overall stuffed with straw on the back and the chest. Large bells hang from the woolen belt, while smaller bells are attached to the collar. The chief feature of the costume is the ostrich-feather headdress.*

Below: *This typical half-timbered building is characteristic of local architecture throughout much of Belgium and the low countries. Despite urban rebuilding in recent decades, such picturesque dwellings remain the rule rather than the exception in rural Belgium.*

quired that each should say five *Pater Nosters* and five *Ave Marias* a day. It cannot have been for this reason alone that the beguinage gained the unflattering name of *"klap-huis,"* or chatter box, but chatter apparently occupied the long hours of the day to such an extent that one of the good women, perhaps to force herself into silence, had herself walled into the little chapel and stayed there until her death, some 40 years later. An opening, still visible to-day, enabled her to look out onto the choir, so as to enable her to take part in the Mass and to receive food and other necessities from her fellow beguines.

FOOD AND DRINK

THE GENERAL CONVIVIALITY OF THE Belgian nature has led to the Belgians' being renowned as great eaters and drinkers, serious rivals to other nations of gourmets.

This is a solidly-based tradition, well borne-out by fact; one finds plenty of evidence for it in history, and indeed in art, as can be seen in certain pictures by Brueghel and the Teniers. This too is a field offering some remarkable contrasts: compare, for instance, the competition in Steenockerzeel known as the "three-times-seven," for which the town was well-known, with the custom according to which—at least until the beginning of the century—the inhabitants of Limburg ate meat only four times a year, on the occasion of the four main festivals. The "three-times-seven" was a spectacle worthy of Rabelais' Pantagruel, a competition in which the victor was he who could do gastronomical justice to the seven exquisite and generous dishes which were each served three times in succession.

Belgian gastronomy was to some degree influenced by the various successive foreign invasions that the country suffered through in its history. Its Gothic cooking, in which sugar was still mixed with salt, was influenced by French taste under the dukes of Burgundy, and this in turn was influenced by old local recipes. Later, the Spaniards, under the Duke of Alba, for all their slaughtering and bloody repressions, brought with them exquisite new ways of cooking fish. One of these, the method called a *l'escavèche,* is still popular today in Entre-Sambre-et-Meuse; and it was on the banks of the Meuse that goose *à l'instar de Visé,* a highly-favored dish, which takes its name from the little town on this river, was perfected.

For centuries French ships have brought cargoes of their finest wines to Antwerp, where they remain for a time to be sorted out, before being taken inland. For this reason connoisseurs say that the best Bordeaux and the Burgundies with the finest bouquets are to be found in the cellars of Flanders and Wallonia. At Nivelles, for instance, the cellars of Burgundy are as well-known as the local *tarte a l'djote,* made with cabbage and cheese from a recipe several hundred years old, perfected by generations of abbesses and beguines; and at Liège the climate, described by the Walloon word *crou* (meaning wet and cold at the same time) with its frequent rains and mists, has an ideal degree of humidity for the renowned "caves" of Burgundy. But Liège is also the city of the hundred fountains, and has balanced the love of good wine with that of water, staging the most spectacular *Fêtes de l'Eau* in the whole of Belgium.

THE "BUTTER AND BEER" COUNTRY

Belgian cooking, and gastronomy in general, therefore, are not strikingly original in any way. Perhaps the most notable feature in this field is the lavish use of butter and beer. These two are not really so ill-assorted a pair as might seem at first sight, for beer is frequently used in the preparation of many dishes and specialities, such as the *carbonnade fla-mande,* a sort of stew, and in certain soups and kinds of ice-cream.

According to statistics on the subject, Belgium is one of the world's biggest per capita consumers of beer and butter, and indeed of foodstuffs and drinks generally. This is often interpreted as a necessity, a physical reaction to the climate, but it is also an indication of the Belgian love of good living, of comfort and, therefore, quite simply, of good food. The phrase the Bible attributes to God after the creation of the world, "and it was good," is used by the people of Liège to express, in their dialect, the blissful satiety that follows a good meal: *"D'ja bin fet!"*

This may be a bit of an exaggeration, even though the delicacies of Belgian cooking include *salade liégeoise*, beans and pigskin in a vinegar dressing, kidneys cooked with juniper berries, *chefneye*, or eggs in bacon fat, and the famous "white sausage." In the little cafés in the older parts of the towns one can eat thick cakes of rice called *dorreyes* usually served with a cup of coffee—and drink a glass of *vieux système*, distilled grape juice which has been brewed at home, matured in vats and then put into earthenware containers.

REGIONAL SPECIALTIES

Ghent contributes to this national interest with one of its most famous dishes, the *Waterzooie*, or roast chicken, the recipe for which dates back to Henry IV's *poule au pot*, with the addition of a few local seasonings. Ghent also has a particularly exquisite beer with the romantic name of *Duivelsbier*, or devil's beer.

Other excellent beers are the *guezelambic* and *krieken-lambic*, both very strong, and the *faro* which is drunk in Brussels. Orval is the home of the wonderful beer with the same name; Namur has *keute*, a blonde and very bitter beer made of barley; Chimay's most famous beer is known as "trappist's" beer; in fact there are innumerable local varieties, certainly enough to justify the existence of the two important hop-markets at Poperinghe and Assche.

Another typically Belgian food is the *boudin*, a kind of black-pudding which can be prepared in various ways and which is usually served in pairs, one white and one dark—"heaven and earth," as the Belgians say. They even go to the extent of having *kermesses aux boudins*, which are served with excellent fruit jam or with sprouts cooked in butter, in which case the *boudins* are more or less green.

The Ardennes might aptly have the pig as its gastronomical symbol, for there pigs are intensively reared and eaten. Pork cutlets are the chief food in this district, but its *jambon fumé* (smoked ham) is even more famous and dates back to the time of the Roman conquest; it is also known for its bacon and sausages. These products are sent to all parts of the world via the market at Bastogne. Other specialities of the region are its game—for the Ardennes is richly forested and game is one of its great resources—exquisitely prepared in a variety of ways. Then, too, there is the *soupe ardennaise*,

The famous Benedictine abbey of St. Hubert was founded in the year 687 and was rebuilt during the middle of the 16th century. The lovely façade, with its two graceful Romanesque-style towers, dates from the early years of the 18th century.

made of vegetables and seasoned with bacon and sausage.

PASTRIES

To return for a moment to the Belgian love of good food—no discussion of this matter would be complete without a mention of Belgian pastries, particularly the simple traditional ones, originally made in the beguinages and old family houses. Such are the *cœurs* of Bruges, which are sugary cakes made in the shape of a heart, eaten after the procession of the Holy Blood; and the *nules*, brightly colored wafer-like biscuits with the shape of a crucifix on them, proffered by the children of Wallonia on New Year's Day and supposed to keep off disease; and, to mention only a few among hundreds of local specialities, the *tartelettes* of Lier, the macaroons of Beaumont and the *avisances* of Namur.

One of the most popular specialties of this kind, and connected with Belgium's considerable production of fruit, are the enormous apple, cherry and pear tarts, which are still cooked in the ovens of those huge kitchens gleaming with copper and pervaded by a hundred unidentifiable smells of past times. It is in these kitchens that the children of St. Trond, in Limburg, sip the delicious stewed cherries in syrup which makes them think, though perhaps without formulating it in so many words, that "one is never better off than in one's mother's kitchen."

Belgium has the dubious distinction of being known as the battleground of Europe. Because of its industrial wealth and strategic location on important trade routes, and because the terrain is generally lowlying and thus vulnerable to attack, it has long been a tempting prize to more powerful neighbors. France, Spain, England, Germany—all have made their bids to control this valuable area. Even when Belgium itself was not the point of contest, the wars of major European powers almost invariably spilled over into its territory.

To complicate the situation, the Belgians were usually too disunited among themselves to act cohesively against threats from without. Beginning in the medieval period, they fought determinedly against interference in their local affairs. Not only did they zealously guard their political liberties from encroachments by foreign rulers, but they were adamantly opposed to surrendering their hard-won privileges to native Belgian leaders in the interest of national unity. Countless rebellions, some against ruling foreign dynasties which made too many demands, some against towns and duchies which had grown too powerful, others against

local governments in which the people felt they had insufficient voice, marked the course of Belgian history down through the first half of the 19th century.

Their determination to maintain freedom of action was indicative of the spirit of initiative which enabled the Belgians to become so extraordinarily successful in commerce and industry. With their comparative lack of restrictions they achieved, from the Middle Ages onward, a prosperity which was the envy of the rest of Europe. There can be no doubt, however, that this same determination frequently kept them from making common cause with one another and brought about much bloodshed and suffering. As a result, the differences between the various elements of the population were accentuated and Belgian national unity was only achieved after a long and painful struggle.

The Belgian nation is a relatively new one (1831), and even the concept of something being uniquely Belgian is of fairly recent origin. From the earliest recorded history until modern times, the Netherlands, or lowlands—the area which now constitutes the states of Belgium, the Kingdom of the Netherlands (Hol-

land) and Luxembourg—was usually considered as a homogenous whole. Frequently the term "Low Countries" has also been used to refer to this area.

Until the latter part of the 16th century, the developments in any one part of the Netherlands were intricately bound up with those in the rest of the area. For this reason, it is virtually impossible to treat the history of the region up to that time in terms of the individual countries into which it is now divided. Instead, this article will consider developments in the Netherlands as a whole until the year 1579, when the Treaty of Arras and the Union of Utrecht established the first clear-cut political division between the southern and northern provinces.

EARLY HISTORY

THE RECORDED HISTORY OF THE Netherlands begins with the Roman invasion of the area in the 1st century B.C. The people that Julius Caesar's armies found there were of Celtic and Germanic stock. These two ethnic etrains were separated from each other by a line which runs roughly from present-day Dunkirk east to Maastricht. In spite of the many invasions to which the Netherlands has been subjected, this division has endured with little change into modern times.

The tribes living south of the Dunkirk-Maastricht line were known collectivively as the Belgae. Caesar, in his *Commentaries on the War in Gaul,* remarked on the courage of these people. In comparison to that of the Roman invaders, their society was an extremely primitive one. Tribes were small and were linked with each other only through their similar religion and language. Social organization was simple and the economy was strictly agricultural.

North of the Dunkirk-Maastricht line were the Batavi; they were concentrated especially between the Waal and the Rhine rivers. Still farther north, between the Rhine and Ems rivers, was the territory of the Frisians. The population in the north was less dense than in the area of the Belgae, and, because of storms and floods from the sea, living conditions there were even more primitive.

The first Roman invasion occurred in 57 B.C., and it was only after a bitter struggle that Caesar succeeded in bringing the Belgae under Roman

The Steen, a famous medieval fortress on the banks of the Scheldt River in Antwerp. Built during the Middle Ages to protect the city against invasions from the north, the Steen later became a prison and now serves as a maritime museum.

domination. In 15 B.C., in the reign of Augustus, their land was made an imperial province—Gallia Belgica— and strong fortifications were built. In 13 B.C. the resistance of the Batavi was broken, but these people were given the status of allies and their land was not made a Roman province. The Frisians retained their freedom throughout the Roman era.

The Netherlands was far distant from the heart of the empire, and as a result the inhabitants did not undergo the intensive Romanization experienced by the conquered peoples of more accessible territories. Although Roman civilization was introduced and provided some measure of

unity, many local customs were retained, and when the Roman power collapsed such unity as there was largely disappeared. The relationship of the Netherlanders to their conquerors was frequently strained; there were a number of rebellions and, although many Netherlandish

The castle of the counts of Flanders at Ghent, a magnificent example of medieval military architecture, was built in the 9th and 10th centuries and enlarged in the 12th century. From here, in the year 1302, the Ghent militia marched to Courtrai where they successfully engaged the French in the famous Battle of the Golden Spurs (so called because of the great number of golden spurs the victors took as trophies from the fallen French knights).

soldiers served in the imperial armies, few thought of themselves as Romans.

Perhaps the most lasting contribution the Romans made to the area was the roads they built linking the urban settlements in the Netherlands with important cities farther inland. This encouraged the development of the industry and commerce which were to play such vital roles in the Netherlands' economy in later times.

The Frankish Period

At the end of the 3rd century A.D., population pressure from the east drove tribes of Salian and Ripuarian Franks across the Rhine and into Roman lands; by the middle of the 4th century they had penetrated deeply into the Netherlands. After the Roman legions were withdrawn to Italy at the end of the 4th century, the Franks gradually took control of the region. The Netherlands then shared in the fortunes of the Frankish empire, first under the Merovingian and later under the Carolingian dynasties.

CONVERSION TO CHRISTIANITY

The Franks, like the Romans, gave the area little real political unity. Far more important, in terms of creating common bonds, was the conversion of the Netherlanders to Christianity, a process which began in the 3rd century. In the southern regions this conversion was carried out by Frankish and Irish priests and met with early success; soon dioceses were established in Liège, Arras, Cambrai and Tournai.

In the north Christianization proved more difficult. In spite of the efforts of such English missionaries as Willibrord and Boniface, conversion was only achieved slowly and with frequent recourse to armed force. The bishopric of Utrecht was not founded until 695, and it took two more centuries before the Frisians and the Saxons, who had settled in the region of the Saale River in the east, were brought to accept either the new religion or the domination of the Frankish empire.

THE MIDDLE AGES

THE DEATH OF CHARLEMAGNE, THE greatest of the Carolingian rulers and the creator of a huge empire, led to drastic political changes throughout Europe. Louis the Pious managed to keep his father's unwieldy empire together, but after his death in 843 his three sons divided it among themselves by the Treaty of Verdun. Louis the German was given East Francia (roughly, Germany); West Francia (roughly, France) went to Charles the Bald; and the so-called middle kingdom went to Lothair (it later took its name from him: Lotharingia, or in its corrupted form, Lorraine).

Unfortunately for the Netherlands, it fell into the middle kingdom, which from the beginning was weaker than the other two. Lothair and his son, Lothair II, were neither vigorous nor long-lived, and when Lothair II died in 869, without an heir, his domains were the object of an intense struggle between the kings of East and West Francia. In 870 the fate of the Netherlands was decided by the Treaty of Mersen; the area was cut in two, with the eastern part going to Louis the German and the western part to Charles the Bald.

This division did not bring political stability, however. Members of the local nobility were offered tempting rewards to switch their allegiance from East to West Francia or vice versa; and they did switch with bewildering frequency. By 925 most of the area was dominated by Germany, under the overlordship of Henry the Fowler. After Henry's son, the German Emperor Otto the Great, inherited the area, it gradually broke up into a number of feudal duchies.

FEUDALISM

The German emperors were not powerful enough to maintain close control over their Netherlands possessions, nor had the French kings the strength to take more than minor advantage of this German weakness. In the 9th and 10th centuries, incursions of Norsemen from Scandinavia demonstrated the vulnerability of the Netherlands to attack and the incompetence of either the Germans or the French to provide protection. Effective defense could only be organized locally, and to accomplish this the most powerful men of the region demanded and were granted special authority. After they succeeded in staving off the Norse threat, they declined to relinquish their privileges. Their rights soon became hereditary, and thus a network of feudal domains came into existence.

Among the most powerful of the feudal lords were the Counts of Flanders. By the 11th century they had managed to amass a considerable territory, which was divided into Crown Flanders, a fief of the kings of France, and Imperial Flanders, a fief of the German emperors. Other leading principalities were Brabant, Limburg, Hainaut, Luxembourg, Holland, Zeeland, Gelderland, and the bishoprics of Utrecht and Liège.

The Growth of the Towns

Important as was the establishment of strong feudal principalities in the Netherlands, this development was eclipsed by the spectacular rise of urban settlements. Cities had been founded in Roman and Frankish times, but most of them had fallen into decline as a result of the chaotic political and economic conditions which followed the breakup of Charlemagne's empire. Toward the end of the 10th century, as order was somewhat restored and the Crusades stimulated the revival of trade, urban

The Cathedral of Notre Dame at Tournai. Tournai, one of the oldest cities in Belgium, was already flourishing in Roman times before the introduction of Christianity into Belgium. Many of the early kings of France were born in the city, and from here they governed their lands to the south and the east.

settlements began to thrive again all over Europe. Nowhere was this development more pronounced than in the Netherlands.

The nature of the countryside, with its flat plains and numerous water routes, had always encouraged dense settlement and thus the establishment of cities. Once trade had revived, the Netherlands' plentiful internal communications and its outlets on the North Sea made it a natural center for commerce. In addition the development of the weaving industries, especially in Flanders, contributed greatly to the prosperity of the region.

CHARTERS

The cities of the Netherlands became centers of wealth, and with wealth came power. Feudal lords had to depend on the urban population for a large portion of their revenues, and in return for their contributions the cities extracted certain privileges. Beginning in the 11th century the townsmen wrested from the feudal lords a series of charters setting forth their rights and obligations. The most famous of these charters, the *Joyeuse Entrée* which was granted to the cities of Brabant and Limburg in 1354, stipulated that trade was to be free from restrictions and that the Duke of Brabant could conduct no war, cede no territory and make no treaty without the consent of his subjects.

These charters, with their recognition of urban privileges, had a profound influence on the course of Netherlands history. This was particularly true in the area that later became Belgium, which was more populous than the northern region and consequently had larger cities. Ghent, Bruges and Ypres, sometimes called the Three Members of Flanders, were especially powerful.

For protection, the medieval cities were surrounded with defensive walls; each had a double center, the commercial quarter *(poort)* and the fortress *(burg)*. Most had a monopoly to import and distribute a particular commodity and, as the medieval period progressed, developed important industries as well. Along with their right to a voice in the affairs of the feudal principalities, the cities also won a large measure of local autonomy. They could organize their own administrations, fix local taxes, raise troops and conclude alliances.

Nevertheless it would be a mistake to conclude that the cities were virtually independent of the feudal princes. They were bound to obey the

Le Rabot (*"the Lock"*), an old fortress at Ghent, was built on the Lieve canal in 1489 in order to fortify the city walls, which had been heavily damaged during a siege by forces of the German emperor Frederick III, of the house of Habsburg.

laws of their principality and to pay taxes; and representatives of the princes were kept in the cities to see that these requirements were fulfilled.

MUNICIPAL GOVERNMENTS

It would also be a mistake to suppose that the governments of the cities, advanced though they were for the times, were basically democratic. Until the 14th century, administration was in the hands of the privileged classes, and local governments were oligarchical in nature. At first the municipal councils consisted of patricians, former merchants who had amassed considerable wealth and had come to form a sort of urban aristocracy. Later, as corporations, or guilds, were organized to regulate specific industries and crafts, the leadership passed to the *dekens* (deans), the guild leaders. Once in power, however, they were no less aristocratic and authoritarian than the patricians had been, and by the beginning of the 14th century the mass of the townsfolk were becoming restive.

A Turbulent Century

The general disorder which prevailed in the Netherlands during the 14th century had both social and political roots. The trouble began in Flanders, where the members of the large and powerful weavers' guild began to agitate for a stronger voice in community affairs. They organized a party called the Clauwaerts, which took its name from the claws of the lion in the coat of arms of Flanders. Arrayed against the Clauwaerts were the urban aristocrats and the feudal nobility, who wanted to protect their entrenched privileges. These forces called themselves the Leliaerts, after the lily in the Bourbon coat of arms.

THE BATTLE OF THE GOLDEN SPURS

Violence erupted at Bruges in May 1302, when hundreds of Leliaerts were massacred. This event, known as the Matins of Bruges, prompted the oligarchs and aristocrats to call on France for aid, and it was not long in arriving. King Philip IV (The Fair) dispatched a company of French knights, and together with the native Leliaert forces, they marched against the Clauwaerts. Considering their superior equipment and training, they should have won an easy victory, but they were resoundingly defeated by the determined Ghent militia at Courtrai

The beffroi, *or bell tower, at Bruges. The tower's 47 bells chime every quarter hour and also give "bell concerts" during festivals and on other special occasions. The idea of connecting the bells with the automatic mechanism of the clocks first arose in the 14th century. Since that time, the towers and their many-belled carillons have been one of the most characteristic and delightful features of Belgian towns.*

(July 11, 1302). This encounter has gone down in history as the Battle of Golden Spurs, so called because of the great number of golden spurs the victors took as trophies from the fallen knights.

Their success at Courtrai immensely strengthened the Clauwaerts' position, and city governments, not only in Flanders but also in the other principalities of the Netherlands, began to be more democratic. Things were relatively quiet for a few years, but disturbances soon flared up again when the Hundred

Years' War between France and England broke out in 1338.

The conflict between these two powers put Flanders in a difficult position. The weaving industries, which were of such economic importance to the region, depended on England for their supply of wool, and the commercial interests naturally did not want this supply cut off. On the other hand, Flanders was still a fief of France, and its count, Louis of Nevers, was in sympathy with that country. He forbade trade with England, and the English king,

Margaret of Parma governed the Netherlands (including modern Belgium) for her half-brother Philip II of Spain from 1559 to 1567. She had to face the first movements in the revolt of the Flemings against the excessive taxation and religious intolerance of the Spanish government. In 1566, during a meeting with the Flemish nobility, one of her courtiers referred to the Flemings as gueux *(beggars). The enraged Flemings adopted this name as a symbol of their revolt and also used it as a battle cry. The Flemish* gueux des bois *(Beggars of the Woods) and* les gueux de Mer *(Beggars of the Sea) did much to weaken Spanish rule.*

wanted to be dominated by Ghent than by the count of Flanders or by France itself. The mistrust Van Artevelde aroused made his alliances at best tenuous ones.

Then, too, in pursuing his external policies he failed to deal effectively with problems in his own city of Ghent. Social unrest there grew, to the point where the same weavers' guild which had put Van Artevelde in power only eight years earlier sanctioned his violent death at the hands of a mob in 1345.

THE DECLINE OF THE CLAUWAERTS

With Van Artevelde's death, Clauwaert strength declined. Cities such as Ghent continued to challenge the counts of Flanders and the aristocracy in general, but they were unwilling to band together and therefore the party steadily lost ground. As their position deteriorated, the weavers of Ghent, ironically enough, called to power Van Artevelde's son Philip. He raised an army to meet the forces of the count of Flanders and the French king, but was decisively defeated at Roosebeke in 1382. Philip died in the encounter, and though sporadic rebellions continued, no other leader arose to give direction to the Clauwaert movement. The political trend was in a quite different direction; the Netherlands was about to pass into a new era.

The Burgundian Period

The unity that the nobility and the Clauwaerts alike failed to bring to the Netherlands was achieved, for a time at least, by the dukes of Burgundy. Louis of Male, who became count of Flanders in 1346, had only one child, a daughter Margaret. In 1369 she married Philip the Bold (1342-1404), duke of Burgundy and brother of the king of France. When Louis of Male died in 1384, his possessions, which included Flanders, Artois and the cities of Antwerp and Malines, fell into Philip's hands. He and his three successors, through a brilliant and intricate series of marriages, inheritances, alliances, purchases and outright annexations, managed to carve out a dominion which included not only most of the Netherlands but a number of outlying areas as well.

One of Philip the Bold's first moves was to court the friendship of the powerful Flemish cities. He even won the support of the hostile citizens of Ghent by granting them the

Edward III, promptly retaliated by suspending wool shipments to Flanders.

VAN ARTEVELDE

It was in this situation that the greatest leader of the Clauwaert forces came to power. He was Jacob van Artevelde (c.1290-1345) of Ghent, who assumed control of that city's government in 1338.

Van Artevelde's goals were to strengthen the power of the Clauwaerts in relation to the count of Flanders, to repair relations with England and to establish Flanders' neutrality in the Hundred Years' War. To achieve these objectives, he brought about an association of Ghent, Bruges and Ypres with the cities of Brabant and Limburg and also concluded various economic and military alliances with cities in Hainaut, Holland and Zeeland. His position was so strong that the count of Flanders fled to France, and Van Artevelde was thus free to draw closer to England. He even proposed that Edward's son become sovereign of Flanders, but Edward rejected this idea.

Van Artevelde was in some ways brilliantly successful, but in pursuing his program he made two fatal mistakes. He was a forceful man, and the power at his disposal aroused the jealousies and suspicions of other Netherlands cities; they no more

Peace of Tournai (1385), which guaranteed their liberties. Next he arranged marriages for his children calculated to add to the family's domains.

The Burgundians were strongly French in their interests and Philip's son, John the Fearless (1371-1419), was more concerned with competing for the French crown than with adding to his Netherlands territories. Toward this end he made an alliance with England, and the result was that the Flemish weaving industries and Netherlands' commerce in general flourished.

PHILIP THE GOOD

The outstanding Burgundian duke was John's son Philip the Good (1396-1467). This second Philip had in mind nothing less than to recreate the Lotharingian kingdom which had broken up over 500 years earlier. In pursuance of this goal, he steadily expanded his territories and his influence.

The county of Namur came to him through purchase (1421), and the counties of Brabant and Limburg through inheritance (1430). In 1433, when his cousin, Jacqueline of Bavaria, violated a family agreement by marrying for the fourth time, he forced her to cede to him the counties of Hainaut, Holland, Zeeland and Friesland. In 1441 he bought the county of Luxembourg, and four years later he succeeded in installing close relatives as bishops of Liège and Utrecht.

Philip the Good realized that he could only maintain control of his domains by establishing a strong central authority. The provincial estates, which had already been in existence for some time, were continued. But a national legislative assembly, the estates general, was created in 1465 and to a large extent superceded the provincial bodies in influence. In addition, a grand council was set up as the supreme authority on financial and judicial matters.

Philip was patient and went out of his way to win the support of his subjects, but it was inevitable that a fair proportion of the population, particularly those resident in the southern cities, would view his every move to consolidate his authority as a threat to their cherished local freedoms. Furthermore, the interests, for example, of the Flemish cities were rather different from those of an agricultural area like Zeeland, and whatever policy Philip chose to pursue in the national interest was likely to antagonize someone.

Philip demonstrated that he was willing to use armed strength if necessary to enforce his decisions—as when he put down uprisings at Bruges in 1438 and Ghent in 1453—but as a whole his reign was a peaceful and prosperous one. The unity of the Netherlands that he achieved, however, was deceptive; it depended not on popular consent but on the ability of one man to maintain his authority. Philip succeeded in doing this, but his son Charles the Bold (1433-1477) soon got into trouble.

CHARLES THE BOLD

Charles was every bit as ambitious as his father, but he lacked Philip's stable temperament and gift for statesmanship. To Charles, power meant military strength, and he lost no time in creating a formidable standing army. He asserted his authority

An old engraving shows the town hall of Antwerp in flames during an episode (Nov. 4, 1576) of the 16th-century struggle between the Netherlands and Spain.

by swiftly and brutally crushing uprisings at Liège and Dinant and rounded out the Burgundian territory by conquering Gelderland.

But Charles' attentions were not confined to the Netherlands; he attempted to expand in other directions and challenged not only the French king but also territories belonging to the German Empire. In spite of the quality of his army, he had neither sufficient manpower nor adequate finances for such large-scale campaigns. The folly of his course of action was all too evident when he suffered a series of defeats at the hands of the Swiss, but Charles stubbornly refused to retire to the Netherlands. He died in battle outside the French city of Nancy in 1477.

THE CULTURE OF THE BURGUNDIAN ERA

The internal peace imposed by the Burgundian dukes greatly benefited commerce and industry. It also stimulated the first real flowering of Netherlandish culture. Fine cathedrals, guild halls and municipal buildings were erected in the cities; such painters as Jan van Eyck, Rogier van der Weyden and Hans Memling became famous and influential throughout Europe. Merchants and traders from all parts of the known world flocked to the bustling commercial centers, bringing new ideas and creating a cosmopolitan atmosphere. It was in such an environment that the leading European intellect of the 16th century, Desiderius Erasmus of Rotterdam, spent his formative years.

The Burgundian court was the most luxurious in all Europe, surpassing even that of France in elegance and splendor. Banquets were lavish, costumes exquisite, rituals unbelievably elaborate. Perhaps the most significant manifestation of this way of life was the Order of the Golden Fleece, created by Philip the Good in 1430 on the occasion of his marriage to Isabella of Portugal. This order established, in effect, an elite within the elite.

The motivation for all this magnificence was an exceedingly practical one—the dukes judged quite accurately that such a display would enhance their prestige, not only in the Netherlands but throughout Europe. And indeed they did win an enviable reputation, one which more than matched their real power. But events following the death of Charles the Bold quickly revealed how unstable their power had been.

THE HABSBURGS AND THE REFORMATION

CHARLES THE BOLD HAD NO SONS; his heir was his daughter Mary, at the time of his death 20 years of age. Hardly had she assumed power when the Flemish cities and the provincial estates of Brabant and Holland forced her to grant the *Grand Privilège* (1477), a charter of liberties which not only reaffirmed their traditional rights but added new ones.

No further evidence of Burgundian weakness was needed, and Louis XI of France, Charles the Bold's old enemy, wasted little time in invading the southern part of the Netherlands. Paradoxically, this action worked to Mary's advantage, for it caused the Flemish cities to rally to the support of her and her husband, Maximilian of Austria. The French incursions were checked, and upon Mary's death in 1482 the rule of the Netherlands passed to Maximilian, a member of the powerful Habsburg family and later German emperor. The Habsburg era lasted far longer than the Burgundian one, but it was not nearly as peaceful nor as beneficial to the Netherlands.

Almost immediately Maximilian's autocratic rule aroused the displeasure of both the southern cities and the northern provinces. The displeasure was militantly expressed; at one time Maximilian even suffered the indignity of being held prisoner in Bruges. In December 1482 he was forced to sign the Peace of Arras, by which his authority was severely curtailed. However, he refused to abide by the terms of this agreement, and civil strife continued.

In 1493 Maximilian ascended the imperial throne, and the following year he entrusted the Netherlands to his son Philip. This young man took little interest in the administration of his realm and generally followed the advice of his Flemish councillors.

The Reign of Charles V

Philip died prematurely in 1506 and was succeeded by his son Charles, then six years old. Emperor Maximilian's daughter, Margaret of Austria, was appointed to serve as regent until the boy reached maturity. She governed judiciously, pursuing policies conciliatory to the local nobility and tried to keep the Nether-

An engraving from a medallion commemorating the counts of Egmont and Hoorn, who were martyrs of the Netherlands' struggle against Spanish rule in the 16th century. They were beheaded by the Spanish in the Grand-Place of Brussels on June 5, 1568. Their deaths were instrumental in bringing about subsequent open rebellion against Spanish rule.

The home of the famous Flemish artist Peter Paul Rubens at Antwerp. The lavishly ornamented mansion was built in an eclectic style that was an architectural reflection of the numerous political, social and cultural influences absorbed by Belgium and the other Low Countries during the troubled years of the 17th century.

lands neutral in the quarrels then developing between the German Empire and France.

The nobility was not convinced that Margaret could successfully maintain the Netherlands' neutrality and felt that a male ruler would be more effective. Accordingly, when Charles was only 15 years old, they persuaded the estates general to declare him of age. This strategy was unsuccessful, however, for through a series of unexpected deaths in his mother's family Charles fell heir to Spain, Naples, Sicily and the Spanish possessions in the New World. Upon the death of his paternal grandfather, the Emperor Maximilian, in 1519, he also became

the head of the House of Habsburg. When he acceded to the throne of the German Empire as Charles V in 1522, he was sovereign of the larger part of the Christian world.

Charles now could scarcely devote his attentions exclusively to the Netherlands. He remained the nominal ruler of the area, but Margaret of Austria was summoned back to act as governor. She was succeeded by Charles' sister Mary of Hungary. Like Margaret, Mary was sympathetic to the local population and promoted economic prosperity.

ADMINISTRATIVE CHANGES

Charles V conducted four major wars against France, and the Netherlands, because of its strategic position, was constantly menaced by the French. After Charles emerged victorious he turned his attention to an administrative reorganization of the Low Countries, to strengthen his dominance. Militant movements for local independence were firmly suppressed, and Charles extended his domains to include Overijssel, Drente and Groningen. He thus brought un-

Alessandro Farnese (1545-92), the son of Margaret of Parma, served as Spanish governor of the Netherlands from 1578 to 1588. A shrewd diplomat and brilliant military strategist, he did much to bring the Netherlands, including most of modern Belgium, back into the Spanish orbit. Among the cities he regained for the Spanish from the rebels of Flanders and Wallonia were Tournai, Maastricht, Bruges, Ghent and Antwerp.

der his authority all of the Netherlands except Liège, and even this area was bound to him by treaty and was only semi-independent. The Netherlands territory was organized into 17 provinces and, although the central authority was clearly established, the provincial estates continued to exist and many traditions of local self-government were preserved. These concessions enabled Charles V to maintain a high degree of popularity.

It appeared on the surface that the Netherlands had at last been effectively united, but within a few decades of Charles' abdication (1556) the region divided once again, this time irrevocably.

The Beginnings of Religious Conflict

Well before Charles turned over control of the Netherlands to his son Philip II, whom he made king of Spain, the religious conflicts brought about by the Protestant Reformation had been felt in the area. Calvinism, Lutheranism and Anabaptism all won converts. Charles V had appointed an Inquisition to root out the reformers in 1522; the first executions took place the following year. But repression only strengthened the movement, and the 17 provinces Philip inherited were seething with unrest.

In character and interests, the new sovereign was badly equipped to cope with the situation. Philip realized that the 17 provinces constituted the richest and most populous part of his realm, but although he appreciated their value he had little understanding of them. His loyalties were to Spain, and in his mind Catholicism and Spanish power were irrevocably linked; he believed it his responsibility not only to maintain his temporal authority but to enforce the religious beliefs on which it was founded.

This inflexible attitude could only meet with opposition in the Netherlands, with its tradition of freedom of thought and action. Even the nobility, which was naturally inclined to be sympathetic to his administrative policies, was alienated.

Philip was not a man to meet his opponents halfway. His response to the unrest in the Netherlands was to dispatch Spanish troops to the area, suspend the meetings of the estates general and step up religious persecutions. He appointed his half-sister, Margaret of Parma, as governor, aided by a three-member council headed by the count of Granvelle.

As the conflict progressed, three members of the nobility emerged as leaders of the opposition to Philip: William I, Prince of Orange (1533-1584) and the counts of Egmont (1522-68) and Hoorn (1518-68). Their followers included not only most of the aristocrats and the commoners who had been converted to Protestantism but, after Philip had reorganized the structure of the Church and removed many of its leaders, the majority of the Roman Catholic clergy as well.

THE COMPROMISE OF NOBLES

In 1566, a "request"—in reality a demand—was presented to Margaret of Parma by some 300 nobles. This document, known as the Compromise of Nobles, called for the easing of religious persecutions, the ending of the Inquisition and the summoning of the estates general. In the interests of preserving the peace, Margaret had no choice but to agree to forward the petition to Philip and in the meantime to suspend some of the most hated royal edicts.

The Compromise of Nobles was handed to Margaret by Hendrik, Lord of Brederode. According to a possibly aprocryphal story, this man was the originator of the name by which Philip's opponents came to be known. The story has it that shortly after presenting the petition Brederode had occasion to attend a lavish banquet, and there he distributed to each guest a beggar's bowl and pouch. These objects were intended as ironic symbols—the nobles would remain loyal to Philip until his policies reduced them to the status of beggars (*gueux*).

Whether or not this was the origin of the term *gueux*, the symbolism was valid enough. Philip was involved in almost constant wars and was continually demanding revenues for his campaigns from the Netherlands. His repressive policies were hardly conducive to the maintenance of a thriving economy, and it was often difficult to raise the monies he asked. There was, in addition, a growing disinclination to do so.

It is possible that in his financial desperation Philip might have been driven to make some of the concessions the Netherlands demanded. However, although the leaders of the nobility were not religious fanatics, many of their followers were. They responded to Philip's persecutions with equally violent actions; the same year that the Compromise of Nobles was presented a number of Catholic churches were sacked. This so enraged Philip that the last hope for compromise was lost.

Repression and Rebellion

One of the few concessions Philip had made to the Netherlands was to withdraw his Spanish troops in 1561. Since she had no army at her disposal, Margaret of Parma first attempted to quell the anti-Catholic riots by granting freedom of worship to Protestants. This measure was of little effect and, backed by high-ranking Catholics, she withdrew all concessions and sent to Germany for mercenary troops to restore order.

Many members of the nobility had been repelled by the excesses of the rioters, and as a result there was no concerted opposition to Margaret's action. By the time the angry Philip dispatched the Duke of Alba to the Netherlands, a state of relative peace prevailed.

THE DUKE OF ALBA

The Duke of Alba's orders were to exterminate the leaders of the Protestant uprisings and to restore strong Catholic rule in the 17 provinces. In this way Philip hoped that the provinces would not only be secured for the Church but could be made to provide the revenues he needed so badly. When Margaret heard that the duke was coming she foresaw the violence that would ensue and asked for her recall. Large numbers of Protestants also accurately predicted what would happen and hastily fled the country. Among the refugees was William of Orange. The counts of Egmont and Hoorn elected to remain, believing that Philip would show clemency, at least to members of the nobility.

The Duke of Alba was enthusiastic about the task which had been entrusted to him; if possible, he was even more fanatically Catholic than Philip. In the summer of 1567 he marched into the Netherlands at the head of an army of 9000 battle-tested soldiers. By obtaining German and Walloon mercenaries he quickly swelled his forces to 60,000. In September he set up the infamous organization known as the Council of Blood and charged it with routing out and prosecuting those who opposed the Catholic faith.

What ensued could justly be called a reign of terror. Between 10 and 20 thousand arrests were made; the death toll is unknown, but it is recorded that on one day alone 84 persons were executed. Executions were well publicized and the property of the victims was confiscated. Among those who met their deaths were the trusting counts of Egmont and Hoorn.

The Duke of Alba did not carry out his program single-handedly. He was supported by Catholic fanatics and at least not opposed by the vast majority of the citizenry, who declined to involve themselves in such violent political and religious quarrels. The spirit of rebellion was exceedingly weak, as William of Orange and his brother, Louis of Nassau, found when they led expeditions into the Netherlands in 1568. Not a single town rose to their support and they were forced to retire.

THE RESISTANCE MOVEMENT

Resistance to the Duke of Alba, and thus to Spain, developed for economic rather than religious reasons. After the first surge of religious persecutions the Duke granted a general amnesty and set about the business of extracting revenues from the provinces. To this end he proclaimed a number of taxes, one of which was a 10 per cent levy on all commercial transactions. This tax was an economic absurdity—it forced prices so high that they were not competitive, and commercial and industrial activities sharply declined. Large numbers of men were thrown out of work, and as the people began to feel the economic pinch they angrily turned against the Duke and Philip.

Prior to 1570, when the tax was enforced, the organized opposition to Spanish policies within the Netherlands had consisted of the *gueux des bois,* outlaws who had found sanctuary in heavily wooded areas and carried out guerrilla warfare, and *gueux de mer,* disgruntled sailors and fishermen who made pirate raids along the coast. They had won little support among the population as a whole, but as dissatisfaction with Spanish policy grew, people became more sympathetic to them.

An old print showing the assassination of William of Orange by Balthasar Gérard, a fanatic French Catholic, at Delft on July 10, 1584 William's efforts to overthrow Spanish rule in the Low Countries resulted in the founding of the Protestant-oriented Dutch Republic. His inability to assuage the distrust of the Catholics in the southern Netherlands, however, resulted ultimately in the separate establishment of the Spanish Netherlands, which later became the nation of Belgium.

THE ROYAL HOUSE OF BELGIUM

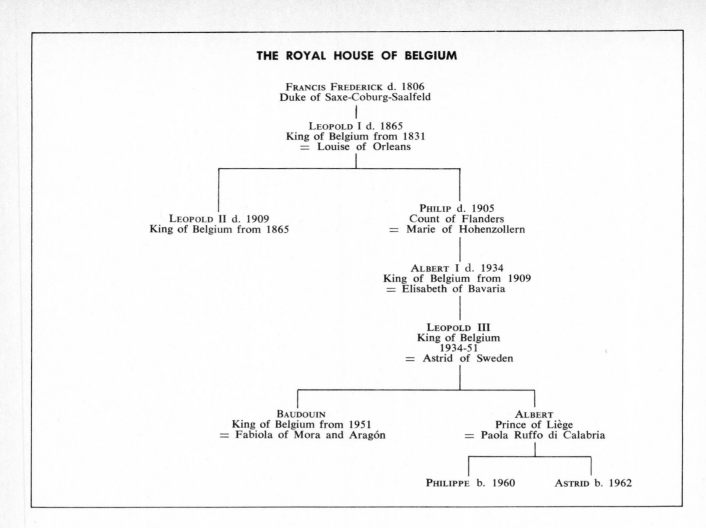

FRANCIS FREDERICK d. 1806
Duke of Saxe-Coburg-Saalfeld

LEOPOLD I d. 1865
King of Belgium from 1831
= Louise of Orleans

LEOPOLD II d. 1909
King of Belgium from 1865

PHILIP d. 1905
Count of Flanders
= Marie of Hohenzollern

ALBERT I d. 1934
King of Belgium from 1909
= Elisabeth of Bavaria

LEOPOLD III
King of Belgium
1934-51
= Astrid of Sweden

BAUDOUIN
King of Belgium from 1951
= Fabiola of Mora and Aragón

ALBERT
Prince of Liège
= Paola Ruffo di Calabria

PHILIPPE b. 1960   ASTRID b. 1962

The Spanish land forces were too strong for the *gueux des bois* to stand any chance of success against them, but Spanish positions along the coast of the North Sea were vulnerable to attack from the sea. In April 1572 a band of *gueux de mer* made a landing on the coast of Zeeland and, meeting support from the local population, was able to move rapidly inland. Soon the entire provinces of Holland and Zeeland were in rebel hands.

This northern stronghold provided a base from which William of Orange could mount an invasion of the south. His armies met with success, and although the hated Duke of Alba was replaced by more diplomatic governors, the Spanish fortunes did not improve. To add to the Spanish governors' troubles, there were no funds to pay their soldiers, and bands of them mutinied and sacked southern towns. Particularly disastrous for the Spanish cause was the looting of Antwerp, which had been loyally Catholic, in 1576.

THE PACIFICATION OF GHENT

Later in the same year, under the initiative of William of Orange, the Pacification of Ghent was drawn up. This was an agreement entered into by representatives of all the provinces except Luxembourg, by which they pledged to band together to drive the Spaniards out of the Netherlands. Both Catholics and Protestants signed this document, and since bitterness still ran high the question of religion was treated circumspectly.

In September 1577 William made a triumphal entry into Brussels, where he was elected *ruwaert* (warden) of Brabant. Victory seemed assured, but William ran into the same sort of difficulties which had plagued Jacob van Artevelde two centuries earlier: his power was suspect, particularly among Catholic nobles of the French-speaking (Walloon) region. Their fears were in no way allayed when a vigorous Calvinist government was set up in Ghent two months after William reached Brussels.

SEPARATION

Once again, diversity prevailed over unity. To strengthen their position in respect to William, the French-speaking southern provinces formed the League of Arras on January 5, 1579; in May they signed an agreement with Philip asserting their allegiance to the Catholic faith and to Spain. The northern provinces countered with the Union of Utrecht. They did not declare their independence, but their opposition to enforced Catholicism was made very clear. These two alliances marked a definite break between the northern and southern Netherlands. (Subsequent developments in the north are dealt with in the article *The Netherlands: The History.*)

THE SEVENTEENTH AND EIGHTEENTH CENTURIES

THE PROVINCES WHICH SIGNED THE Arras agreement represented only

the southern extremity of the territory destined to became the Spanish Netherlands and, two and a half centuries later, the nation of Belgium. Flanders, Brabant, Antwerp and Limburg had entered the Union of Utrecht; the Spaniards were determined to win back not only these areas but the whole of the north.

Fortunately for the Spanish cause, Philip had at last appointed a governor, Margaret of Parma's son, Alessandro Farnese, who was a leader of the caliber of William of Orange. By 1585, through shrewd diplomacy and brilliant military strategy, Farnese re-established Spanish authority as far as the northern parts of Flanders and Brabant. Spanish wars with England and France prevented further advances.

Farnese offered the reconquered provinces and cities many guarantees, but there were no concessions on the question of religion: Protestantism was expressly forbidden. Protestants were allowed to sell their property and emigrate, however, and many did so. Most of them moved further north, and they contributed significantly to the prosperity of the Dutch Republic.

DECLINE

The 17th century was indeed a properous one for the northern provinces; the reverse was true for the Spanish Netherlands. Philip, in a move to win the friendship of the people, granted them nominal independence under the rule of his favorite daughter, Isabella, and her husband, the Archduke Albert. In reality, however, Spanish control remained as firm as ever, and when Isabella died in 1633 even the nominal independence was ended.

In spite of the promises which had been made, most of the organs of local self-government were suppressed or greatly reduced in power. The royal council in Brussels constituted a strong central authority, and the provinces were placed under the administration of royal governors. Adherence to Catholicism was strictly enforced. Spain itself was in decline at this time, and its policies in no way helped the economy of its Netherlands possessions.

These developments had the effect of demoralizing the population, and their spirit was further weakened by a series of wars fought on Belgian soil. The Thirty Years' War, the campaigns of the French king Louis XIV. the War of the Spanish Succession—all these cost Belgian lives and property.

THE AUSTRIAN HABSBURGS

BY THE TREATY OF UTRECHT (1713), which ended the War of the Spanish Succession, Belgium came under the control of the Austrian branch of the Habsburg family. The change signified no improvement. The Dutch

A scene along the Lys River in Ghent. The two buildings at center and right are the guild buildings of the Free Boatmen and the Grain Weighers. Ghent, for centuries a stronghold of the various guilds, has been a rich and prosperous trading town almost continuously since the 12th century. The city was the site of the signing of the Treaty of Ghent, which ended the War of 1812 between Britain and the U. S.

had seized on the opportunity the war afforded to close the Scheldt River to Belgian trade. They steadfastly refused to reopen it and Antwerp, a thriving city which had depended on this river as its outlet to the sea, fell into decline.

In addition, the Dutch and the British imposed high tariffs which cut further into Belgian trade. So strong was the determination to eliminate Belgium as a commercial rival that when merchants in Ostend and Antwerp formed a company to trade in the Far and Middle East the Dutch, French and British compelled the Austrian emperor to suspend the company's charter.

Austria had too many pressing concerns elsewhere in Europe to pay much attention to its Netherlands possessions. The Emperor Charles VI was a strong believer in authoritarian government, and he was genuinely surprised when his Belgian subjects protested the highhanded policies of the governors he appointed. In 1718 a serious uprising broke out in Brussels, but it was quickly crushed.

When Charles VI died in 1740, the War of the Austrian Succession broke out, and five years later Belgium again found itself a battlefield for the major powers of Europe. The French occupied much of the country, but under the Treaty of Aix-la-Chapelle, which ended the war in 1748, they were required to withdraw.

Charles VI was succeeded by his daughter, Maria Theresa, who was popular in Belgium, though she was not greatly interested in this corner of her domains and never visited it. In 1753 she appointed as governor her brother-in-law, the count of Coblenz. He was an able administrator and skillfully carried out the reform policies Maria Theresa decreed for her empire. Although the distinctly anticlerical spirit of these policies antagonized the Church, popular support was won by the granting of more freedom to the provincial and local governments. Long needed financial reforms were instituted and a program of road and canal building was undertaken to stimulate an economic revival.

JOSEPH II

When Maria Theresa died in 1780 her son became emperor as Joseph II. He had still more reforming spirit than his mother, but though his intentions were good his methods were authoritarian and he was soon at odds with the Belgian people.

In 1781 Joseph issued the Toleration Edict, which granted freedom of worship to all; he also permitted mixed marriages, disbanded monasteries and in general weakened the power of the Catholic church. This naturally won him the enmity of the clergy. Popular resentment was aroused when he tried to regulate fairs and festivals so that the number of holidays in the year would be fewer and productivity would be increased. Then he carried out administrative and judicial reorganizations which made for more efficient government but cut into cherished local freedoms.

THE BRABANÇON REVOLT

Joseph responded to the growing dissatisfaction with his policies with a show of force. This only strengthened the resistance and the opposition began to organize. Two important political groups were formed, one led by the conservative Henrik Van der Noot and the other by Francis Vonck, who espoused the ideals of the French Revolution. Their ideas on government differed widely, but they agreed on one point: the Austrians must be driven out of Belgium. In 1789 they published a manifesto declaring that Joseph II, by his repressive actions, had forfeited his right to rule. Revolution followed, and the Austrian forces were compelled to retreat. The province of Brabant declared itself independent, and the other provinces quickly followed suit.

Once victory had been achieved the two political parties had no further point of agreement. The Van der Noot faction, by far the more numerous, wanted to set up a confederation, with the ancient privileges guaranteed to the local branches of government. The Vonckists, on the other hand, wanted a strong central government. The Constitution of the United States of Belgium, issued on January 11, 1790, embodied the ideas of the Van der Noot forces. The Vonckists declined to support it and were soon forced out of the government.

This split in effect destroyed the confederation when it had barely gotten started. Joseph II died in February 1790, and his successor, Leopold II, sent an army to retake the Belgian provinces; in December his forces entered Brussels.

During this same period the prince-bishopric of Liège, which had not been united with the rest of Belgium though it was under Austrian domination, was also the scene of a popular uprising. A liberal government was established, based on the principles of the French Revolution. The Austrians restored the old regime in 1790, but the revolutionary spirit remained strong and the men of Liège were to play an important part in the coming French intervention in Belgium.

FRENCH DOMINATION AND UNION WITH HOLLAND

THE REVOLUTIONARY FRENCH GOVERN-ment at first declared that it had no designs on the Low Countries. This position quickly changed, due in part to the Belgians and men from Liège who had fled to France after the Austrians put down their uprisings.

In January 1792 the two groups got together in Paris and formed the Committee of the United Belgians and Liègeois. Shortly afterward they published a manifesto calling for a free Belgium and proclaiming a liberal constitution based on the French model. Their violent speeches and pamphlets against the Austrians influenced French opinion on the matter of invasion, at least to the point of making it possible to carry out such an operation as a war of liberation, which the Belgians themselves wanted.

Both the Belgian exiles and the Liègeois were prominent in the French forces which entered Belgium in November 1792 and secured an easy victory over the Austrians. The returnees were warmly welcomed, and attempts were made to establish a new government along French lines. However, the liberal programs aroused the opposition of the still powerful conservatives, and a political impasse developed.

The French resorted to force in their attempt to create a sympathetic government, and this aroused sufficient opposition to allow the Austrians to triumph again. Control changed hands several times until, on October 1, 1795, Belgium was formally annexed to France. Liège was joined to the Belgian provinces and ceased to exist as a semi-independent principality. In the same year the French asserted their domination over Holland, though this nation was allowed to retain nominal independence.

French rule was generally unchallenged; the only serious exception was an uprising which began in Flanders in 1798, inspired by the anticlericalism of the new regime. This rebellion was quickly put down. The country benefited from the administrative reforms and expanded civil rights instituted by the French, but any show of Belgian nationalism was firmly discouraged and attempts were made to convert the people into good French citizens.

THE NAPOLEONIC ERA

When Napoleon came to power, legal reforms were introduced and industry and agriculture developed rapidly; in 1801 a concordat was signed which settled the major differences between the French regime and the Catholic church. But in spite of these developments the population grew increasingly hostile to the French. The reasons were much the same as in other countries subject to Napoleon's rule—as his fortunes declined his demands on the manpower and resources of the country grew excessive. Belgium once more became a battlefield—it was at Waterloo in Belgian territory that Napoleon's power was finally crushed.

The people were for the most part relieved that French domination had ended. As things turned out, however, they were only to exchange foreign rule for something not much more appealing.

The United Netherlands

William I, a prince of the House of Orange-Nassau, had become the first king of the Netherlands in 1814, and it was his ambition to unite the northern and southern provinces once again. His argument that such a state would act as a barrier to French expansion appealed to the allied powers. Accordingly, the delegates to the congress which met in Vienna in 1815 to redraw the map of Europe after the collapse of Napoleon's empire dictated the inclusion of the southern provinces in the Kingdom of the Netherlands.

Neither the Dutch nor the Belgian citizenry was given a choice in the matter: the new state was forced on them. The Congress of Vienna stipulated that the constitution contain guarantees to protect the interests of the two populations—equal Dutch and Belgian representation in all branches of government, freedom of religion and the press, and well-defined civil liberties. Like the new state itself, the guarantees soon proved artificial.

Both the Dutch and the Belgians were less than enthusiastic about union. The Belgians even refused to ratify the constitution (Grondwet), and William put it through only by maneuvering to create an artificial majority in the Belgian legislative assembly. Since the two parts of the Netherlands had split in 1579, their differences had become entrenched. Economic rivalry was intense, and the religious bitterness between the Catholic south and the Protestant north remained strong. From the first the two sides were suspicious of each other.

CAUSES OF OPPOSITION

William I tried to formulate policies which would benefit the kingdom as a whole, but his programs were always more popular in the north than in the south. His religious reforms and his attempts to bring education under state control were violently opposed by the southern Catholics, who saw these programs as infringements on their freedom. A compromise was reached in the Concordat of 1827, but it did not really solve the problem.

Much antagonism was aroused among the Belgians over the filling of important government offices. Although in theory the two popula-

tions were to be equally represented, in practice the Dutch held the majority of the top positions. Another cause of dissatisfaction was the national debt—it was divided equally between the two populations, but it had been disproportionately high in the northern provinces and the Belgians resented the added burden the equal division imposed.

A further grievance developed from the fact that the Belgian economy had become based on industry, while in Holland commercial interests prevailed. The south wanted high protectionist tariffs, the north low ones which would stimulate trade. At first the Belgian interests were favored, but in 1821 the Dutch got their way. The result was that the Belgian industrialists who had supported William because of his economic policies were now disenchanted.

As southern opposition to his policies grew more vocal, William reacted by curtailing the freedom of the press. Nothing could have served his cause less well.

REBELLION

Though he failed to unite the Netherlands, William at least succeeded in uniting the Belgians. Since the abortive Brabançon revolt there had been two clearly defined political factions—the conservatives, who were strongly Catholic, and the liberals, who tended to be disinterested in religious issues. They finally made common cause in the former's objection to William's controls of education and the latter's objection to his restrictions on the press. Petitions were presented, but the king yielded only on minor points.

The impetus to rebellion came from the popular revolution in Paris in July 1830. Spontaneous disturbances broke out in Brussels on the night of August 25, after a performance of the opera *The Mute of Portici*, the story of a Neapolitan uprising against the French. Members of the audience took the mes-

sage to heart, and demonstrations began.

The risings spread to other cities, and although William offered concessions if peace was restored the Belgians were beyond considering anything short of administrative separation of the two sections of the kingdom. William could not agree to this, and he sent Dutch forces to Brussels, where they were defeated in a battle which raged from September 23 to 27. The Belgians established a provisional government, and on October 4 independence was proclaimed.

BELGIUM THROUGH WORLD WAR I

THE NEW STATE HAD TWO PRESSING problems—the establishment of a permanent government and international recognition. The former was solved comparatively easily. The Catholic-Liberal coalition agreed that the nation would be a constitutional hereditary monarchy, and on February 7, 1831, a constitution was issued which was one of the most advanced of its times.

International recognition was a different matter. Since there was no native noblemen of sufficient stature to be king and since there was adamant opposition to the selection of a representative of the House of Orange, the Belgians had to look elsewhere in Europe for a monarch. This necessarily involved the interests of the great powers, and it was only after difficult negotiations that a German prince, Leopold of Saxe-Coburg, was chosen.

The French, who had supported the Belgian revolution, wanted to strengthen their influence over the new state; Louis Philippe even contemplated annexation. This aroused the opposition of the other powers, and in the complicated negotiations that ensued Belgian independence was agreed upon, provided that the new nation abided by a number of regulations. These regulations, embodied in the Eighteen Articles drawn up in London, were not entirely favorable to the Belgians, but they saw no choice other than to accept them.

Right: *The 13th-century* Broodhuis, *or* Maison du Roi, *in Brussels, the capital of modern Belgium. Once a center of government, the building today houses an historical museum.*

The Dutch, however, did not assent to the Eighteen Articles, and in the summer of 1831 William's army crossed the newly established frontier and routed Belgian forces. France intervened in favor of the Belgians, England in opposition to the French, and the fate of the new nation went back to the conference table. A new set of 24 stipulations was worked out in the Treaty of London (November 15, 1831), and once again the Belgians had to give their assent. Though this treaty was more advantageous to the Dutch than the Eighteen Articles had been, William I refused to accept it until 1838. There was, however, no more armed conflict.

Major Problems of the New State

In spite of its initial difficulties, the new nation quickly proved to be a stable one. This was in part due to the fact that the Liberal-Catholic coalition held together until government was firmly established. The popularity of Leopold I and his successors was also of considerable help. Serious domestic problems arose, but they were settled peacefully.

EDUCATION

Although the Belgian liberals, in the interest of union with the Catholics, had denounced William I's moves to bring education under state control, most of them privately favored such action. They introduced similar programs in the new nation and met with strong Catholic opposition. The issues caused the Catholic-Liberal coalition to break up, and after 1846, ministries alternated between the two parties. First one and then the other side scored temporary victories; the question of state versus parochial education has not been resolved to this day.

SOCIAL ISSUES

Demands for expansion of the suffrage and effective labor legislation also divided the two parties. The Catholics were in general opposed to both, the Liberals mostly in favor. However, support was not strong enough to satisfy some segments of the population, and in 1885 the socialist Belgian Workers' Party was formed. This quickly became an important political force in the nation. But in spite of increasing pressures, it was not until the 1890s and the first decade of the 20th century that significant progress was made in the areas of labor legislation and expansion of the suffrage.

THE FLEMISH QUESTION

A problem which transcended party lines was the division of the nation into two distinct ethnic groups —the Flemings in the north and the Walloons in the south. The latter, though fewer in number than the former, dominated the government, and their language, French, was the official one of the state. Flemish protests grew so strong that some even advocated partition of the nation, but a series of government concessions kept this movement from becoming dangerous.

INTERNATIONAL RELATIONS

The Treaty of London had guaranteed Belgium's neutrality, a status which proved difficult to maintain. Both France and Germany tried to win the new nation as an ally, and as relations between these two powerful countries deteriorated, Belgium was hard pressed to avoid taking sides. When it became increasingly likely that war would erupt, the Belgian army was reorganized and strengthened. Hopes of preserving neutrality through armed defense, however, were quickly shattered.

World War I

On August 2, 1914, Germany demanded that the Belgians allow its troops to move across their territory to France. The Belgian government firmly refused, but the troops came anyhow. This violation of Belgian neutrality served as the official reason for Britain's entry into World War I.

In spite of heroic resistance, the Belgian forces were no match for the German invaders. Within two months the entire country, except for a small region in the southwest around Yser, was in German hands. The Belgian army, under the leadership of King Albert I, was able to hold this area, but it could not advance until the General Allied offensive began in October 1918.

The German occupation was a harsh one. Industries were dismantled, huge tributes were exacted, necessary food supplies were requisitioned, public opinion was strictly regulated and Belgians who resisted the German authority were deported, imprisoned or executed. The war left the land devastated and the economy in ruins. Because of their sufferings the Belgians made harsher demands for peace terms than did some of the victorious nations which had been less directly affected.

MODERN BELGIUM

BETWEEN THE WARS

The rehabilitation of the country was the most pressing problem in the years following World War I. Recovery was helped by revenues from the Congo, which had been organized as an independent kingdom in 1885 under Leopold II and annexed to Belgium in 1908. The B.L.E.U. (Belgium-Luxembourg Economic Union), formed in 1921, was also beneficial.

A serious setback occurred in 1926. Belgian economic planners had counted too heavily on reparations from Germany and when these were not forthcoming there was an inflationary crisis. Hardly had the currency been stabilized when the world-wide depression began in 1929. This time recovery was slow and painful, but by the late 1930s finances were again in good order and industry was rapidly expanding.

The foremost political problem of the years betweeen the wars was the growth of a number of minority parties. Government coalitions became complex, and cabinet turnovers were frequent, though orderly.

Social legislation made considerable progress during this period. However, the educational question remained troublesome, and the conflict between the Walloons and the Flemings grew in intensity, with the Flemish nationalists winning many adherents to their cause.

On the international scene, Belgian relations with the Kingdom of the Netherlands improved significantly. Modest tariff agreements were concluded, and the two nations began to draw closer together in political matters as well.

WORLD WAR II

Immediately after World War I Belgium abandoned its policy of neutrality and concluded pacts with the Allied powers. In 1936, when it became evident that German strength was once more on the rise, King Leopold III withdrew from these pacts and tried to re-establish the nation's neutrality. Such a position was impossible to maintain, and in 1940 Belgium was once again overrun by the Germans. They controlled the country until late in 1944, and although many Belgian soldiers escaped to join the Allied forces, no major action was possible on Belgian soil before this time.

The Postwar Years

The second German occupation, though not so costly in terms of material destruction, was still more troublesome to Belgium than the first had been. Thousands of citizens were deported, never to return; Nazi requisitions kept basic commodities in desperately short supply. More important, in terms of the postwar years, was the fact that the Nazis had won a sizeable number of collaborators. The majority of these were Flemish nationalists, but there were also many Walloons. Bitterness ran high, and the identification and punishment of collaborators after the war created a tense atmosphere.

Another cause of tension was the controversy over King Leopold III. He had surrendered to the Germans in the belief, he said, that this would ease the sufferings of his people; many citizens attributed his action to less admirable motivations. During the last phase of the war he had been taken to Germany, and there was much opposition when he wanted to return to Belgium and resume his reign. The population was almost equally divided on the matter, and when the issue threatened to split the country, Leopold was persuaded to abdicate in favor of his son Baudouin.

Belgian recovery was rapid after World War II; both industry and agriculture have flourished since the late 1940s. Although the education question and the differences between the Flemings and the Walloons have flared up from time to time, there is every indication that the nation remains a stable one.

The most serious problem of the postwar period concerned the loss of the Congo. In the late 1950s African leaders began to demand political independence and public disturbances broke out in the colony in support of these demands. Rather than become involved in an all-out armed conflict, the Belgian government agreed to grant independence; it went into effect on June 30, 1960. The loss of revenues from the Congo created financial difficulties, and the Belgian government embarked on an austerity program. The people responded to this program with a wave of crippling strikes and public demonstrations, but gradually the crisis passed.

FOREIGN POLICY

In international affairs, the policy of neutrality was again abandoned after World War II. The Brussels Pact of 1948 allied the Low Countries with Britain and France, and in 1949 the Brussels Pact powers entered NATO. Belgium was a charter member of the United Nations and has been active in movements to secure international peace.

The most significant development of Belgian foreign policy in the postwar years has been the advocacy of international cooperation in the economic sphere. This policy was first manifested in the Benelux Union concluded in 1947 with Luxembourg and the Netherlands. Many problems have occurred in this attempt to integrate the economies of the Low Countries, but considerable progress has been made.

The desire for economic union extends beyond the Netherlands region to include all of Western Europe. The Coal and Steel Community, the Common Market and the other organizations set up to increase cooperation among European nations number the Belgians among their most ardent supporters. It is too early to estimate how successful such unions will be, but it is clear Belgium will play a leading role in their future development.

FUNDAMENTAL DATES

15 B.C. Belgium becomes the province of Gallia Belgica in the Roman Empire.

400 A.D. The Netherlands comes under Frankish domination.

843 The Netherlands becomes part of the Kingdom of Lotharingia.

870 The Treaty of Mersen divides the Netherlands between Louis the German and Charles the Bald of France; feudal duchies rise in importance.

1302 Popular forces defeat the aristocrats in the Battle of the Golden Spurs and local governments become more democratic.

1382 The aristocrats triumph at Roosebeke and the popular forces decline in power.

1421-45 Philip the Good, Duke of Burgundy, unites most of the Netherlands under his rule.

1482 Control of the Netherlands passes to the House of Habsburg.

1567 The Duke of Alba arrives in the Netherlands to put down Protestant rebellions.

1579 The League of Arras and the Union of Utrecht are formed, marking the separation of the southern and northern provinces.

1713 Control of the south (Belgium) passes to the Austrian Habsburgs.

1789 Belgium declares its independence, but internal weaknesses in the new state allow the Austrians to regain control.

1795 The Belgian provinces are annexed to France.

1815 The Congress of Vienna joins the Belgian provinces to the Kingdom of the Netherlands.

1830-31 Belgian independence is proclaimed, and, after concessions are made, the new nation is recognized by the major European powers.

1908 The Congo is annexed to Belgium.

1914-18 Belgium is under German occupation during World War I.

1921 An economic union (B.L.E.U.) is formed with Luxembourg.

1940-45 During World War II Belgium is again under German occupation.

1947 The Benelux Union between Belgium, Luxembourg and the Netherlands is formed.

1951 A bitter controversy over King Leopold III is resolved when he abdicates in favor of his son Baudouin.

1960 The Congo is granted independence.

Left: The Virgin Enthroned with the Child, *painted by the great Flemish master Jan van Eyck (c. 1370-c. 1440).*

INTRODUCTION

THE TERMS "THE NETHERLANDS" (literally, the "lands down under") and "The Low Countries" have frequently been used to designate the entire region wedged between Germany and France which now comprises the countries of Belgium, the Netherlands and Luxembourg. Throughout history, the area's strategic coastal position and extensive lowlands, with their lack of natural barriers, have encouraged invasions. The Low Countries have survived the successive domination of the Romans, the Burgundians, the Spanish, the Austrians, the French and the Germans, and these compounded layers of political influence are naturally reflected in the artistic output of the region. Generally speaking, the Germanic influence predominates in the area of the present-day Netherlands (often called Holland) and northern Belgium (Flanders), while the French influence is strongest in southern Belgium.

Belgium and Holland have played significant roles in European artistic development. The arts of the two regions developed along similar lines until the 15th century, when various conflicts arose which resulted, in the following century, in political separation. After this, both countries developed distinct national art forms. In order to clarify the course of artistic development as much as possible, the general characteristics of the early art of the Low Countries as a whole will be treated in this article, while the first portion of *The Netherlands: The Fine Arts* will treat Dutch-born artists and the variations which were peculiar to that region.

THE FINE ARTS

THE ROMANS AND THE FRANKS

THE ROMAN PERIOD

THE NAME BELGIUM DERIVES FROM the Roman "Gallia Belgica," after the

Right: The Madonna of the Firescreen, *probably painted by Robert Campin, the so-called "Master of Flémalle" (c. 1375-1444), although sometimes ascribed to Rogier van der Weyden (c. 1399-1464). Campin is thought to have been an early teacher of Van der Weyden.*

Belgic tribes of Celtic origin who first inhabited the region. The Netherlands became known to the Romans during Julius Caesar's successful thrust to the North Sea in 57 B.C. In 15 B.C., under the reign of Augustus Caesar, the Netherlands was formally added to the long list of imperial provinces and the region underwent a process of Romanization. The frontiers were strongly fortified, roads were laid and buildings were erected, but successive invasions later destroyed almost all traces of Roman civilization.

Even in these ancient times, Belgium was a manufacturing center, and the ladies of Rome prized the famous Manapian cloth woven in Flanders of wool brought from England. Roman roads contributed to the economic development of the Netherlands, linking interior manufacturing centers with the seacoast cities of Leiden and Bruges.

THE KINGDOM OF THE FRANKS

Germanic tribes from the north and east known as the Franks had penetrated deep into the Netherlands by the 4th century. During the period of Frankish rule (c.400-800), Christian religion and civilization spread throughout the Netherlands. The region was unified briefly under the Frankish Merovingian dynasty, but soon disintegrated into a number of unstable, petty kingdoms. In the 8th century Charlemagne re-established a semblance of unity and strengthened French influence upon the culture of the Netherlands, but after his death in 814 a series of Nordic invasions destroyed the churches and monasteries that had been built under Frankish rule. The unsettled conditions of the time were not conducive to artistic development.

THE MIDDLE AGES

THE INABILITY OF THE FRENCH AND German kings to protect their sub-

The Ghent Altarpiece, one of the most ambitious works of religious art ever produced in Belgium, was executed by the brothers Jan and Hubert van Eyck between the years 1420 and 1432. A polyptych of twelve hinged panels, the altarpiece is divided into two main sections: the upper seven panels being devoted to portraits of God the Father, saints, angels and Adam and Eve; the lower five panels being a representation of The Adoration of the Lamb. *Although it has never been fully determined which of the brothers was responsible for which parts of the masterpiece, it is generally agreed that Hubert conceived the plan of the altarpiece, while Jan, the greater artist of the two, was responsible for the final unification of the many parts through the use of light-filled space surrounding the various objects and personages represented. The altarpiece was commissioned for the Cathedral of St. Bavon in Ghent. Its various panels were separated in 1816, but were brought together again, by one of the terms of the Treaty of Versailles, in 1920.*

Romanesque Architecture

Architectural development in the Netherlands followed the general pattern of all of western Europe during the Romanesque period (800-1100). Although the Roman Empire had long since passed into extinction, the Roman principles of construction continued to dictate the general shape and composition of the structures raised until the 10th century, when a daring new use of balance and stress appeared. The Romans had built solidly and without mortar, but later architects learned to use smaller stones imbedded in thick mortar. This technique resulted in lighter and sturdier frameworks which allowed greater freedom of design, larger internal spaces and more complex vaulting systems.

As a whole, the character of Romanesque architecture in Europe was sober. It was, above all, a religious architecture, and decoration was limited. This restraint often gave Romanesque buildings a powerful and impressive appearance.

TWELFTH-CENTURY ARCHITECTURE

In the 12th century, the introduction of an improved system of vaulting greatly simplified the construction of roofs. Where the Romans has used heavy barrel and cross vaults, Romanesque architects arched the four corners of a crossing with stone ribs in what is known as the rib-and-panel system. They then laid thin stone slabs against these ribs to lighten the load carried by the vaults. In the Gothic period, this system was further elaborated by the addition of more ribs and high-pointed arches.

The particular character of Netherlandish Romanesque architecture was largely determined by the materials available to the builders. Throughout the region there was a plentiful supply of red clay for bricks, and granite-like stone and marbles were found in the Belgian hills. Wood was abundant, providing material for roofers and sculptors alike.

The few Romanesque buildings still standing in Belgium were constructed during or after the 10th century, and all are overlaid with successive enlargements and embellishments· of the Gothic period. The most notable of these buildings are the churches of St. Vincent at Solgnes and St. Pierre at Ypres and parts of the cathedral of Tournai. The most important remaining Romanesque secular building in Belgium is the massive castle of the counts of Ghent, built in 1080. Its powerful and severe central tower is characteristic of early Romanesque architecture.

Romanesque Sculpture

Sculpture during the Romanesque period was devoted almost exclusively to the enhancement of architecture. Wood-carving was decidedly crude, and the most typical motifs were stylized animal and plant forms. The cathedral door at Tournai, called the *Porte Mantile,* is the most important work of early Flemish sculpture. Romanesque baptismal fonts have survived in churches at Bastogne, Zedlichen and Gossau, and the magnificent copper font in the church of St. Bartholomew at Liège (made by Ranier de Huy in 1113) indicates the high level of craftsmanship reached by the artisans working in the mineral-rich regions of the southeast.

Ivory-carving was also highly developed. The best existing example of this delicate art is. the 9th-century Bible-cover of St. Nicaise, in the cathedral of Tournai.

Romanesque Painting

Painting during the Romanesque period was limited to fresco decorations in churches and illuminated manuscripts. Unfortunately, none of the frescoes have survived the ravages of time and the damp climate of the region.

The art of illumination was brought to Belgium directly from England and Ireland by missionary monks, as early as the 6th century. The Celtic

jects after the collapse of Charlemagne's empire led to the rise of the feudal system. Local noblemen built the sturdy fortifications which later became towns and cities. Bruges, then connected to the North Sea by a long arm of the river Zwijn (now filled with silt), became a central market for European trade. Liège developed into a center of iron forging and manufacture, while Ghent and Ypres were lively, prosperous cloth-manufacturing cities. All of these communities grew up on the ruins left by the Norsemen, and their buildings were frequently composed of fragments gathered from the destroyed buildings of the past.

monks had developed an extraordinarily individual kind of illumination consisting of intricate initial letters that often covered an entire page. These letters are composed of incredibly delicate interlacing spirals, bands and knots which surround bird and animal motifs. Other manuscripts were brought from Rome, and large numbers of illustrated religious books of this period are still in existence.

THE GOTHIC PERIOD (1100-1500)

BY THE 12TH CENTURY, FLANDERS had become a region of considerable economic importance, and a prosperous middle class had grown up. The wealth of the region attracted the French, who finally broke the back of Flemish resistance in 1328 and made Flanders a fief of France. With the marriage of Philip the Bold, of the house of Valois, to Margaret of Flanders in 1384, the Low Countries came under the rule of the Burgundian dukes. Political unity and economic prosperity created a climate which was extremely favorable to artistic development, and there ensued what is known as the "golden age of medieval culture" in the Low Countries, centered around the luxurious Burgundian court.

Gothic Architecture

With the rising prosperity of the towns, secular architecture became increasingly important, and these types of buildings began to benefit from the care and attention to detail previously reserved for religious structures. The powerful guilds (unions of craftsmen) built magnificent guild halls, and weavers and

merchants of competing towns vied with each other to raise town halls which reflected the social progress and wealth they had won through hard work and shrewd management of their businesses. The assorted municipal and domestic buildings of the Gothic period stand as monuments to the ideals of the freedom-loving burghers of the Netherlands and the relatively stable political conditions of the times. Designed for commerce, exchange and good living, they contrast sharply with the forbidding fortresses erected during the same years in Italy by rival mercantile families.

Special features of secular architecture in the Netherlands were dictated by the climate. Extremes of cold and heat, a heavy annual rainfall, frequently overcast skies and forceful sea winds had to be taken into consideration by the architects. Therefore, roofs were pitched at steep angles to throw off rain and snow, many windows pierced the façades to admit all possible light and warmth from the sun, solid shutters were provided to shield the windows against the wind and cold and walled courtyards offered airy shelters protected from the winds.

Brick was the most practical and most frequently used material.

One of the most interesting examples of secular architecture in Flanders was the Cloth Hall at Ypres, built between 1200 and 1304, which was probably the finest medieval mercantile building in all of Europe. Its long, dignified, horizontal lines and rhythmically repeated windows and statues were crowned with a high, pitched roof and a massive, turreted tower. The Cloth Hall was destroyed by the Germans during World War I, but it has since been partially rebuilt.

TOWN HALLS

The rich embellishments of the town hall at Bruges (1377) demonstrate the importance of this city in the commerce of the times. The façade is pierced with elegant traceried windows, and a series of statues of the counts of Flanders stands in niches between them. The huge upper room, where the burghers and citizens gathered to conduct the affairs of their city, is a typical feature of town halls in the Netherlands. Bruges, meaning "city of bridges", is webbed with canals which once transported raw goods and industrial products to and from the sea. Although Bruges is now a slow-moving and delightful museum of a town, it was once the busy, wealthy and cosmopolitan capital of the dukes of Burgundy, where the riches of England were bartered for the riches of the East. The beautiful and ornate houses, halls and streets echo Bruges' Gothic hour of glory.

Other impressive town halls are found in all parts of Belgium. The 15th-century hôtel de ville in Brussels is the masterpiece of two of Belgium's finest architects, Jacques van Thienen and Jan van Ruysbroeck. The Gothic tower which divides the façade into two parts is often considered the most beautiful in the entire country. The town hall in Louvain, designed by Mathieu de Layens, was built in the general shape of a chapel. The intricacy of its sculptured decoration makes it resemble an enormous carved jewel box.

RELIGIOUS ARCHITECTURE

Although most innovation and attention during the Gothic period in the Netherlands was concentrated upon secular architecture, several impressive ecclesiastical structures were erected. Gothic ecclesiastical architecture of the Middle Ages was characterized by the use of spires, belfries and towers, and these elements were especially effective against the backdrop of the relatively flat landscape of the Netherlands. The bell tower was often the most elaborate feature of a Belgian Gothic church, and elaborate carillons announced the time of day, summoned people to worship and also signaled danger. The high-pointed ogive arch became a characteristic mark of Gothic style, while stained-glass windows formed the chief decoration for church interiors.

The black-marble Tournai Cathedral, built between 1066 and 1338, exhibits both Romanesque and Gothic architectural styles, while the cathedral at Antwerp, begun in 1352 and completed in 1411, is probably the most imposing of all Belgian churches. Its nave rises 92 feet into the air, and its interior is lighted by magnificent stained-glass windows. A single enormous bell tower (400 feet high) on the west front is richly adorned with the florid sculptured detail typical of late Gothic architecture.

Gothic Sculpture

During the Gothic period, sculpture occupied a prominent position among the arts. The rigorous training required by the guilds raised Belgian sculpture and masonry to a high level of accomplishment, and these crafts were influenced by the styles imported from France by the Burgundian dukes. Ornamentation in wood, stone and metal was applied to every possible area on the façades and interiors of both secular and ecclesiastical buildings. Wood-carving was a highly developed craft, and the best-known of the Gothic wood-carvers was Jan Borreman (c.1479-1522).

The excellent workmanship of this time is exemplified by Quentin Massys' beautiful, late-Gothic, iron well-head in the city of Antwerp. The fireplace, a traditional gathering place in homes and civic halls, became a decorative focal point in architecture. Chimney pieces became as elaborately carved as the cathedral altar screens, and were decorated with heraldic emblems and niches containing effigies of noblemen.

One of the most beautiful pieces of medieval craftsmanship in the world is the small Shrine of St. Ursula in the Hospital of St. John in Bruges. This exquisitely carved and painted miniature Gothic chapel stands about three feet high, and its steeply pitched roof is delicately ornamented with lacy crests and pinnacles. The arcaded sides frame six miniature paintings by Hans Memling which depict episodes from the life of St. Ursula. This shrine represents a superb unity of sculpture, architecture and painting.

Hunters in the Snow, one of the most memorable paintings of Pieter Brueghel the Elder (c. 1520-69), universally considered one of the greatest artists in European history. The mountains in the background were painted from the artist's memory of the Alps, which he had visited as a youth. The remainder of the scene is typical of the Flemish landscape in winter.

Stained Glass

The art of stained glass became popular during the Gothic age and achieved its highest expression in the 13th-century French cathedrals. The French cathedral workshops enjoyed such renown that their craftsmen were much in demand in other European countries as expert consultants. Some naturally went to Flanders in the service of the dukes of Burgundy, and Gothic liturgical writers described their windows as "lights of grace and crystals of the Faith." As the medieval cathedral grew taller and more delicate, the glass window became an increasingly essential part of the structure. Cathedral walls grew lighter, stone was balanced more precariously and the richness of the colored windows increased as the Gothic style developed.

The stained-glass technique, like painting, depends upon a knowledge of color, line, drawing, modeling and the handling of paint. Thus, the stained-glass windows may be viewed as the earliest paintings of Gothic times. In the Low Countries, the best examples of this French-inspired art are the windows of the cathedral of Antwerp and the cathedral of St. Gudule in Brussels.

Tapestry

In the cool climate of the north, the warmth and richness of wall tapestry was favored over fresco art, and Belgium played a leading role in the production of this magnificent Gothic art form. Tapestry weaving is an extremely slow and costly operation, requiring the services of a painter-designer and many weavers whose sensitivity to myriad variations of color and texture is equal to the task of translating the painter's ideas into wool and silk. Because of their tremendous costliness, tapestries were available only to royalty or to the very wealthy.

Belgium had been a center of weaving since Roman times. During the Gothic period, this long tradition was raised to the level of a fine art, inspired by the French *tapisseries*

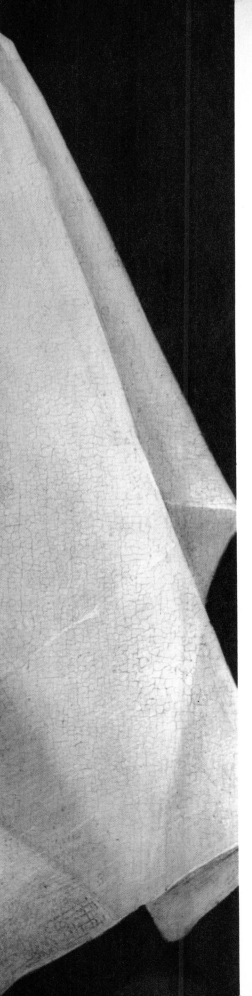

and spurred by the demands of the well-to-do Burgundian dukes. The earliest and largest of surviving tapestries is the *Apocalypse*, made for the castle at Angers in 1375 by order of the duke of Anjou and now preserved in the museum of Angers. This masterpiece was woven by French workmen, but was designed by the Flemish artist Hennequin de Bruges (sometimes called Jean de Bandol). De Bruges was famous as an illuminator, and his designs for the Angers tapestry are apparently derived from late 13th-century French illuminated manuscripts. The huge *Apocalypse* (432 ft. long) consists of 7 separate tapestries containing 90 pictures. Seventy of the pictures are still intact.

The theme of the *Apocalypse* is religious, but most Gothic tapestries were devoted to secular subjects. Their purpose was to delight the eye and the imagination, and they reveal the life and thoughts of the times in their curious blending of myth and reality.

Book Illumination

In the Gothic period, the art of illumination was directly influenced by stained-glass windows. In style and composition, the pages of illuminated manuscripts are often miniature adaptations of the shimmering splendor of the church windows; even the frameworks are replicas of the architectural elements surrounding the windows. Typical motifs, such as stylized flowers and foliage, transposed from stone and glass to gold-leaf and paint, filled the brightly colored pages.

The art of illumination owes much of its glory to the patronage of the art-loving dukes of Burgundy and Anjou. The famous Jean de France, Duc de Berry, was especially fond of calendar books (Books of Hours), and the greatest French and Flemish illustrators were on his payroll. After commissioning a book, the duke would hover about the artist, supervising every page. If his affairs suddenly called him elsewhere, the Duke would snatch the unfinished book from the hands of the artist and take it to his next stopping place, where he would order another of his illuminators to take up the work. Thus, his books are frequently the product of several artists.

Without question the supreme achievement in the field of illumination during this period is *Les Très Riches Heures du Duc de Berry* (The Very Rich Hours of the Duke of Berry). The pages of this manuscript, painted for Jean de France by the three Flemish brothers Pol, Jan and Hermann Limburg, are covered with enchanting landscapes which describe the various seasons and aspects of contemporary life in detail. The exquisite works of the Limburg brothers have the same elegant sophistication which characterized the works of the Italian painters of the Sienese school.

When the Duc de Berry died in 1416, Pol de Limburg was working on *Les Très Belles Heures de Notre-Dame* (The Most Glorious Hours of Our Lady), but he died a year later before completing the manuscript. Experts sometimes attribute the completion of this beautiful work to the two famous Van Eyck brothers, who inaugurated a new era in Belgian painting.

Early Gothic Painting

In the Low Countries, architecture was extremely influential in determining the course taken by the painter's art. The many windows which pierced the walls of Netherlandish buildings discouraged the creation of frescoes and promoted the development of miniature painting and small easel pictures. Furthermore, the wealthy art patrons of the Netherlands were frequently on the move for commercial or political reasons. They therefore preferred transportable art: tapestries which could be folded, books and jewels which could be packed in a box and small pictures which could be slipped into a casing in any emergency.

During the prosperous years of Burgundian rule, the princes replaced the priests as the leading patrons of the arts and introduced the refined and rather secular tastes of the French court into the Netherlands. At the same time, the many wealthy Italian merchants who visited the Flemish cities were likewise in the market for fine art. These demands prompted the painters to expand and enrich

Detail from Portrait of a Young Woman, *by the Flemish master Rogier van der Weyden (c. 1399-1464). Similar to his older contemporary, Jan van Eyck, in his exquisite attention to detail, Van der Weyden was the warmer and more human of the two artists. A deeply spiritual quality, which is enhanced rather than overshadowed by his technical mastery, pervades his portraits and religious works.*

their craft. In previous times, the art of painting had been limited to the illumination of manuscripts, to frescoes (which have since disintegrated because of the damp climate) and to designs for stained-glass windows or tapestries. In the late 14th century, as the secular spirit burgeoned, Flemish painting finally began to come of age.

The earliest identifiable artist from Flanders, Melchior Broederlam, was in the service of Philip the Bold. His only undisputed work, the shutters of an altar screen in the Carthusian House of Champol near Dijon, was painted between 1394 and 1399. His treatment of the Presentation at the Temple and the Flight into Egypt in this work show his familiarity with Parisian courtly tastes, while his bright and charming vistas of the countryside paralleled the techniques and spirit of manuscript illuminators.

THE GOLDEN AGE OF PAINTING

BY THE 15TH CENTURY, THE PICTORIAL arts of the Low Countries vied with those of Italy in excellence. A long tradition of miniature painting and manuscript illumination was expanded into the field of altar panels, and subsequent Netherlandish painters manifested a singular love for delicate detail. Due to the rise of the mercantile classes and the development of the oil technique, the subject matter chosen by the 15th-century painters dealt increasingly with the common man and his way of life.

The Van Eycks

The greatest painters of the century were Jan van Eyck (c. 1370-c. 1440) and his brother Hubert (c. 1366-1426). Jan and Hubert often collaborated in their work. Both were extraordinarily talented, but most experts agree that Jan was the more significant artist.

Although oil had been used in painting for at least a hundred years before the time of the Van Eycks, the technique was a very primitive one. The quality of the oils was so poor that they could be used only for backgrounds; tempera paints had to be employed to depict human flesh. Jan van Eyck immensely widened the possibilities of pictorial art by developing oils and varnishes which could convey rich, golden colors and a jewel-like precision of detail. His exact technique is not known, but it is usually thought that he combined tempera and oils.

The Van Eyckian style, which continued almost unaltered until the time of Rubens, depended directly upon the development of a technique in which light penetrated the surface of the picture and was refracted from the opaque layers beneath the topmost glazes. The flat, opaque quality of the conventionally used, water-based tempera made stylization necessary, but the depth of color and spatial effects possible with the oil technique permitted realism.

THE GHENT ALTARPIECE

One of the most famous works of the Van Eyck brothers was the *Ghent Altarpiece*, commissioned in 1420, which consists of 12 separate panels hinged together. The upper

Portrait of a Man, *by Joos van Cleve (c. 1480-1540). One of the so-called Antwerp Mannerists, Van Cleve became well-known for his realistic portraits and religious paintings. Highly talented but not the most original of artists, he usually copied the styles of other masters, particularly Leonardo da Vinci.*

7 panels are devoted to portraits of God the Father, saints, angels and Adam and Eve, while the 5 lower panels form a panorama called *The Adoration of the Lamb* (see pages 74 and 75). As far as experts can determine, the original concept of the altarpiece was Hubert's. In addition, Hubert is credited with the painting of the lower part of the central panel of *The Adoration of the Lamb,* while the upper part—which depicts groups of bishops and virgins against an exquisitely detailed rustic background—is attributed to Jan. It is virtually impossible to determine which brother painted the rest of the panels, but it is fairly certain that Jan finished the elaborate composition after the death of Hubert and is responsible for achieving the final unification of the many parts by surrounding objects with light-filled space.

JAN VAN EYCK'S PORTRAITS

Jan van Eyck was trained as a book illuminator, and a number of his pages show early evidence of his genius ; the rendering of detail is masterful, the hand is sure and the eye is selective. Later, Jan turned to portraiture, creating highly realistic studies of individuals in their natural surroundings. The details found in these portraits, whether of saints or of common man, reveal his subjects' patterns of life.

One of the most beautiful portraits in the history of painting is *Giovanni Arnolfini and His Wife* (National Gallery, London), painted by Jan van Eyck in 1434 (see page 76). Arnolfini, a wealthy Italian merchant, ordered this picture to commemorate his marriage. In the Netherlands at that time, a couple might contract a marriage without the presence of a priest. This solemn and tender picture shows the couple standing in their home, in the subdued light from the windows. The single candle which burns in the chandelier above their heads symbolizes the presence of God, while the small dog on the floor between them is a symbol of fidelity. A spherical mirror reflects the couple from the back, while the wooden clogs, the furniture, and the light coming through the leaded window panes are painted in an amazingly realistic manner.

Jan van Eyck's work may be regarded as an early harbinger of the new idea of the world growing out of the Gothic age: the celebra-

A view of the Grote Markt, Antwerp's main square, showing the famous 16th-century Town Hall on the left and, at center, the Brabo fountain erected in the late 19th century. The Town Hall, designed by Cornelis Floris and constructed during the years 1561-65, displays the architect's debt to the Italian style then so much in vogue throughout Europe.

tion of man and his life on earth as significant and beautiful. Van Eyck lived in a very religious time, despite its emphasis upon commerce and good living. In both his sacred and secular paintings, there is a perfect balance of the spiritual and physical worlds. Above all, his art sweeps aside traditional conventions dictated by the Church and depicts reality.

Petrus Christus and the Master of Flémalle

After Jan van Eyck's death, his position as leading painter of Bruges was taken over by his follower Petrus Christus. His works lack originality, but his portraits are competent and sometimes charming. He often presented holy personages as simple folk, and his *Portrait of a Monk* (Metropolitan Museum, New York) is one of his most successful paintings in the Van Eyckian style.

One of Jan van Eyck's contemporaries was the Master of Flémalle, now identified as Robert Campin (c. 1375-1444), who represented the Latin-influenced art native to the region of Tournai. In about 1420, Campin was elected head of the guild of painters in that city. His earliest paintings are vigorous, severe and almost primitive in character, in the tradition of the Franco-Flemish illuminators (see page 73). The realistic landscapes and interiors in typical portraits such as *St. John the Baptist and Heinrich Werl* and *St. Barbara* describe the world of his time. The works of the Master of Flémalle, which have only recently come to light, influenced those of Jan van Eyck, and Rogier van der Weyden.

Van der Weyden

Next to Jan van Eyck, Rogier van der Weyden (c. 1399-1464) is one of the most significant and influential Belgian painters of the 15th century. Although data on his early years are scarce, there is reason to believe that he entered the workshop of Robert Campin in Tournai in 1427 and became a master painter in 1432. Later, he set up his own workshop in the city of Brussels.

The art of Van der Weyden is an intellectual and spiritual one. Although he worked in a more traditional framework than Van Eyck, his concepts are more poetic and richer in personal interpretations. Van der Weyden carefully selected and controlled his backgrounds, to make them represent the mood of his religious scenes.

In his earlier works, executed soon after 1430, Van der Weyden's technique is similar to that of the Master of Flémalle. Later, he painted terse and almost abstract images of nature. One of the best known of his earlier compositions is the stunning *Descent from the Cross* (The Prado, Madrid). This work is rendered almost in the manner of a relief sculpture, with the subjects isolated from the background. Indeed, there is no attempt to depict natural surroundings. The ten figures are "carved" in a tightly packed arrangement against a plain gold field. They display a restrained, almost poised grief, like players in a classic tragedy. *Descent from the Cross* was painted soon after the artist settled in Brussels, and gained immediate fame throughout Europe.

Van der Weyden visited Italy around 1450, and his contact with the late-Gothic and early-Renaissance artists of Rome, Florence and other centers gave an aristocratic flavor to his art. The knowledge he acquired from the Italian masters subsequently led to his subtle use of space and color.

In Van der Weyden's mature religious works, he detaches his sacred figures from the world by placing them in theatrical surroundings designed to emphasize his mystical concept of the Christian legend. During this later period, he painted many sober and formal portraits in which the details of the costumes, the positioning of the hands or the fall of a veil became so carefully studied that they vied with the facial expression for the attention of the spectator. This style may be seen in his *Portrait of a Young Woman* (National Gallery, London). The beauty of the girl is as precise as the mathematical arrangement of hands, clothes and accessories (see page 80). Prints and copies popularized Van der Weyden's style in Germany, Spain and France, and he was the most imitated Netherlandish artist of the 15th century.

St. Jerome in the Wilderness, by Joachim de Patinir (c. 1475-1524). Patinir, a pioneer in landscape painting, often reduced the specifically human or religious content of his works to a minor scene or episode set against a vast and overwhelming landscape. His figures and small towns seem all but lost in the grandiose and dramatic natural environment of which they form a small, though significant, part.

Late Fifteenth-Century Painting

Few of the artists of the late 15th century known as "Flemish masters" were actually born in Belgium. Most were natives of Germany and Holland who settled in the artistic centers of Bruges, Louvain and Antwerp to gain the advantages offered to artists in those thriving cities. During this period, most painters devoted themselves to refining and perfecting the ideas of Van Eyck and Van der Weyden rather than cultivating original forms of expression.

DIERIK BOUTS

One of the most influential painters of the late 15th century was Dierik Bouts (c.1410-75), whose early art is strongly reminiscent of the work of Van der Weyden. There is evidence that Bouts was born in Haarlem, but it is known that he left his home at an early age to live in Louvain, where he did most of his work. After reaching maturity, Bouts managed to free himself from the powerful domination of the Van der Weyden cult, and his attention to detail and textural variations in works such as *Annunciation, Adoration of the Kings* and *The Nativity* was closer to the work of Van Eyck.

The figures in Bouts' larger compositions and portraits were drawn realistically, rather than being lean, angular and emaciated like those of Van der Weyden. Although Bouts was never very original, his passionate attention to landscape, his delight in color and his precise attention to detail make his competent art noteworthy.

VAN DER GOES

With the exception of Jan van Eyck himself, Hugo van der Goes (c.1440-82) was the greatest pioneer of the 15th-century realistic devotional picture, and his intensity of expression was new in Flemish art. While most northern painters confined themselves to small surfaces, Goes stretched out the spaces, enlarged the patterns and created monumentality where others were content with preciosity. His style forecasts the Brueghel manner in landscape painting.

Goes became a master painter in the city of Ghent in 1465, and began his largest and most significant work, the *Portinari Altarpiece,* in about 1475. The dimensions of this painting, which was commissioned by the Italian merchant Tommaso Portinari,

The Money Changer and His Wife, *by Quentin Massys (c. 1466-1530), one of the greatest of the Flemish* genre *painters. Massys was little influenced by Italian painting, which markedly altered the style of many of his contemporaries. Throughout his career he remained faithful to local artistic traditions. His scenes of everyday life and domestic interiors are characterized by a strong sense of realism. Massys, like many of his Flemish contemporaries, depicted numerous objects and everyday accessories in his paintings, to help define the social status of the persons depicted.*

are vast for a northern painting. The central panel alone measures 10 feet by 8 feet 2 inches.

In this work the artist has presented an original and daring interpretation of the timeworn story of the adoration of the shepherds (see page 77). In the center, the Virgin looms over the emaciated and helpless Christ Child. Arranged about her are three groups of magnificently dressed angels, drawn to a smaller scale than the mortals, while on the fringe to the right is a group of shepherds and on the left is Joseph. Goes' presentation of the devoted shepherds is especially interesting; the serenity of their facial expressions contrasts sharply with their rugged appearance. Portraits of the Portinari family decorate the wings on either side of the central panel.

The *Portinari Altarpiece* was painted at the height of Goes' creative powers, and his confidence in his

own technical control was unhesitating. Some of his later works are less moving. In the last years of his life, Goes left Ghent and entered a monastery near Brussels, where he was treated as a celebrity. Before his death, his mind became totally deranged.

MEMLING

Hans Memling (c.1430-95) was born in Mainz in Germany, but spent at least half of his life in Bruges, where he was steadily and profitably employed. Memling's art is at its best in his many serene portraits and placid biblical scenes. He tended to submerge all else in the over-all decorative effect, and his works show the influence of Van der Weyden. His renown and wealth surpassed even that of Jan van Eyck, and Goes' patron, Tommaso Portinari, had no less than three portraits of himself done by Memling.

Detail from **The Fall of Icarus,** *by Pieter Brueghel the Elder. The narrative content of the painting is almost wholly subordinated to the treatment of the landscape and the incidental figures of men and animals. Icarus himself, already fallen into the sea after his plunge from the heavens, can be partially seen, with his legs kicking out of the water, in the lower right-hand corner between the boat and the shore.*

The *Madonna and Child with Angels* (National Gallery, Washington D.C.) is one of Memling's successful pictures. Its scenic background is representative of the Flemish countryside, and the castle seen in the distance may well be that of the nobleman who commissioned the painting for his private chapel. The Madonna sits in the center foreground, slender and unruffled, holding the lean and helpless Christ Child. Angels on either side attend the Child.

The aristocratic and graceful composition of this painting is full of the symbolism typical of Gothic art. One angel offers an apple, the symbol of man's fall, to the Child, while the Child points to a passage in the open Bible on the Virgin's lap, fore-telling his own appearance on earth. The second angel plays a harp, symbolizing the music of the spheres. Above the heads of the group is an arch carved with grapes, a symbol of man's redemption. As in all of Memling's work, the surface of the panel is enamel-like and flawless, and the colors are cool and restrained.

Some of Memling's most charming work appears in the famous Shrine of St. Ursula in the Memling Museum at St. John's Hospital in Bruges. This work has been discussed under Gothic sculpture.

DAVID

The work of Gerard David (c. 1460-1523) is typical of the competent, conservative and imitative style which prevailed in Belgian art at the end of the 15th century. David left his birthplace in southern Holland at an early age and went to Bruges, which was then the liveliest center of art in the north. His paintings, although obviously derived from the works of Rogier van der Weyden and Jan van Eyck, are on the whole well integrated and structured. His figures are solid, lacking Memling's sentiment, and he commonly mingles devotional and genre themes.

His *Rest During the Flight Into Egypt* (National Gallery, Washington D.C.) is harmonious and painstaking in its depiction of nature. The figures of the Madonna and the Child are delicately drawn, and the subdued colors create an atmosphere of calm and meditation. In this scene, nature, as a manifestation of the divine, is neat and orderly. This concept of nature, introduced during the early part of the 15th century, was fully accepted by David's time.

THE SIXTEENTH CENTURY

Architecture and Sculpture

IN RELIGIOUS AND SECULAR ARCHItecture and sculpture, the ardent Gothic spirit remained a dominant influence in Belgium well into the 16th century, while the rest of Europe was already responding to the Italian Renaissance. At the end of the 15th century, to escape French domination, the Belgians allied themselves to the Spanish royal family through a series of prudent political marriages. As a result, Spanish influence began to be felt in the arts of Belgium.

The Bourse (exchange) at Antwerp, built in 1531, stubbornly retains the Gothic inspiration in the intricately webbed vaulting of the ceilings, while the trifoil arcading around the courtyard is a Moorish characteristic resulting from the Spanish political ascendency. Another example of Spanish influence is the bulbous turret covering the crossing in the famous cathedral at Antwerp.

Sculpture of the period also continued to follow Gothic styles. It was generally realistic, but grew more and more decorative. In the latter part of the 16th century, sculptors began to introduce Italian-inspired classical motifs.

Painting

By the 16th century, the bold achievements of Van Eyck, Goes and Van der Weyden had gone through two generations of refining and reshaping. Lesser painters began to imitate the 15th-century geniuses with blatant carelessness—not simply repeating their techniques poorly, but aping their compositions in a slipshod manner. At the same time, there was a great demand for Flemish painting in Spain, Germany and Scandinavia. In the tide of easy money, painters were guided more by ambition than inspiration, artists vied with one another in search of novelty and styles changed like the weather. The Gothic style began to degenerate into a kind of mockery of itself and the classical forms of the Italian Renaissance were popularized but hardly assimilated. The names of Massys, Patinir and Brueghel stand out against the general mediocrity of this transitional period.

MASSYS

The refined and elegant Quentin Massys (c.1466-1530) spent most of his life in the city of Louvain. His early works were patterned upon the style of Dierik Bouts, while his more mature paintings show the influence of the Van Eycks and in their treatment of the human figure foreshadow the style that was to become popular in the 17th century. In examining Massys' work, it is interesting to note that he deforms and distorts characters of a brutal nature, such as the mob in *Christ Presented to the People,* equating evil with ugliness. In contrast, the majority of his "nice" people are handsome and reserved, and bear a marked similarity. It is thought that Massys designed models for tapestries, and that this work influenced his painting.

One of Massys' more famous works is the *Altarpiece of St. Anne* (Brussels Museum). Although this painting has lost much of its rich color from overcleaning, Massys' composition and realistic treatment of personalities have been preserved. The carefully posed arrangement of the beautifully costumed Virgin and Child and their attendants in the central panel is reminiscent of tapestry design.

The Money Changer and His Wife (1514) is one of Massys' most interesting paintings (see page 85). The figures are almost lifesize, and the details of the composition reveal much about their way of life. The wife is reading a fine illuminated manuscript while the husband weighs the value of coins in a balance scale, and the couple is surrounded by valuable objects appropiate to their manner of existence. This picture is in the best tradition of Flemish *genre* painting, in which accessories help to define an individual's character.

PATINIR

Joachim de Patinir (c.1475-1524) was the first Netherlandish painter to devote himself exclusively to landscape painting and his wonderful mixture of fantasy and naturalistic detail presages the more naturalistic landscapes of Brueghel. Patinir's ability in this relatively untried field of

Detail, showing Mary Magdalene, from Rogier van der Weyden's The Crucifixion, *painted in about 1440. The simple yet startlingly realistic rendition of the face and figure conveys in full the artist's compassion for the event and persons portrayed. Yet, despite this communication of emotion, Van der Weyden displays extraordinary artistic restraint, a coolness in the midst of passion, that allows the observer simultaneously to participate in the tragedy and to stand apart from it in contemplation.*

painting was so famous in the north that two of his greatest contemporaries, Joos van Cleve and Quentin Massys, provided the figures for his spacious and fantastic vistas.

Patinir was greatly influenced by his near-contemporary in Holland Hieronymus Bosch (see *The Netherlands: The Fine Arts*). He usually placed his horizon very high, giving the spectator a grand view which encompassed all sorts of incidental episodes. He was the first painter to introduce clouds of every shape and color, and their formations emphasize his wide country vistas by receding in stripes parallel to the picture plane. Three of the finest paintings from his mature period are now in the Prado Museum: *The Temptation of St. Anthony* (painted with the co-operation of Quentin Massys), *Rest During the Flight into Egypt* and *St. Jerome in the Wilderness* (see page 84).

Patinir's landscapes reflect his subjects. For example, he accents the trees and the soft massing of foliage when painting the Virgin, while he emphasizes the clumps of dry and inanimate rocks when depicting the ascetic St. Jerome. Although the achievements of this first Flemish landscape artist are less memorable than those of Heironymus Bosch, he had a profound influence upon later painters of idyllic and descriptive landscapes. His small, cool landscapes have much in common with Antwerp Mannerism.

THE ANTWERP MANNERISTS

During the 16th century, the styles of the Italian Renaissance became increasingly important in Belgian painting. There was a growing interest in the hitherto ignored nude figure, landscapes and in Italian architectural forms and figure types. The Antwerp Mannerists, along with their contemporaries in Bruges and other cities, were among the earliest painters who attempted to merge the formal style of the High Renaissance with northern Gothic naturalism.

Joos van Cleve (c.1480-1540) became a master painter in the Antwerp guild in 1511. He was known for his sober and realistic portraits and his paintings of the Virgin and Child. He was a skillful colorist, but usually copied the styles of other masters, particularly the delicate style of the Italian Leonardo da Vinci.

Van Cleve was at his best in formal portraits of royalty. Contemporary chronicles reveal that he was summoned to Paris by King Francis I to paint a number of members of the royal family. One of these portraits, *Queen Eleanor of France,* is now in the Kunsthistorisches Museum in Vienna, while his well-known portrait *Henry VIII* is now at Hampton Court Palace, near London. For an example of his style, see *Portrait of a Man* (page 82).

The Death of the Virgin, which closely follows the Italian style in religious painting, is typical of Van Cleve's larger and less successful compositions. His exaggerated use of movement in the posturing of the figures destroys much of the dignity of the scene and shows that the Renaissance forms were not yet properly assimilated into the northern tradition.

Bernaert van Orley (c.1492-1542) was called in his time the "Raphael of the Netherlands", though his interpretation of that great painter's style has been judged something less than successful by later critics. Two of his better portraits, *Georges de Zelle* (Brussels Museum) and *Charles V* (Budapest Museum), are precisely

A view of part of the house of Peter Paul Rubens in Antwerp. Rubens designed the building himself and lived in it from 1615 until his death in 1640. Despite his enormous productivity as a painter, Rubens found time to design and decorate numerous buildings and churches that won recognition as architectural masterpieces.

executed in the tradition of finely detailed Netherlandish art. Orley was a prolific designer of tapestries and stained glass as well as a painter. His altarpiece *The Ruin of the Children of Job* (Brussels Museum) clearly reflects the influence of Raphael. The work is an example of the exaggerated movement favored by the Italian Mannerists, which began to show itself in Flemish painting at this time.

PROVOST AND GOSSAERT

Jan Provost (1462-1529) became a master painter at Bruges in 1494, and introduced a taste for pleasant religious scenes into the conservative calm of that city. His works were frequently charming despite the fact that his desire to please resulted in rather overcrowded and monotonous compositions. *The Virgin and Child with Angels, Prophets and Sibyls* (The Hermitage, Leningrad) is typical of his works.

Jan Gossaert (c.1478-c.1533), also called Mabuse (after his birthplace), joined the St. Luke's guild in Antwerp in 1503. In the service of Philip of Burgundy, he traveled to Italy, where he was strongly influenced by the Italian interest in the nude figure and ancient Greek and Roman sculpture. He was the first Belgian painter to introduce classical subjects with nude figures into Flanders, a contribution of profound importance to Flemish artistic development. Gossaert's understanding of the Italian forms was superficial, however, and he often tacked them almost haphazardly onto the traditional styles of Van Eyck. He introduced flamboyant, overabundant detail, particularly in architectural settings, and was more successful with his portraits than with his showy figure compositions.

PIETER BRUEGHEL THE ELDER

The most original Belgian painter of the 16th century was Pieter Brueghel the Elder (c.1520-69), who reflected the growing secularization of his time in complicated paintings which blended mythical and realistic qualities. Sometimes called the "Peasant Brueghel," he was the founder of a family of painters. His sons, Pieter Brueghel the Younger and Jan Brueghel, did not approach their father's genius. A marked relationship between the landscapes of Pieter

Brueghel the Elder and Hieronymus Bosch has been cited by many critics, and it is possible that Brueghel was trained by a student of Bosch.

In 1551, when Brueghel became a member of St. Luke's guild in Antwerp, the city's tastes were dominated by second-rate painters working in a florid style imitative of the Italian Mannerists. Brueghel's satiric and illustrative art was conspicuously lacking in "the grand manner," and was not appreciated by the great majority of his contemporary critics and fellow artists. The warmth and robust humor of his paintings, however, made them popular with the Humanists and the German princes.

Brueghel began his career as a designer of engravings. This early training, coupled with his keen intelligence and ironic humor, stood him in good stead when he took up painting. In spite of the fact that Italian art was well known in Belgium by this time, Brueghel seems to have been little influenced by it.

It is probable that many of Brueghel's works, particularly his watercolors painted on fine linen, have been lost in the course of time, and there are now only about 50 in existence—including 15 in Vienna and 6 in the United States. It is not easy to separate these paintings into distinct categories; his biblical pictures, for example, are given the same local Flemish flavor found in his landscapes and illustrations of Flemish life and popular proverbs. Brueghel scanned the horizon of human activity, interpreting and transposing it in a realistic manner. He does not tell his stories as he has heard them, but picks them to bits and reconstructs them in a novel and illuminating fashion. Thus, he brought the sacred scene down to man's level and gave a larger dimension to the common daily routine.

One of Brueghel's most charming renditions of Flemish life is the *Wedding Dance*, painted in 1566 (Detroit Institute of Arts). In this work, crowds of people dressed in simple, brightly colored peasants' costumes echo the rhythm of folk music in their interlocking postures, while the pattern of colors forces the eye to dart from one point to another on the canvas as though responding to the whirl of the dance. The blunt features and squat figures of Brueghel's peasants give them a solid, almost brutish appearance, but their movements are sprightly and gay.

Hunters in the Snow (see page 79), is one of Brueghel's most memorable paintings. The grandeur of the vista reflects the influence of Patinir and Brueghel's own memory of the Alps which he had visited as a youth. Hunters and dogs are silhouetted as they plod through the blank white snow: all unessential detail is sacrificed to the pattern of their forms and the broad color areas of their clothes. Their direction and the march of the trees carries the eye down the steep slope and over the housetops to the ice, with its sprinkling of skaters and children. In the air, a bird accents the sweep of the picture's movement, while the jutting, snow-covered peaks of the distant mountains create a counter-thrust to the strong diagonal momentum of the rest of the picture.

Hunters in the Snow is one of several paintings of the months of the year. Another of the group is *The Harvesters* (Metropolitan Museum, New York), which shows peasants eating and napping under the hot, mid-day sun during the summer harvest.

Unlike Patinir, Brueghel does not idealize his landscapes. He presents the season as it is, with all the aspects of its beauty or its harshness. Likewise, when painting a human being, Brueghel scans the actual man behind his would-be virtues, neither mocking nor glorifying. "This is a man," his painting says. There is no precedent in Belgian art for this kind of unbiased observation, and it is significant that Brueghel never occupied himself with straight portraiture. The specific individual held no interest for him: he preferred to explore the situation and attitudes of mankind. For this reason, he painted from memory rather than using models.

The *Triumph of Death* (The Prado, Madrid) is typical of Brueghel's panoramic pictures. There is no moral in this gruesome scene other than the simplest and most obvious: death is an enemy no man escapes. In a bare, surrealistic landscape, a crowd of the living are being surrounded and overcome by an advancing army of skeletons. Noblemen and peasants

alike succumb to inexorable attack by every kind of weapon and torture —from arrows and scythes to fire and gallows. In the distance, two skeletons gleefully ring the death knell with a pair of bells hung high in a barren tree.

Brueghel's broad range of interest and lively imagination prompted him to record the world with the enthusiasm of a discoverer. He did not dwell on the exquisite surface, the decorative fabric or the charming accessory. His style was broad and flat, and depended upon line and color rather than modeling and linear perspective for its impact. He followed his fancy, not the established vogue, and is considered one of the greatest and most original of the northern painters.

THE BAROQUE PERIOD

IN 1569, THE YEAR OF BRUEGHEL'S death, the arts of the Low Countries reached the end of an era. The northern provinces revolted against

The Church of St. Michael in Louvain, built during the mid-17th century, is a fine example of the richly ornamental Italian Baroque style of architecture. The Baroque influence pervaded nearly every aspect of the arts in Belgium during the post-Renaissance period.

Spanish rule and Catholic religious persecution and their independence was formally recognized in the Treaty of Westphalia in 1648. The name "The Netherlands" was thenceforth used in reference to these northern provinces rather than to the whole area of the Low Countries. The new nation developed its own distinct art styles, while Belgium remained under Spanish domination and adopted the Baroque art and architecture popular in Spain and Italy.

Baroque Architecture

The Baroque movement in architecture began in Rome and ultimately spread throughout Europe. The style varied from country to country, but Baroque forms were essentially a reaction against the regulations laid down by Renaissance architects who devotedly copied the architectural styles which had been developed in ancient Greece and Rome. Baroque architects violently rejected the strict rules of this classical architecture; they advocated unrestrained independence in design and ornamentation.

This spirit of freedom which characterized the Baroque was frequently carried to extremes. Novel and flamboyant decoration was rampant, and the disunity of structure and accessories was frequently glaring. Because of its complex and elaborate lines, the Baroque style has been called "the architecture of the curved line" and "the pictorial architecture." Despite its faults, the style set forth many architectural innovations and explored many daring ideas.

The beginnings of Baroque influence in Belgian architecture are difficult to distinguish, for since the Gothic period the Belgians had displayed a taste for the ornate in their building. Many of the secular and religious structures raised during the 17th century show the better characteristics of Baroque architecture, but by the end of the 18th century the style had degenerated into superficiality and disharmony.

ECCLESIASTICAL ARCHITECTURE

During the early 17th century, splendid ecclesiastical buildings were raised in Bruges, Namur and Antwerp. The Beguinage church at Brussels and the opulent churches in the pilgrimage center of Malines feature classical cornices combined with rich, complex carvings superimposed upon the broad façades. The major architects of the period were Jacques Francuaert, Wenceslaus Coberger, François Augillon and Pierre Huyssens.

SECULAR ARCHITECTURE

The guild halls in the Grand-Place in Brussels, erected by various organizations of craftsmen, present a group of magnificent connecting Baroque façades. No one of these tall, narrow and ornately trimmed buildings is like any other.

The guild halls were constructed primarily of brick or stone. Their outstanding feature, the elaborately scrolled gables on the topmost story, once contained cranes and hoists for lifting raw materials and equipment for the guild workers and lowering their finished products. The walls are pierced with as many windows

The Four Ages, by Anthony Van Dyck (1599-1641), after Rubens one of the greatest masters of 17th-century Baroque painting. Van Dyck, who spent the last years of his life as court painter to King Charles I in London, was strongly influenced first by Rubens and later by the Venetian master, Titian. In the allegorical work shown here, Van Dyck depicts the four ages of man, from early childhood to old age.

Peter Paul Rubens' Portrait of Isabella Brandt, *the artist's first wife, whom he married in 1609. Isabella died in 1626, and four years later Rubens married the beautiful 16-year-old Helena Fourment, whom he also immortalized in a number of famous portraits.*

as possible to admit the light and warmth of the sun, and the roofs are steeply pitched against snow and rain.

Baroque Sculpture

Since painting dominated the arts in the 17th century, sculpture tended to take its cue from the works of Rubens. Figures took on pictorial effects, with their swirling garments seemingly suspended in mid-air. However free the motifs seemed, they were carefully calculated to accord with architectural elements. Three families of sculptors, the Quellins, the Noles and the Du Quesnoys, stand out among the many craftsmen of the period.

In the full flush of the Baroque era during the early 18th century, Belgian wood-carvers created a new vogue in church furnishings which was quite unlike anything else in the world. Choir stalls, screens, pulpits and other sorts of accessories began to be heavily encrusted with carvings which had no relation to religious subject matter in the medieval sense. These carvings substituted contrasting textures and grains for paint and apparently echoed the notion that heaven is a place literally filled with fruits and flowers.

The most astounding of these creations is the wooden pulpit by Michael Vervoot in the Antwerp Cathedral (1713). Two twisting, realistically carved trees support the canopy of delicately draped wood which covers the pulpit itself, and cupids, angels and various birds cluster around the leafy bower. The nature of these carvings illustrates the combination of materialism and deep spirituality which characterized the Belgian people of the age.

Baroque Painting

Baroque painting was especially concerned with space and dramatic effects of light and shade, and color and illumination were used in expert and imaginative ways. During a time when all other arts had fallen into a serious decline, painting reigned supreme, producing such masters as Peter Paul Rubens and Anthony Van Dyck.

RUBENS

It is no exaggeration to say that the Flemish artist Peter Paul Rubens (1577-1640) is the chief representative of European Baroque painting. He was the last of the great masters to base his art upon the human figure, and his style dominated 17th-century Flemish painting.

Rubens began painting at the age of 14, and was recognized as a master of his craft at Antwerp in 1598. He lived in Italy between 1600 and 1608, spending part of his time as court painter to the Duke of Mantua. While in Rome and Venice, he absorbed the lessons of the great 16th-century Italian painters, and his own genius was strenghthened by what he assimilated. Rubens was the most successful artist of his century in synthesizing Italian influence into the Baroque style.

After his return from Italy, Rubens showed a decided preference for large canvases and dramatic themes. He treated subjects of all kinds and attempted to paint "all there was" in a world which never failed to excite him. His technique was an adaptation of Jan van Eyck's, perfected by a combination of varnishes which allowed a marvelous transparency of glazes, layer after layer, until an incredible richness of depth and variation of color was attained. His skill as a colorist is particularly evident in his rendering of flesh tones.

Portrait of James Stuart, Duke of Lennox, *by Anthony Van Dyck. Van Dyck's long residence at the royal court in London resulted in a large number of finely executed portraits of English and European nobles. The refinement and subtlety of his portraits have seldom been surpassed. He is credited with founding the English school of portraiture.*

Rubens organized a great workshop in Antwerp, where he kept a string of assistants busy turning out his grandiose schemes. These assistants would lay out compositions from his sketches and paint in the broad underlayers. Afterwards, the master applied the finishing drawing and glazes. For most of his smaller works, Rubens used no collaborators, and he customarily repeated attitudes, poses, gestures, motifs and designs when treating wholly dissimilar incidents. Because of his remarkable energy and efficient system of collaboration, Rubens' total output is staggering—some 3000 paintings, many of enormous dimensions.

In about 1618, Rubens produced one of his most famous works, *Castor and Pollux Seizing the Daughters of Leucippus* (Alte Pinakothek, Munich). The painting shows the handsome and strapping twin sons of Leda and Jupiter kidnapping the lush daughters of Leucippus, while a pair of horses rear against the cloud-swept sky behind them. The mythological figures are every bit as alive as those painted from life, and illustrate Rubens' imaginative power. The work is a treasure-trove of Rubenesque textures: the soft, luminous flesh of the women, the sun-burned skin of the men, the satins and glinting metals and the tensed sinews of the horses make it a veritable feast for the eyes. Another example of Rubens' mythological works is *Bathsheba* (see page 88).

Between 1621 and 1625, Rubens produced the monumental *Life of Marie de Medici,* a series of huge paintings combining history, flattery and fantasy to please his patroness. The group now occupies an entire salon in the Louvre. In 1630, four years after the death of his first wife, Rubens married the young and beautiful Helena Fourment. Thereafter he painted some of his most moving and intimate canvases, and several portraits of his young wife and her sister Susanna stand among the highest achievements in portraiture. In these later pictures, Rubens refined his use of color and movement (see page 93).

Rubens is represented in all the sizeable art museums in the Western world. He remains the hero of the Baroque era, for his inventive and powerful work captures the essence of those restless times.

VAN DYCK

Sir Anthony Van Dyck (1599-1641) began painting when he was only 10 years old. At the age of 18 he joined the thriving workshop of Rubens, and collaborated closely with him for many years. He learned Rubens' technical skills, and his style represented an elegant and refined development of his master's more robust art. Van Dyck used thinner paint, and his works often reflected his own introspective melancholy.

In his later years, Van Dyck turned from the grandiose schemes of Rubens to specialize in portraits of the nobility of Europe such as the *Portrait of James Stuart, Duke of Lennox* (see above). He saw and recorded the refined personalities and subtle temperaments of his clientele, and is credited with the founding of the English school of portraiture.

After his early years in Antwerp, Van Dyck worked in Genoa and Rome, where he was influenced by the pictorial style of the Venetian master Titian. In 1632 he emigrated to London, where he became a favorite of King Charles I. In these courtly surroundings he found an almost inexhaustible supply of models for his languid, aristocratic portraits. One fine work, chosen at random from his impressive output, is the *Portrait of Queen Henrietta Maria with Her Dwarf* (National Gallery, Washington D.C.). In this work, the costumes, the pose, the pallid, decadent expression and the accessories combine to produce a memorable effect of melancholy in the midst of abundance.

THE MONUMENTAL SCHOOL

The two major mainstreams of 17th-century Belgian painting were the monumental and the intimate. Rubens, who served as a model for all Belgian painters of the period, is the only major artist to incorporate the theories of both groups.

The adherents of the monumental school were considered the "moderns" of the day, and tended to choose dramatic subjects. They were inspired by Italian styles, and expressed the revolutionary ideas of the Baroque. Historical scenes were placed boldly in the foreground, while architectural elements and landscapes were used simply as decorative settings.

Jacob Jordaens (1593-1678), a disciple of Rubens, was the most famous member of the monumental group. He was greatly influenced by the objective paintings of Caravaggio; his paint is thicker than that of Rubens and his colors contrast light and shade emphatically. Cornelius de Vos (c.1585-1651), a student of Van Dyck, is known for his vigorous portraits, while Van Thulden specialized in historical subjects and Frans Snyders and Paul de Vos were expert painters of animals and elaborate Flemish still lifes. In addition to his own works, Snyders painted most of the animals, fruit and flowers in the pictures of both Rubens and Jordaens.

THE INTIMATE SCHOOL

The intimate school continued native traditions, presenting a close-up view of local life, particularly in a satiric vein. The school contained no outstanding individuals, but included a number of very competent painters. Jan Brueghel (1568-1625), also called "Velvet" Brueghel, was the leading intimate painter (see page 96), and the popular David Teniers (1610-90) was noted for his competent, if superficial scenes of peasant life. Adriaen Brouwer (1605-38) was trained at the studio of the Dutch painter Frans Hals, where he developed a fine sense of color and an opulent technique. He produced a large number of scenes from peasant life, and commonly selected tavern scenes and the shrewd humor of the farmers as his topics. His realistic style is illustrated in *A Quarrel* (see below).

The landscape tradition begun by Patinir, typified by its high horizons, was continued by other members of the intimate group such as Joos de Momper and Jan Brueghel. Jan Siberechts (1627-96), who drew in a primitive and rigorous manner and substituted grays and cold greens for sensual colors, was the only 17th-century landscape painter uninfluenced by Rubens.

Both the monumental and the intimate schools were extremely active until about 1680, when a series of political upheavals led to a stultification of the arts. The fire of the Baroque era flickered out, and 18th-century art largely reiterated the ideas and techniques of the 17th century. Subject matter quickly became academic, observing strict conventions and rules. During this century, Belgium produced no outstanding painter, sculptor or architect.

THE NINETEENTH AND TWENTIETH CENTURIES

IN 1830, BELGIUM GAINED POLITICAL independence and the remainder of the 19th century was a period of industrialization and colonial expansion. Economic prosperity and political stability created conditions which encouraged the resurgence of art. During this time, Belgian architecture and sculpture were generally dominated by French models, but the painter James Ensor symbolized the tensions of his era and again gave Belgium a leading role in European artistic development.

Architecture

The flamboyance and pompousness of French Neoclassicism had a negative effect on the art of neighboring countries. In Belgium, the native traditions begun in the Middle Ages were ignored, and 19th-century architecture was generally characterized by a lack of discipline. One of the few Belgian architects to make effective use of French Neoclassicism was Joseph Poelaert (1817-79). His impressive Palais de Justice (1866-83), with its four-square plan and colonnaded central tower covered by a circular peristyle and dome, stands on a hill overlooking the city of Brussels.

L'Art Nouveau, promoted by a rising interest in the architectural possibilities of iron and glass, swept Europe at the end of the 19th century. A major example of this style in Belgium is the Maison du Peuple (Brussels), built by Victor Horta

A Quarrel, *by Adriaen Brouwer (1605-38), who was a member of the so-called intimate school that flourished in Belgium and elsewhere during the late 16th and the 17th centuries. Brouwer, a student of the great Dutch painter Frans Hals, produced numerous paintings of peasant life, specializing in tavern scenes where the roughhouse antics of the local carousers provided him with fascinating subject matter for his paintings. According to available biographical sources, Brouwer himself lived a life much like that of the ruffians and boors he so often depicted.*

(1861-1947), which illustrates the modern architect's search for new styles and new materials to meet new conditions.

Sculpture

Through most of the 19th century, the styles and themes in sculpture were dominated by Paris.

Among the more talented 19th-century Belgian sculptors were Matthieu Kessels (1784-1836) and the early Romantic sculptor Paul Bouré (1823-45). Constantin Meunier (1831-1905) specialized in figures of miners. Inspired by their hardened muscles, he emphasized the dignity of labor. The early work of Rik Wouters (1882-1926), shows the influence of the French Impressionistic sculptor Auguste Rodin.

Nineteenth-Century Painting

Painting of the 19th century, like sculpture, fell under the influence of Paris. Wouters was a painter as well as a sculptor, inspired by the works of the French Impressionist painters Edgar Degas and Auguste Renoir. The painters Van Rysselberghe (1862-1926) and Vogels (1836-96) were also followers of the Impressionists. They selected from nature and improvised upon reality rather than imitating it, and were interested in the fascinating possibilites of ordinary objects viewed from unexpected angles. The Impressionists often applied primary colors directly to the canvas, blending colors in the eye of the viewer rather than on the painter's palette.

Toward the end of the 19th century, Europe was overtaken by a profound spiritual restlessness. Economic prosperity and industrialization had produced a materialistic society whose hallmark was security and a prevailing faith in technology and progress. Poets and painters criticized the lack of spiritual and moral direction in their society, and symbolism arose as an attempt to relate the spiritual world to the material one. The Symbolists reacted against Impressionism; they felt that a picture should be thought out and organized in advance rather than present the artist's instinctive reactions when faced with the subject.

ENSOR

In Belgium, the spokesman for the anti-Impressionist movement was James Ensor (1860-1949). Ensor, Munch of Norway and Van Gogh of Holland formed the trio of Germanic artists who best expressed the insecurities of the modern age.

Born in Ostend, Ensor attended school in Brussels and then returned to his native city for the rest of his life. His artistic development was rapid, and by the age of 20 he was an accomplished craftsman with an exceptional color sense. His early works are vigorously realistic, but he soon began to give free rein to his lively imagination, combining the macabre with the farcical. His well-known ghosts and masked men reflect his own sense of isolation from the world; even titles of his works— *Indignant Masks, Skeleton Examining Chinoiseries* and the drawing *Demons Tormenting Me*—convey this feeling.

In his later works, Ensor painted human beings only to ridicule them —to reveal their ugliness and stupidity. He represented people as skeletons and masks, but endowed them with disquieting vitality.

In a series of paintings on the life and death of Christ produced between 1885 and 1900, Ensor explored the quality of light as a medium of communication. The subtle irridescence of these pictures marks them as major technical achievements. *The Entry of Christ into Brussels* (1899) represents the culmination of Ensor's use of light and color and his phantasmagorical interpretation of the world (see right). During his years of productivity Ensor created a powerful, original and influential art.

Twentieth-Century Painting

Although Belgium's modern artists cannot be classified rigidly into "schools," art historians point to three major trends in contemporary Belgian painting: emotional realism, surrealism and non-figurative (constructive) art. The first is closely related to earlier Expressionism and includes such artists as Constant Permeke, Léon Spillaert and Gustave

Still Life, by Jan Brueghel (1568-1625), the leading exponent of the 17th-century Flemish intimate school. The son of Pieter Brueghel the Elder, Jan was called the "Velvet" Brueghel. Although a highly competent artist and much admired by his contemporaries, he lacked the depth and scope of his father's genius.

Detail from **The Entry of Christ into Brussels,** *painted in 1899 by the precursor of modern Expressionism, James Ensor (1860-1949). Ensor's work, often macabre and grotesque, had considerable influence on European painting of the 20th century. The painting shown here formed part of a series of works on the life and death of Christ produced between 1885 and 1900. Although he continued to paint for many years (he lived to the age of 89), Ensor produced his greatest work before the year 1900.*

de Smet, while the second, whose best-known exponents are Paul Delvaux and René Magritte, explores the world of fantasy. The non-figurative artists formed a group known as *Jeune Peinture Belge* (Young Belgian Painting) which pulled away from both realism and fantasy to emphasize abstract forms. This last group, which arose about 1947, has become one of the most productive and significant in Belgium today, and includes such artists as Antoine Mortier, Roger Dudant and Gaston Bertrand.

CONTEMPORARY REALISM

Expressionism, from which contemporary Belgian realism is derived, is emotional and self-centered. The artist expresses his emotions on canvas by purifying and intensifying them. Expressionism reflects the new attitude of the modern artist, who views his subject matter as personal and highly charged with emotions. Today's realists attempt to discover the "hidden aspects of reality," rather than copy in a photographic manner, and individual techniques within the movement have varied greatly.

One of the most interesting modern realists is the sculptor-painter Constant Permeke (1886-1952), who created massive figures and powerful landscapes which possess a brooding, primitive gravity. In his drawing *Woman Cutting Bread* (see page 98), he uses physical deformity to reflect the hard life of the peasant.

Another realist, René Quiette (1893-), uses many rare and strange materials to make each work a unique tactile and visual composition. Floris Jespers (1889-1962) is known today as "the painter of the Congo," while War van Overstraeten (1891-) has found the ideal subject for his austere style in the fierce and barren Spanish landscape.

SURREALISM

Belgian Surrealism is based primarily upon the works of earlier painters such as Brueghel and Bosch. The symbolism of these two artists is picked up in the skeleton continually found in the works of one of the leading contemporary Surrealists, Paul Delvaux (1897-). His works resemble waking dreams, with people wandering like sleepwalkers amid strange, moonlit surroundings. René Magritte (1898-) attempted to illustrate the interrelationship of image and objects through such devices as the superimposition upon a landscape painting of a window opening out onto this same landscape. Both Delvaux and Magritte use deliberately old-fashioned techniques, but attempt to show mysteries hidden in familiar things.

Surrealists such as Maxim van de Woestijne (1911-), Paul Renotte (1906-), Louis van de Spiegele (1912-) and René Lambert (1925-) paint dream experiences—abolishing the distinction between the "real" world and the world of dreams in an attempt to express the lack of spiritual balance of the modern age. Belgian Surrealists have often used collages to depict incongruous associations with greater effectiveness.

CONSTRUCTIVISM

Constructivism, an outgrowth of Cubism, is essentially three-dimensional. It grew up largely in reaction to the realism of the Expressionists and the fantasies of the Surrealists, and was influenced by the unsentimental abstract painters of the School of Paris. Belgian Constructivists often use collages, round sculpture and reliefs constructed of wood, glass, string and other materials.

The works of a somewhat earlier artist, the Belgian sculptor Georges van Tongerloo (1886-), had a great effect upon the evolution of the *Jeune Peinture Belge* group. Like Mondrian, he discarded all diagonals and curves and all secondary colors in an attempt to create an art as rigorous and impersonal as a science. His work is a studied manipulation of cubic and rectangular forms, which are sometimes related to mathematical formulae. One example of his work is the nickle and silver construction entitled $Y = 2x^3 - 13.5x^2 - 21x$ (Kunst Museum, Basel).

Some members of this group favor stark geometric constructions, while others have a strong sense of the dramatic, using brilliantly colored constructions of circles and waves. For example, Roger Dudant (1929-) seeks order in the precise designs of scaffoldings, airports and shipyards, while Antoine Mortier (1910-) uses the cross as the dramatic focal point of his compositions. Many constructivists, such as the influential Gaston Bertrand (1910-), initially produced figurative works and shifted to abstractionism in the 1950s.

The constructivist School of Laethem-Saint-Martin, founded in 1910, attempts to express the essential spirit of objects by simplifying natural appearances to the utmost. Two painters of this school, Gustave de Smet (1877-1943) and Edgard Tytgat (1879-1957), tried to recapture the unsophistication of a child in their stylized scenes of everyday life. All the non-figurative artists try to shed all similarity with natural form in their works, to evoke an emotional response from the observer rather than a visual or intellectual one.

CONCLUSION

WITHOUT QUESTION, THE MOST OUT-standing examples of Belgian art have been in the field of painting. There are, of course, fine sculptures and works of architecture, but building has largely followed tradition and sculpture has been primarily an anonymous, highly skilled craft practiced as an adjunct to architecture.

The arts in Belgium enjoyed two great eras. The first, the Burgundian period, lasted from the 13th to the 15th century and produced the realism of the Van Eycks and the expressionism of Rogier van der Weyden. These two approaches continued to dominate Belgian art well into the Baroque era. During the Burgundian period, architecture also flourished, and the magnificent Gothic churches and town halls were characterized by a typically Netherlandish attention to detail. The development of tapestries, illuminated manuscripts and small painted altar panels also reached a peak during this time.

The second great period of Belgian art stretched from the mid-16th to the mid-17th century, and its genius is epitomized in the works of Pieter Brueghel the Elder and Peter Paul Rubens. Brueghel's unbiased observation of Flemish peasant life was unprecedented in Belgian art, and shaped the work of later realistic genre artists. Rubens is sometimes viewed as the epitome of the Baroque spirit. He perfected the glaze techniques of the Van Eycks, and his use of color was widely imitated. His imaginative style dominated the art of the 17th and 18th centuries.

The most significant movement in contemporary Belgian art is constructivism. Young non-figurative artists are exploring new techniques and approaches in an attempt to achieve a rational order. They have abandoned forms which carry conventional visual and intellectual meanings, in order to strive for an emotional content which will give new vitality to art.

Throughout Europe, modern art has taken two major directions: abstractionism and expressionism. Whatever the future, the vigor of Belgium's young artists seems to promise that the country will continue to play a leading role in European artistic development.

Woman Cutting Bread, an ink and charcoal drawing by Constant Permeke (1886-1952), one of the better-known Belgian artists of the 20th century. Permeke's work, generally classified as "emotional realism," combines numerous elements and styles to create a highly original and often powerful artistic expression.

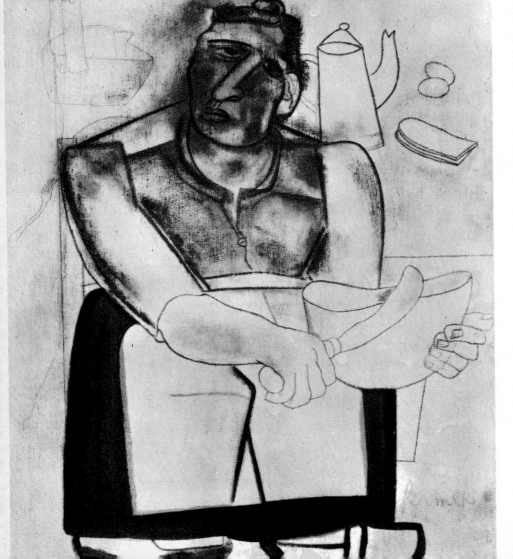

Above: *Illustration for the medieval*
Legend of St. Alexius, *a moral work
written in the Walloon dialect.*

The literature of Belgium has been written in two major languages, Flemish and French. Flemish is the spoken and written language of the northern provinces of East and West Flanders, Antwerp and Limburg and the upper half of the province of Brabant. This language, which developed from Low German, is identical with the Netherlandsch (Dutch) of Holland, and literary developments in the two regions have often followed similar courses (see *The Netherlands: The Literature*). Many authors of the Flemish-speaking region are bilingual, and the area has developed impressive bodies of literature in both Flemish and French.

French is the spoken and written language in the southern half of Brabant and the provinces of Hainaut, Namur, Liège and Luxembourg. In general, the literature of this region is more refined and cosmopolitan than that of the north.

THE MIDDLE AGES

Flemish Secular Literature

THE EARLIEST EXTANT FLEMISH writings date from the 12th century, and the Flemish-speaking region of Belgium produced almost the entire body of Flemish-language literature during the Middle Ages. A good many of the ancient Flemish writers were highly didactic and encyclopedic, while others are noted for their delightful ballads, love lyrics and mystical writings.

The earliest known example of Flemish secular literature is *Carel ende Elegast* (Charles and Elegast), derived from the French Carolingian epic cycle. The Arthurian legends became widely known in Flanders, and Prince Philip of Alsace (d.1191), an enthusiastic supporter of the Crusades, encouraged his subjects to translate these legends from French into Flemish. The most representative Flemish work of this genre is the 12th-century *Walewein,* which treats celebrated Arthurian legends such as the love of Lancelot and Queen Guinevere and the death of King Arthur.

Below left and right: *Two illustrations for the late medieval satirical allegory*
Roman de Renart, *a French version of the popular Flemish tale* Van den Vos
Reinaerde (Reynard the Fox).

The poet Jacob van Maerlant (c. 1235-c.1300), the founder of the Flemish didactic school, is known for his many rhymed Flemish versions of Latin and French poems and didactic works. His numerous works include a rhymed Biblical history (*Rhyme Bible,* 1271) and a rhymed chronicle of world history, *Spiegel Historiael* (The Mirror of History) c.1282. Van Maerlant's poetry, with its harsh and labored versification, began a trend away from sentimental poems of love and chivalry. He was most successful with his political satires, and his numerous followers included the poet Jan de Weert and the historian and moralist Jan van Boendaele.

The decline of chivalric poetry led to a rising production of folk literature, particularly love and work songs, dance tunes and religious songs. Two of the most famous secular ballads are *Sire Halewijn,* which tells the legend of a Belgian Blue Beard who killed all the maidens attracted by his singing, and *Van de twee Koninghs Kinderen* (The Royal Children), a moving and tender account of the legend of Hero and Leander.

At about this time, many Flemish

An early 16th-century illustration for a book of moral fables published at Antwerp. The skeleton, as a symbol of Death, figured prominently in many early Flemish works, most notably in Van der mollen feeste (The Mole's Festival) by the poet Anthonis de Roovere (1430-82). In this work, Roovere depicts Death in the guise of a skeleton leading the souls of the living and dead in a danse macabre.

writers began to adopt the best works of the time into the vernacular in an attempt to bring literature to the common people. The noted Van Veldeke, for example, based his *Eneïde* (Aeneid) c.1185 on Vergil's epic, while Diederic van Assenede's extremely popular *Floris ende Blanchefloer* relates the love story of the son of a Moorish king and a Frankish girl of noble birth.

The most important piece of Flemish secular literature in the Middle Ages was Henric van Veldeke's *Van den Vos Reinaerde* (Reynard the Fox) c.1150, which expressed the popular discontent of the peasantry. Van Veldeke likened the peasant to the fox, because his survival in the face of persecution by both nobility and clergy depended upon his cunning. The satirical tone of this pungent social treatise does not hide the author's sensitivity to his characters and their surroundings, and *Van den Vos Reinaerde* is considered a work of European importance—the finest expression of the spirit of the Belgian people written prior to the Renaissance.

Flemish Religious Literature

While *Van den Vos Reinaerde* was the most important Flemish contribution to the secular literature of the time, the 13th-century poem *Beatrijs* (*The Tale of Beatrice,* Eng. trans. 1943) elevated Flemish religious literature to a great height. The work brings profound psychological insight to the legend of the aristocratic Beatrice, and is considered a European masterpiece.

During the Middle Ages, religious writing was the most highly developed Flemish literary form. One of the most beautiful of the many works based upon the lives of various saints was *Lutgarde der Afflighem* (Lutgarde of Afflighem). *Van Seven Marieren van heiligher Minnen* (The Seven Ways of Loving), written by the mystic Beatrijs van Nazareth (c. 1200-c.1268), was one of the first Flemish prose works. The *Visioenen* (Visions) and *Brieven* (Letters) of

Hadewych, another early woman mystic, present the most perfect example of early Flemish literature in this genre. Hadewych's descriptions of the various experiences and states of mystic life began a trend toward imaginative, speculative writing in Flemish literature.

This trend culminated in the 11 brilliant philosophical treatises of Jan van Ruysbroec (1293-1381). During his lifetime, the clergy became highly corrupt, and he withdrew from a regular religious order in protest. Despite his deeply religious themes, he was skilled in his use of picturesque vernacular language and folk humor, and his works remain in touch with life about him.

Early French Literature

The earliest known Belgian literature was written in the French-speaking southern provinces. The medieval epics (*chansons de gestes*) *Reynaud de Montauban* (Renard of Montauban) and *Les Quatre Fils Aymon* (The Four Aymon Sons), for example, take place in the Ardennes, while the knightly hero Hugo of Bordeaux occupies a prominent place in the folklore of Hainaut. These works form part of the so-called Crusade cycle, which concerned itself primarily with the deeds of the Flemish lords who led the first Crusades.

Prince Philip of Alsace was influential in popularizing the Arthurian legends in both the French and Flemish-speaking regions of Belgium. One of the best known Arthurian romances was Manessier's *Perceval le Gallois* (Percival the Welshman), which introduced the saga of the Holy Grail into Belgian literature. His equally well-known *Le Chevalier à la Charette* (The Knight in the Little Cart) was the first Belgian work to tell the story of Sir Lancelot.

The southern region also made several important contributions to Belgian literature of the Middle Ages. *Gilles de Chine* (Chinese Clowns) 1250, is attributed to Gautier of Tournai, and Adenet le Roi treated the basic themes of the *chansons de gestes* in two long poems, *La Chanson de la Chevalerie Ogier de Danemarche* (The Youthful Enterprises of Ugger the Dane) and *Berte aus grans piés* (Bertha of the Big Feet), toward the middle of the 13th century. Satirical literature was very popular among the people of the southern regions, and many French versions of the popular Flemish tale *Van den Vos Reinaerde* were produced during the Middle Ages, including *Roman de Renart* (The Tale of Renard) and *Le Couronnement de Renard* (The Crowning of Renard). Two other popular works were Gautier le Leu's *La Veuve* (The Widow) and *Les Augures* (The Omens).

THE BURGUNDIAN PERIOD

THE DUKES OF BURGUNDY SET UP their court in Belgium during the 14th century, and their patronage influenced the course of Belgian literature throughout the 15th century. The luxurious and brilliant Burgundian court attracted many talented writers, particularly chroniclers, but the establishment of clear-cut classifications led to the mechanization of many forms of literature, particularly poetry. "Pious" poems, for example, were often pedantic, "amorous" ones were commonly coarse and vulgar and "gay" ones were frequently trivial. But despite the adverse effects of Burgundian literary conventions, the dukes of Burgundy provided a center for Belgian writers and founded the Burgundy Library, which remains one of the most valuable parts of the Belgian National Library.

The 16th century in western Europe was also the time of the "Chambers of Rhetoric," which were organized as dramatic and literary centers. One could be found in almost every Belgian town and village. These groups set up literary competitions, gave official prizes and generally concerned themselves with the production and development of poetry and drama.

Flemish Literature

One popular type of verse during the Burgundian period was the *refrein* (refrain), a form developed by a group of Flemish poets which included the rhetorician Matthijs de Castelein (c.1488-1550) and the poet Anthonis de Roovere (1430-82). Castelein was most famous as a critic, but he was also the author of many plays and poems. His *Const van Rhetorikan* (Treatise on Rhetoric) 1555, was the first treatise on Flemish versification.

French Chroniclers

The Burgundian period also saw the development of a significant body of French-language historical writing.

Two of the most popular chronicles were Philippe Mousket's *Une Chronique des Rois de France* (A Chronicle of the Kings of France) and Jean d'Outremeuse's *Le Geste de Liège* (The Heroic Deeds of Liège). Another Burgundian chronicler, Jean Froissart (c.1333-1400), covered European history from 1325 to 1400 in his classic *Chronique de France, d'Angleterre, d'Ecosse et d'Espagne* (History of France, England, Scotland and Spain), which has been influential in the development of British historical writing.

THE SIXTEENTH CENTURY

DURING THE 16TH CENTURY, BELGIAN literature came under the influence of the Italian Renaissance. Belgian Humanists, under the leadership of the Dutch scholar Erasmus, advocated a return to Classical culture. The College of the Brothers of the Common Life, founded in the middle of the 15th century, served as the Belgian Humanist center, and the invention of printing helped spread Humanist doctrines throughout the country.

Flemish Literature

During the 16th century, the intellectual center of the Flemish-speaking region of the Low Countries shifted from Flanders to the Netherlands, and the great wars of religion that devastated the area hindered artistic activity in the latter part of the century. The religious wars produced many anonymous battle songs known as *de Geuzenliederen* (the Beggar's Songs), which boiled with passion for religious reform, and vernacular literature became a religious weapon. One of the most noted polemical writers of the time was the Antwerp schoolmistress Anna Bijns (1494-1575), who is famous for her strong and eloquent poems in defense of orthodoxy. Another Antwerp poet, the Calvinist Philips van Marnix van Sint Aldegonde (1538-98), was a fierce and vigorous defender of the Reformation. His *Biencorf der H. Roomsche Kercke* (Beehive of the Holy Roman Church) was one of the most striking works in a large body of literature protesting the corruption of the Catholic church. Marnix also translated the *Psalms* of David into Flemish and wrote the Flemish national song, *Wilhelmuslied.*

French Literature

The Flemish poet Marnix also wrote in French, and his long *Tableau des différends de la Religion* (Description of Religious Differences) defends the ideas of the Reformation with extraordinary vigor and verbal richness. Most of the Belgian Humanists came from southern Belgium and many of them gathered about the court of the Regent Margaret of Austria, who ruled the Netherlands for the house of Burgundy from 1507 to 1530.

Margaret was the patron of one of the most noted Belgian Humanists, Jehan Lemaire de Belges (1473-1516), whose *Le Temple d'honneur et de vertu* (Temple of Honor and Virtue) and *La Plainte du Désiré* (Lament of the Desired) are perfect models of scholastic allegory. Lemaire first came into contact with Humanism during a trip to Italy, and expressed his admiration for the Italian Humanists in his *Concorde des deux Langages* (Concord of Two Languages). He was one of the first Belgians to propose a fusion of ancient pagan beliefs and the Christian tradition and he revealed his pagan vein in the revolutionary *Le Temple de Vénus* (The Temple of Venus).

THE SEVENTEENTH AND EIGHTEENTH CENTURIES

DURING THE 17TH AND 18TH CENturies, Belgium experienced a period of decline. The country had been drained by the wars of religion, and the great past seems to have died away and been forgotten. French culture and literature overshadowed all of Europe, and Belgian authors devoted much of their time to academic attempts to establish the superiority of French over Flemish as the national literary language.

Flemish literature of the period was scant, and many Flemish authors fled to The Netherlands to escape persecution. One of the best 17th-century Flemish writers was the popular moralist Adriaan Poirters (1605-74), who wrote picturesque tales of life in Flanders. As the upper classes came increasingly under French influence, the popular character of Flemish literature became more marked. During this time, the work of the "Chambers of Rhetoric" helped to preserve Flemish literature.

The second half of the 18th century saw the founding of the Société de Lettres de Bruxelles, which was the beginning of the present Royal Academy of Science and Letters. One of the most varied and interesting personalities of the time was Prince Charles Joseph de Ligne (1735-1814), author of numerous poems, essays, biographies, moral works and letters. His cosmopolitan attitude was typical of the dominant French culture, but his fashionable social life did not prevent him from ironically criticizing the follies of his age.

THE EARLY NINETEENTH CENTURY

IN 1830, AFTER A BRIEF AND ILL-fated union with The Netherlands, Belgium achieved political independence. The 19th century was a period of literary revival; literature was at last given a chance to freely express national characteristics, and the young authors of the Romantic movement looked to the Belgian history and countryside for their inspiration.

Flemish Literature

During the first quarter of the 19th century, Romanticism domin-

ated Flemish literature, and Flemish authors and scholars such as Jan Frans Willems (1793-1846) rediscovered the treasures of Flemish literature of the Middle Ages.

The novelist Hendrik Conscience (1812-83), author of more than a hundred novels and short stories, was typical of the young Romantics. Although he was not a great genius, Conscience restored the vernacular to high popular favor as a literary language. It is often said that "he taught his people to read," and he is regarded as the founder of modern Flemish literature. His numerous ardent historical novels include *Die Loteling* (The Conscript) and his masterpiece *De Leeuw van Vlaanderen* (The Lion of Flanders), which presents a lively, patriotic and ultra-Romantic picture of the Battle of the Spurs, in which the Flemish people defeated the French.

Other important Flemish Romantics included poets such as Karel Ledeganck (1805-47), Theodoor van Rijswijck (1811-49) and the sentimental Jan van Beers (1827-88). Ledeganck's *De Drie Zustersteden* (The Three Sister Cities)—a tribute to Ghent and her rivals Antwerp and

Bruges—is the best-known poem in the Flemish language. Rijswijck is known for his fiery political satires and his influential repudiation of classical concepts and forms in literature.

In about 1860, a realistic reaction set in against Romanticism. The works of the anti-Romantics were characterized by pessimism, humor and realistic descriptions of characters and scenes.

GEZELLE

During the mid-19th century, a remarkable revival occurred in West Flanders, and the name of the poet Guido Gezelle (1830-99) overshadowed all others. For some time, Flemish poetry had been characterized by the dry and cold formalisms of the rhetorical tradition; Gezelle liberated it from pedantry and academism by combining a gift for melodious language with a profoundly mystical view of life. He drew his inspiration from God, nature and his country, and possessed great powers of observation and sensitivity and an extraordinary imagination. His skillful use of form and sounds to evoke the desired mood are unequaled in Flemish poetry, and he helped to revive the use of Flemish as a literary language.

Gezelle was widely imitated. The natural and supple style of one of his pupils, Hugo Verriest (1840-1922), influenced Flemish prose writers, while the strongly nationalistic and idealistic works of the poet Albrecht Rodenbach (1856-80) had both political and literary significance.

French Literature

During the early part of the 19th century, the groundwork was laid for the great revival of the 1880s. The appearance of the periodical *La Sentinelle des Pays-Bas* (Sentry of the Netherlands) in 1827 heralded the arrival of Romanticism in French-speaking Belgium. Young Romantic writers were also given leading space in the *Revue Belge* (Belgian Review), founded in 1830.

By the mid-19th century, political nationalism had become a definite part of the Belgian cultural climate, and both literature and the visual arts looked to the history of the country for inspiration. Patriotic and Romantic poets such as André van Hasselt and Théodore Weustenraad attempted to create a specifically Belgian national spirit, while other young writers of the time took an interest in German literature and

Illustration for Floris ende Blanchefloer, *a 12th-century love epic by the Flemish poet Diederic van Assenede. The story revolves around the love of a Moorish prince for a Frankish girl of noble birth.*

folklore. The poet and playwright Édouard Wacken (1819-61), for example, published an anthology entitled *Les Fleurs d'Allemagne* (Flowers of Germany).

One of the most noted Belgian poets of the early 19th century was André van Hasselt (1806-74), who contributed to the periodical *La Sentinelle*. He was definitely a Romantic, and his *Primevères* (Primroses) 1834, shows the influence of Victor Hugo. Hasselt is famed for his metrical experiments in which he used regular accents (as in German and English) rather than the traditional French counting of syllables. He was a prolific writer, and his works include several histories—such as *Les Belges aux Croisades* (The Belgians during the Crusades) 1846 —as well as his many volumes of verse. Another poet of the times was Théodore Weustenraad (1805-49), a follower of the French socialist Saint-Simon.

DE COSTER

The two leading prose writers of the early 19th century were Charles De Coster and Octave Pirmez. De Coster (1827-79) first published two series of tales on national themes, *Les Légendes Flamandes* (Flemish Legends) 1858 and *Contes Brabançons* (Tales of Brabant) 1861. He then wrote his epic work *La Légende de Thyl Eulenspiegel et de Lamme Goedzak au pays de Flandre* (The Legend of Till Eulenspiegel and of Lamme Goedzak in the Land of Flanders) 1868, which was not fully recognized until after his death.

Although this work was derived from an old and well-known German tale, De Coster adapted it to the requirements of the Flemish setting. Traditionally, Till Eulenspiegel was a fat man of the people of dubious uprighteousness, but De Coster turned him into a symbol of the Flemish spirit. In his work, Till Eulenspiegel longs to liberate Flanders and has a vision of the country's future glory. He represents the heroic resistance of the Belgian people during the 16th century, for he uses his calculating intellect and subtle wit to trick the Spanish and other neighboring powers who had dominated his nation. De Coster realized, however, that many facets of Flemish society were not represented in the character Till Eulenspiegel, and thus he depicted the grosser side of man through Till's fat, lazy and comic companion Lamme Goedzak. De Coster used French art and civilization as models to stimulate and refine his own talent, but his work stands apart from French literature. Some critics have declared that his works made it fashionable to be Flemish.

De Coster was not only a patriot and skillful author, but also a patient scholar. His command of old French in his *Légendes Flamandes*, for example, won him a reputation as a medievalist, and he carefully documented his anarchisms in *Till Eulenspiegel* to give his epic a solid scholarly foundation. Like *Renard the Fox*, *Till Eulenspiegel* took its inspiration from the political helplessness of the serf in the Middle Ages. Both lack a consecutive narrative, but are rich in variety and detail.

PIRMEZ

The second great writer of this period, Octave Pirmez (1827-83), was known to his contemporaries as the "hermit of Acoz" because he spent most of his life shut up on his estate in meditation and in contemplation of nature. Pirmez was regarded chiefly as a thinker by his contemporaries, and his inner search for truth made him more of a philosopher than an artist. Indeed, he once declared that he wished to be described and remembered only as a moralist. His style was extremely lyrical, and his poems are filled with melancholy and rich reflections. Pirmez' rejection of the conventions of his day and his unremitting search for truth were overzealously admired by the young writers of the following generation.

A group portrait by Peter Paul Rubens, including a self-portrait of Rubens himself, center left. At center right is Justus Lipsius (1547-1606), one of the leading Belgian scholars, Classicists and Humanists of the late 16th century. The Belgian Humanists, like their counterparts in other countries, advocated a return to Classicism in literature and art. Their doctrines had a strong influence on Belgian literature, both in Flemish and French, during the 16th and 17th centuries.

THE LATE NINETEENTH CENTURY

THE LATE 19TH CENTURY WAS ONE of the greatest periods in Belgian literature. The writers of the early part of the century had helped to make Belgium conscious of its own literary potentialities, and this awareness sparked a great literary and intellectual ferment in Belgian life in about 1880.

The Flemish Renaissance

In the Flemish-speaking region, the literary revival of the late 19th century is sometimes known as the Flemish Renaissance. It was dominated by a group of young writers centered about the literary review *Van Nu en Straks* (From Then and Now, 1893-1901), which emphasized sensuality, individualism and art for art's sake. Under the influence of these young writers, style liberated itself from the classical conventions and became more fluid and colorful. Writers became more interested in probing human nature, and a true revival of Flemish letters occurred.

'VAN NU EN STRAKS'

The reaction against the provincialism of Flemish letters by the poet Pol de Mont (1857-1931) is extremely important to the development of Belgian poetry. The principles he derived from the style of the French symbolists were enunciated in *Van Nu en Straks,* and his fresh and complex modern poems widened the horizons of Belgian poetry.

Three of the major writers who grouped themselves about this review were Prosper van Langendonck (1862-1920), August Vermeylen (1872-1944) and Karel van de Woestijne (1878-1929). Van Langendonck's lyrical poems are few in number, but they show a highly refined form and a great sensitivity to the pain of life. The cosmopolitan August Vermeylen is viewed by some as the leader of the *Van Nu en Straks* movement. Although chiefly known as an essayist and critic, he wrote the notable symbolic novel *De Wandelende Jood* (The Wandering Jew) 1906, which describes a conflict between duty and passion. His works contain a strange mixture of rationalism and sentimentalism.

Woestijne, known as the *poète maudit* (accursed poet) of Flemish literature, expressed the typical attitude of the *Van Nu en Straks* group. He was deeply influenced by the French poet Baudelaire, and his chief goals were individualism, frankness and artistic liberty. His writings form a symbolic autobiography in which

he viewed his life as a torment and a problem. He made skillful use of highly aristocratic language, and is noted for his ability to unify disparate sensory images into an artistic whole.

Another writer associated with *Van Nu en Straks* was the essayist Emmanuel De Bom (1868-1953). His novel *Wraken* (Wreckage), a study of the character of the people of Antwerp, was the first modern Belgian psychological novel.

STREUVELS

Stijn Streuvels (Frank Lateur, 1871-   ), a nephew of Gezelle and another contributor to *Van Nu en Straks,* represented the more provincial tendency in Flemish writing. During the early part of his career he worked in a bakery, and was considered mad by many of his fellow townspeople. His first realistic writings were overshadowed by a vague pessimism. Streuvels isolated himself in a lovely country villa, and during his later life the peace which he found in these beautiful surroundings lent a happier tone to his short stories.

The writer was more concerned with the impression he could create through his powerful verbal rhythms and pictorial energy than with story line; his colorful and varied prose echoes the great Flemish painters, and his stories and novels present broad canvases of life among the Flemish peasants. His most powerful epic, *De Vlaschaard* (The Flaxyard) 1907, is an impressionistic account of the influence of environment upon man. Streuvels is one of the most powerful of all Flemish novelists. Although he wrote in the language of everyday life, his tales demonstrate a mastery of style and a deep understanding of human nature.

TEIRLINCK AND BOELAERE

Two younger writers of the Flemish Renaissance were Herman Teirlinck (1879-   ) and F. Toussaint van Boelaere (1875-1947). Teirlinck's novels, dramas and essays departed from the strict realism which has characterized earlier prose. He had a great deal of imagination, and his comments upon his world are benevolently ironic. Boelaere was more refined and intellectual than Teirlinck, viewing rural topics as if from a distance. His intense and compressed themes often contain a sense of underlying tragedy.

OTHER TRENDS

Apart from the development of *Van Nu en Straks,* the 19th century in Belgium also saw the rise of Naturalism, the regional novel and cosmopolitan poetry. Naturalism reached its height with the works of Cyriel Buysse (1859-1932), author of some 40 volumes of robust tales and novels treating the life of the poor in Flanders. His early novels were dark and harsh, reflecting the fury of his exposure to peasant oppression. As he matured, his writing grew more fluid and accomplished, and he began to analyze the vices and failings of the provincial petit-bourgeoisie. His best work is probably the novel *Tantes* (Aunties) 1930. The leading regional novelist of the 19th century was Maurits Sabbe (1873-1938), who gave a romantic and idyllic view of the city of Bruges.

During the latter part of the 19th century, poets such as the elegiac Jan van Nijlen (1884-   ) tried to be more cosmopolitan than those of the *Van Nu en Straks* group. Van Nijlen's melancholy poetry contrasted sharply with the tormented emotionalism of Woestijne and his followers.

French Poetry of the Revival

In the French-speaking region, the literary revival of the late 19th century began in the university towns. There young poets were inspired by the work of the French Symbolists and young novelists produced harshly realistic and colorful pictures of peasant life and mystical sketches of their country filled with patriotic and religious symbolism. The young southern artists centered about *La Jeune Belgique* (Young Belgium, 1881) and other literary and philosophical reviews which declared that a Belgian should think and write as a Belgian.

The poets identified with the review *La Jeune Belgique* were generally classed as Symbolists or as Parnassians. The Symbolists were primarily concerned with the creation of a mood through the use of powerful symbols, while the subtle poems of the Parnassians were characterized by a highly refined use of language and attention to classical forms.

One of the most important Belgian Symbolists was Emile Verhaeren (1855-1916), who filled his works with terror, agony and destruction. Verhaeren, who has been called the poet of Belgian moods, began his career with a violently realistic volume of verse entitled *Les Flamandes* (The Flemish Women). His later works became less aggressive, and he is most noted for his elegiac and social trilogies. Emile Verhaeren's style was aggressively masculine. He coined words from the Flemish to give new vigor to the French language, and his works included elements of violence and brutality.

MAETERLINCK

Three of the major Belgian Symbolist poets belonged to what is known as the School of Ghent. The first of these, Maurice Maeterlinck (1862-1949), had a harsh style which resembled that of Verhaeren. He was, however, more mystical than Verhaeren, and formed most of his verses through contrasts. Maeterlinck's use of contrast and unusual word associations in his first collection, *Serres Chaudes* (Hothouses), was extremely influential in the development of the Symbolist movement. He was preoccupied with the mystery and strangeness of things, and had a fear of "dark and evil forces." Some of his poems presaged Surrealism, and even his *Douze Chansons (Twelve Songs)* and his early theatrical works show this same nightmare quality and horror of waiting for the unknown (see *Belgium: The Theater*).

Maeterlinck's meeting with Georgette Leblanc in 1895 caused a change of direction in his literary work; he began a long series of philosophical treatises—starting with *Le Trésor des Humbles* (The Treasure of the Humble) 1896, which describes the heroic nature of everyday life. Maeterlinck was awarded a Nobel prize in 1911.

LERBERGHE AND LE ROY

The second poet of the Ghent group was Charles van Lerberghe (1861-1907), a childhood friend of Maeterlinck. His pictorial gifts and mystical bent were linked to a fundamental sense of balance and technique. The variations and developments which he used to express his

ideas, the fragile delicacy and lyricism of his verse and the dreamy and mysterious quality of his mood make his poetry perhaps the most original in the entire body of French-language Belgian literature. He felt that his perceptions lay on the borderline between the real and the mysterious and ungraspable, and indicated this belief in calling his first collection *Entrevisions* (Glimpses). The intensely personal and subjective nature of his verse may be seen in his long *La Chanson d'Eve* (The Song of Eve), in which Eve represents his thoughts and his soul.

The third member of the Ghent group was the gentle and sentimental Grégoire Le Roy (1862-1941) who described his life of suffering in

melancholy tales and poems. His expression was highly musical, and he assumed the attitude of a wise and gentle sage in his later works.

RODENBACH AND FONTAINAS

Georges Rodenbach (1855-98), another Symbolist poet associated with *La Jeune Belgique*, was perhaps the best-known of the Belgian poets abroad. Rodenbach has been called "the singer of Bruges," for he described the gay, haunting beauty of the capital of West Flanders in many poems and in his well-known novel *Bruges-la-morte* (Bruges-the-Dead). Rodenbach saw silence and solitude beneath the surface of modern life and his later works, in which he described the twilight atmosphere

Portrait of Cardinal Guido Bentivoglio (1579-1644), by the Flemish painter Anthony Van Dyck. Cardinal Bentivoglio served as papal nuncio (representative) in Flanders from 1605 to 1617. He wrote Della guerra di Fiandra *(1632-39, a history of the war in Flanders which contains a wealth of valuable information on events of the time.*

of the old Flemish cities, are considered his best. The Symbolist poet and novelist André Fontainas (1865-1948) has won critical acclaim for his skillful use of words, his refined themes and his musical expression.

THE PARNASSIANS

The Parnassian poets advocated art for art's sake, and divorced themselves from the world of the Belgian bourgeoisie to concentrate upon the purification of the Classical style and the French language. One of the major Parnassians poets, Iwan Gilken (1858-1925), refused to allow free verse in *La Jeune Belgique* when he became its editor in 1891. He had studied with Verhaeren at the University of Louvain, and together they were responsible for the gloomy mood of a large part of the poetry of the young Belgians. Other members were Albert Giraud (1860-1929) Valère Gille (1867-1921) and Fernand Séverin (1867-1931), who was noted for his almost morbid concentration upon solitude.

OTHER FRENCH REVIVAL POETS

The poems of Albert Mockel (1866-1945), founder of the review *La Wallonie* often imitated the rhythms of old folksongs, while Georges Marlow (1892-1947) combined Parnassian sonorousness with symbolistic musicality in his *Ame en Exil* (The Soul in Exile). One of

Maurice Maeterlinck (1862-1949) was perhaps the best-known Belgian writer of the late 19th and early 20th centuries. A poet and dramatist, he was awarded the Nobel prize for literature in 1911. Maeterlinck, along with Charles van Lerberghe (1861-1907), and Grégoire Le Roy (1862-1941), belonged to the School of Ghent, a group of Symbolist poets whose work tended toward the musical and melancholy.

the most noted poets of the time was the colorful and unique Max Elskamp (1862-1931), who blended themes drawn from old ballads and local customs with simple, childlike imagery and delicate humor. Elskamp has sometimes been called a miniaturist because of his many graceful and charming word-portraits, and his works enjoyed a great popularity during the 1920s and 1930s.

French Prose of the Revival

The national character of French-language prose in Belgium has become strikingly evident since 1880. As young writers turned to realism and naturalism, the tempo of the development of the Belgian novel was accelerated.

The recognized leader of Belgian prose writers during the literary revival was Camille Lemonnier (1844-1913), who has sometimes been called "the awakener." His large and rich body of work includes realistic novels and stories of peasant life, psychological novels, works for children, descriptive novels and critical works. His masterpiece was undoubtedly *Le Mâle* (The Male), which presents the romantic and defiant story of a poacher who falls in love with the daughter of a nobleman. Lemonnier fused lyrical passion with a typically Flemish love of color, and his works are noted for their fiery and impetuous language and picturesque and evocative scenes. His earliest works, such as *Le Mâle*, are his most romantic and lyrical.

Lemonnier later came under the influence of French naturalism, and wrote a series of stark novels depicting the life of the workers in the iron and steel mills around Charleroi. He expressed his hatred of war in the novel *Les Charniers* (The Burial-Chambers) 1871, while works such as *L'Ile Vierge* (The Virgin Island) and *Au Cœur de la Forêt* (In the Heart of the Forest) described his love of nature. Contemporary critics prefer his calmer and more intimate later works, such as *Comme va le Ruisseau* (As the Brook

Flows) and *Le Vent des Moulins* (The Wind in the Vanes), which have regional themes.

EEKHOUD AND DEMOLDER

Another leading novelist of this time was the vigorous and realistic Georges Eekhoud (1854-1927), one of the founders of *La Jeune Belgique*. An extremely prolific author, he produced collections of Romantic poems, realistic and historical novels and short stories of Flemish life. Eekhoud seemed to find ordinary life flat, vulgar and tasteless, and his characters are the outcasts of society. He viewed life as wholly tragic, yet he pitied his characters and had a profound love for his country. His style reproduced the harsh and guttural sounds of Flemish in the French language; and his finest work is the substantially autobiographical *La Nouvelle Carthage* (The New Carthage), a vivid series of sketches describing the teeming life of the port of Antwerp.

The colorful Eugène Demolder (1862-1919) expressed his love of life in a series of realistic sketches and novels. His style is often unruly, uncontrolled and violent, and his works are weighted with patriotic and religious symbolism. He was, above all, a painter with words; his *La Route d'Emeraude* (Emerald Road), for instance, is the life story of a painter. Demolder often used primitive symbolism to popularize his stories, which he drew from the Gospels, and wrote many quaint sketches of judicial and literary life in Belgium.

REGIONAL NOVELISTS

The late 19th century also produced a great number of regional novelists. Georges Virrés (1869-1946) told of his warm affection for the Campine and its people in a style characterized by great precision and delicate irony. The Brabant regionalist Léopold Courouble (1861-1937) gave expression to Belgian humor in his *Famille Kaekebroeck* (The Kaekebroeck Family) series, while Louis Delattre (1870-1938) presented a simple and poignant image of the Walloon character. The prolific and colorful Maurice des Ombiaux (1868-1941) concentrated on the history, architecture, folklore and scenery of his native Hainaut.

CRITICS AND SCHOLARS

In the latter part of the 19th century, literary criticism, the essay and history were also well represented. One of the most notable literary critics was Firmin van den Bosch (1865-1949), author of *Impressions de littérature contemporaine* (Impressions of contemporary literature) 1905, while the well-known art critic Jules Destrée (1863-1936) also wrote a collection of socialist essays entitled *Semailles* (Weeklies) 1913 and a collection of pessimistic poems, *Les Chimères* (Fantasies) 1889. Among the most prominent 19th-century essayists were nationalistic dramatist Edmond Picard (1836-1924) and art critic Arsold Goffin (1863-1934) who criticized the follies of his age.

Godefroid Kurth (1847-1916) is considered principally responsible for the revival of historical studies, but his work was surpassed by his pupil Henri Pirenne (1862-1935), one of the most noted medieval scholars in the world. Pirenne's seven-volume *Histoire de Belgique* (History of Belgium) 1899-1932, enjoyed a popular success unequalled by any other Belgian historian, but he is most noted among fellow-historians for shifting the date of the end of Roman civilization from the time of the Germanic invasion to the time of the 8th and 9th century Nordic and Islamic invasions and presenting evidence of a 10th-century European economic revival.

THE TWENTIETH CENTURY

BY THE END OF THE 19TH CENTURY, Flemish letters were in full bloom and a mature French literature reflected both national and universal characteristics. The upheavals caused by two world wars and the influence of German Expressionism led to a 20th-century revolt against Symbolism and Classicism. Young authors tried to integrate the social and political aspects of life into their writings, while poets sought expression in free verse. Some authors, both Flemish and French, searched for a more universal means of expression through the use of fantasy and psychology.

Flemish Literature

During and immediately after World War I, there was a sudden new flowering of the picturesque regional or rustic tale. One of the chief regional novelists was Felix Timmermans (1886-1947), who was inspired by the folklore and spirit of the Flemish people. His celebrated prose poem *Pallieter* (1916), with its gay, roistering hero and Flemish vistas, is reminiscent of Brueghel's paintings. His use of comic themes and his complacent view of peasant life were copied by novelists such as Ernest Claes (1885-   ), who used dialect to describe rural life. Another regional novelist, Jozef Simons (1888-   ), was a master in the use of humor and sarcasm. His hero is a Flemish Milquetoast with great, impractical dreams who is always forced to fall back upon the resources of his family.

After World War I, poetry and drama were particularly influenced by German Expressionism, and Belgian Expressionists gathered about the review *Ruimte* (Space, 1920-21). They declared that the community was more important than the individual and that ethics were more important than aesthetics. The Expressionist movement was led by the poet Paul van Ostaijen (1896-1928). His *Music Hall* was more political than poetical, but his experiments in form and content had a great deal of influence upon the development of modern Flemish poetry. The poets who have followed in his footsteps include the social revolutionary Achilles Mussche, the delicate and refined Paul Verbruggen, the experimental Victor J. Brunclaire and the

A picturesque setting in Bruges (Brugge), the city so often and so movingly celebrated by the Symbolist poet Georges Rodenbach (1855-98). Rodenbach, who has been called "the singer of Bruges," described the haunting beauty of the West Flanders capital in numerous poems and in his well-known novel Bruges-la-Morte *(Bruges-the-Dead), published in 1892.*

modern Humanists Marnix Gijsen and Wies Moens.

In prose, a group of novelists opposed the regionalists' stereotyped pictures of country vistas and peasants. These writers were often moved by social misery and concerned with the psychological motivations of their characters.

After 1930, the novel reigned supreme in Flemish literature. Young writers such as Willem Ellschot, Maurice Roelants, Gerard Walschap and Lode Zielens sought to describe man's inner conflicts and weaknesses. Poetry also became increasingly personal after 1930. Social and ethical themes became less common, and poets split into a traditional school and an experimental school. Members of the latter group have created poems containing elements of both the real and the unreal. The most powerful of the young Flemish poets is the visionary Bert Decorte (1915-), while Pieter Bucknix and Paul Jonckheere, the religious poet Albe, René Verbeeck and Jan Vercammen have shown great promise.

After World War I, several other novelists rose to prominence. These young writers include the vigorous Louis-Paul Boon, the delicate and subtle Paul Aeken, the intellectual and poetical Hubert Lampo and the lively and interesting Johan Daisne. The novel in recent years has covered a wide range of subjects and styles.

Twentieth-Century French Poetry

During the early years of the 20th century, French-language poetry continued to be dominated by the sometimes violent other-worldliness of symbolist poets such as Maeterlinck, Lerberghe and Verhaeren and by the refinement of the Parnassians. This period saw the rise of a number of young symbolists including Théodore Hannon, Thomas Braun and Jean Dominique. Braun (1876-) was a lawyer and a Roman Catholic, and his poems present Catholicism as a pleasant, almost jolly peasant religion.

Hannon (1851-1916) is noted for his wordplay and exotic sensuality, while Jean Dominique (1875-1957), whose real name was Marie Closset, is known as a poet's poet. She modeled her symphonic and affected style upon the work of the French Mallarmé in many sharply observant poems.

After World War I, Marcel Thiry (1897-) united conservative and experimental forms in his famous *La Mer de la Tranquillité* (Sea of Tranquillity), which presented the drama of man lost and powerless among the anonymous forces of modern business and trade. The founding of the *Journal des Poètes* (Poetic Journal) in 1930 stimulated the production of lyric poetry. Some poets, such as Maurice Carême (1903-) and Jules Minne (1889-), believe poetry should address itself to the common people. Others, such as Georges Linze (1900-), Henri Michaux (1899-) and Robert Vivier (1897-), wrote in a more personal and religious vein.

Since World War II, a number of other young poets have shown great promise. Among these new talents are Charles Bertin, Liliane Wouters, Gérard Prévot, Jean Tordeur and Arthur Haulot. These modern poets are drawing upon both old and new themes and forms in an attempt to portray the Belgian nation and find answers to the problems which face modern man.

Twentieth-Century French Prose

During the early part of this century, French-language prose was dominated by the writers of *La Jeune Belgique*. The orientation of the young writers became increasingly psychological, however, and a number of new novelists and short-story writers appeared after World War I. These young writers were led by André Baillon, Jean Tousseul, Charles Plisnier, Franz Hellens, Marie Gevers and Pierre Nothomb.

The intensely personal André Baillon (1875-1932) wrote bitter accounts of his amoral life, his unhappy childhood and education and his bad health. The novel *Jean Clarambaux* (Eng. trans., 1939), by Jean Tousseul (1890-1944), presents a lovely, sad and simple tale of the quarrymen of the Meuse which makes the author's love for the common people clearly evident. The calm, orderly and lyrical works of Marie Gevers (1883-) concentrate upon form, while Pierre Nothomb (1877-) is noted for his powerful style and imagination.

Two of the best-known authors of this period were the poet, novelist and critic Franz Hellens (1881-) and the prolific and successful Charles Plisnier (1896-1952). Hellens edited the important Franco-Belgian review *Le Disque Vert* (The Green Disc), and his first novel, *En Ville Morte* (In the Dead City), followed the style of the 19th-century symbolist Georges Rodenbach. In his later works, Hellens turned to imaginative realism and surrealism; many of his books contain harsh self-revelations and vague forebodings of doom and anguish. He freely mingled hallucination and reality in works such as *Réalités Fantastiques* (Fantastic Realities)

Plisnier has divided his attention between psychological novels and studies of the atmosphere in Europe between the two world wars. His poetry has moved toward a revolutionary surrealism, and his most moving works are undoubtedly the short stories *Faux Passeports* (False Passports) and the novel *Mariages* (Marriages), which were awarded the Goncourt Prize for Literature in 1937.

Another popular novelist of this period is Georges Simenon. Many of his series of detective stories centered about the fictional Inspector Maigret have been translated into English. The names of Robert Goffin (1898-) and Armand Bernier (1902-) should be added to this list. The period between the wars produced many noted historians and essayists.

Since the end of World War II, authors such as Alexis Curvers, Stanislas Dotremont, Daniel Gilles, Françoise Mallet-Joris, Albert Ayguesparse, Paul Dresse, Arthur Nisin and Maud Frère have gained prominence, as have the historians Georges-Henri Dumont and Jean-Didier Chastelain.

The novelist Francis Walder (1906-) received the Goncourt Prize in 1958, while the poet Roger Bodart (1910-), literary adviser of the Ministry of Public Education, was awarded the National Triennial Prize for literature in the French language in 1947.

CONCLUSION

THE MOST NOTABLE QUALITY OF BELgian literature is its diversity. Not only is it written in two languages, but it expresses both a profound nationalism and most of the major trends which have appeared in European literature. The truculence and fatalism of Eekhoud and Lemonnier the reserved mysticism of Rodenbach, the *joie de vivre* of Demolder, the regionalism of Virrés and the national folklore of De Coster have all been incorporated into the mainstream of Belgian literary thought. The pronounced degree of individuality of the Belgian authors has contributed to the creation of a vigorous body of modern Belgian literature of exceptional quality.

THE THEATER

BELGIAN DRAMA, LIKE BELGIAN LITER-ature, has been written in both the French and the Flemish languages. During the Middle Ages, the emphasis was upon religious drama, and the playwrights of Flanders dominated the production of both religious and secular works. Mystery plays and liturgical dramas, for example, were performed from the 10th century and Passion and Resurrection plays and dramas based upon Old Testament stories were popular throughout the Middle Ages.

Early Flemish Drama

The theatrical genre known as *abele speelen* (artistic plays) dates from the 14th century, and the four surviving Flemish texts of this genre —*Esmoreit, Gloriant* (Gloria), *Lansloet van Danemarken* (Lancelot of Denmark) and *Vanden Winter ende vanden Somer* (Winter and Summer) —are viewed by some historians as the earliest examples of European secular drama. The period also produced a comic theater, characterized by folk earthiness, which extended the tradition of the popular farce. One of the best-known of the medieval farces was *The Witches.*

The best-known morality play of the time was *Elckerlyck,* from which the famous *Everyman* was taken. Other important early mystery plays were *Die Eerste Bliscap van Maria* (The First Joy of Mary) and *Die*

Sevenste Bliscap van Onser Vrouwen (The Seventh Joy of Our Lady).

The "Chambers of Rhetoric," which date back to at least the 12th century, took special interest in the theater and sponsored many theatrical competitions in which the competitors treated a given theme *(regel).* The activities of these groups reached a height in the 16th century. No less than 19 morality plays were performed on the theme "What is the greatest consolation of a dying man?" at a *landjuweel* (festival of competitions between the various chambers) held at Ghent in 1539.

During the 16th century, Cornelis Everaert (c. 1480-1556) produced about 30 works which satirized scandal and vice. His license was tolerated because he always concluded his works with a moral application. The Chamber competitions also produced a number of farces and plays upon classical themes such as *Venus, Palas ende Juno,* and the famous rhetorician Matthijs de Castelein is also known for his play based upon the legend of Piramus and Thisbe *(Historie van Pyramus ende Thisbe).* Several other plays with classical themes were produced at Antwerp during the mid-16th century.

Early French Drama

During the Middle Ages, the French-speaking region of Belgium also produced a large number of religious and secular plays. The first farce in the French language, *Le Garçon et l'Aveugle* (the Boy and the Blind Man), was performed at

Tournai in 1275. The most noted French-speaking Belgian playwright of the 16th century, Louis de Masures, worked in France. His famous trilogy, *David* (1563), had the qualities of both a mystery play and a tragedy, and expressed some of the ideas of the Reformation. A number of scholarly dramatic works written during this century, such as Pierre Heyns' *Comédies et Tragédies du Laurier* (Comedies and Tragedies of the Laurel) and Gerard de Vivre's *Trois Comédies Françaises* (Three French Comedies), reveal a measure of imagination.

The Seventeenth and Eighteenth Centuries

FLEMISH DRAMA

The most noted Flemish authors of the 17th century fled to Holland to escape religious persecution by the Spaniards. One of the best of these was the poet and dramatist Joost van den Vondel (1587-1679), whose works include over 30 dramas (see *The Netherlands: The Literature*). Van den Vondel wrote most of his tragedies and biblical dramas for the "Chambers of Rhetoric," and his best-known religious dramas are *Pascha* (an Easter play), *Adam in Ballingschap* (Adam in Exile) and *Joseph in Egypten* (Joseph in Egypt). He also wrote a number of historical plays, such as *Gijsbrecht van Aemstel,* and cultivated many different styles with great success. His contemporaries regarded Van den Vondel as one of the greatest dramatists of all time.

The "Chambers of Rhetoric" were active in the countryside throughout the 17th century, although they began to disappear from the cities. During the 18th century, the French language dominated Belgian literature, and most Flemish plays of the time were crude versions of French originals. The most noted 18th-century Flemish playwright was the prolific J. B. Hofman (1758-1835), who introduced the middle-class tragedy into Belgian theater.

FRENCH DRAMA

During the 17th and 18th centuries, French-language drama in Belgium was kept alive primarily through per-

A scene from an anonymous 15th-century farce of the type produced in Flanders and Wallonia during the Renaissance, as a reaction against the solemn liturgical dramas and mystery plays that dominated the theater of the time.

formances held in the Jesuit colleges. The comedy became popular among the upper-class members of Belgian society and formed part of the festivities staged for the visits of foreign princes and the entertainment of the royal court.

During the 18th century, the Jesuit colleges continued to present sacred tragedies such as *Abimelech*, which was performed in the Jesuit college at Mons in 1722. This century also saw the rise of the secular theater. In 1698, the Elector of Bavaria erected a building in Brussels which later became the national opera house, and other playhouses were erected at Ghent and Antwerp during this same period. This development led to the rise of permanent, settled acting companies, which had become well established by the end of the 19th century.

The most important 18th-century French-language dramatist was the spirited and talented Blaise-Henri de Walef (1661-1734). Only one of his tragedies, *Electre*, was published during his lifetime; his *Mahomet II* was not published until 1870, while a third play, *Hannibal à Caporie* (Hannibal at Capua), remains in manu-

script found among his family papers.

The Nineteenth and Twentieth Centuries

The most noted Flemish playwrights of the 19th century were Albrecht Rodenbach (1856-80), Alfred Hegenscheidt (1886-1964) and Cyriel Buysse (1859-1932). The youthful and impassioned Rodenbach's *Gudrun*, a drama in verse, served as a model for young post-Romantic poets of his time. Hegenscheidt's sole drama, *Starkadd* (Stars), has a subject which is related to the theme of *Hamlet*. The play's language is beautiful and poetic, and was later used by Oskar de Gruyter in his efforts to revive Flemish-language theater.

Cyriel Buysse, the most famous of the three, was also a realistic novelist, and his writings were influenced by the naturalism of Emile Zola. His plays enjoyed great success in Flanders and Holland, and his masterpiece was the comedy *De Plaatsvervangende Vrederechter* (The Deputy Justice of the Peace) 1895, which caricatured the Belgian judiciary.

Buysse stated that he chose to write in Flemish because there were so few literary works for the common people in that language.

'LA JEUNE BELGIQUE'

During the early part of the 19th century, few plays were written in the French-speaking region of Belgium. At the end of the 19th century, however, drama shared in the general revival of Belgian culture. Like the outstanding poets and novelists of the revival, the most noted Belgian dramatists of the time also gathered about the review *La Jeune Belgique* (see *Belgium: The Literature*).

One of the earliest members of the 19th-century poetic theater was the Symbolist poet Charles van Lerberghe (1861-1907), whose *Les Flaireurs* (The Sleuths) 1892, was a sort of mystery play depicting the horror of a young girl confronted with death. The modern dialogue in his drama *Pan*, which presents the conflict between Pan and the established order, foreshadowed the work of the leader of the poetic theater, Maurice Maeterlinck.

Maeterlinck (1862-1949) centered his plays about the idea of fatality. His extremely symbolical early plays, such as *La Princesse Maleine* (1899) and *Pelléas et Mélisande* (1892), maintain an oppressive, uneasy and mysterious atmosphere. His later plays, which include *Monna Vanna* (1902) and *L'Oiseau Bleu* (The Blue Bird) 1909, are more realistic, and contain elements of humor and fantasy. Other noted playwrights of the late 19th century include the poets Paul Spaak, Henri Maubel, Emile Verhaeren and Iwan Gilken.

MODERN FLEMISH DRAMA

The most significant impetus to the modern revival of Flemish theater was given by an organization called *Vlaamse Volkstoneel* (Flemish Popular Stage) 1923-29, led by Dr. Oskar De Gryter. This group renewed contact with Flemish traditions by staging miracle plays, farces and moralities, as well as producing the best of the modern dramas. From 1919 to 1930, theater in the Flemish-speaking region followed the ideas of German Expressionism, which stressed the importance of the author's inner emotions and sensations.

The most influential dramatist of the period was Herman Teirlinck (1879-   ), who first won fame as a novelist. His *Ik Dien* (The Servant) is a modern version of the famous Flemish legend *Beatrijs* (see *Belgium:*

The Literature), while *De Man Zonder Lijf* (The Man Without a Body) is patterned upon a medieval allegory. The two major characters of *De Man Zonder Lijf* represent the two facets of man: the part which is satisfied with what it has and the part which pursues an unattainable ideal. This work is considered Teirlinck's best, and its dialogue is fresh, warm and humorous.

Another noted playwright of the period between the wars was Pol de Mont (1895-1950), whose beautiful *Nuances* (1922) is a bitter denunciation of false patriotism. *Het Geding Van Ons Heer* (The Lawsuit of Our Master) 1925, is a modern version of the Passion story. The best work of Anton Van de Velde (1895-1964) is his battle story *Tyl I*, an extravagant, witty, lively and sometimes irritating play which has enjoyed great success.

During the German occupation of Belgium in World War II, Johan Daisne (1906-   ) demonstrated the new freedom which Expressionism had given to the Flemish theater. Herwig Hensen (1917-   ) also gained prominence at this time. Hensen's characters challenge death and rush to test their strength against it. His most famous play is *Lady Godiva*, a version of the famous English story. Hensen has won great praise for his inventive, vigorous and skillful dialogue.

Since World War II, three young dramatists have come to the fore in the Flemish theater. Tone Brulin's works deal with the anguish created by the war and the postwar period, the precocious Hugo Claus opposes conformity and bourgeois morality, and Jozef van Hoeck's famous *Voorlopig Vonnis* (Tentative Judgment) explores man's egoism. Another notable trend in modern Flemish drama is the growing number of massive productions generally based upon religious themes growing out of the medieval mystery plays. The mass theater attempts to raise and broaden the level of the theater and to reanimate religious and national traditions.

TWENTIETH-CENTURY FRENCH DRAMA

Between the two wars, the drama in French-speaking Belgium was dominated by Fernand Crommelynck (1885-   ), Henri Soumagne (1891-1951), Michel de Ghelderode (1898-1962) and Herman Closson (1901-   ).

Crommelynck won world fame with *Le Cocu Magnifique* (The Magnificent Cuckold) 1920, and *Tripes d'Or* (Guts of Gold). He presents a basically moral theater, pointing out the danger of foolish people who spend their lives wrapped up in idle worries. Henri Soumagne became famous overnight with his play *L'Autre Messie* (The Other Messiah) 1923, in which a group of drunken men discuss the existence of God in a miserable Warsaw saloon.

The prolific and experimental Ghelderode has written some 50 plays characterized by excesses, contrasts and strange images. He shaped language to suit his dramatic purposes and—like Crommelynck—often built his works upon the idea of sin. The fourth major playwright between the wars was Herman Closson, who believed that man could achieve greatness only in the act of creation. His cold and critical works presented heroes haunted by the idea of grandeur, and the manner in which he reduced a Belgian national hero to the level of a weak, scheming and insecure modern man in his *Godefroi de Bouillon* created a scandal.

Since World War II, a number of other Belgian playwrights have risen to prominence. Suzanne Lilar (1901-   ) won fame with her analysis of the Don Juan theme in *Le Burlador* (The Trickster). *Chemins Menant au ciel* (Roads Leading to Heaven) reveals her preoccupation with the supernatural, while *Le Roi Lépreux* (The Leper King) 1951, alternates between the personal conflicts of the actors and the events of a medieval drama in a play-within-a-play. Jean Mogin (1921-   ) creates dramatic interest through the personalities of his characters rather than through his situations, and was awarded the Lugne-Poe prize for the best play of the year with his firm and vigorous *À Chacun Selon Sa Faim* (To Each According to his Hunger). Other noted modern playwrights include Georges Sion, Paul Willems, Marie-Thérèse Bodart and Charles Bertin.

Although modern Belgian theater has played a major role in contemporary literary movements such as Symbolism and Expressionism, it still illustrates a kinship to the dramas of the Middle Ages. The sense of tragedy which pervaded Belgian medieval plays has been applied by modern playwrights to the drama of modern man, torn between his earthly aims and his spiritual ideals.

A scene from the dramatic opera **Montus,** *by the Belgian composer Marcel Poot (1901-   ). Poot, director of the Brussels Conservatory, has been responsible for numerous artistic triumphs on the Belgian musical stage.*

During the 13th century, the Belgian-born Francus of Paris wrote *Ars Cantus Mensurabilis* (The Art of Measured Singing), the oldest work of its kind in existence. Monks and abbots such as Olbert, Estienne, Heriger, Hingobrand and Damian contributed to 13th-century Belgian church music, while the troubadour Adenez (born c.1420) is noted for a number of secular songs.

From the second half of the 14th century on, there was active exchange between Flemish and Italian music. The Belgian-born Johannes Ciconia (c.1340-1411), who studied music at Avignon and spent much of his life traveling and working in Italy, wrote two important treatises, *De Nova Musica* (The New Music) and *De Proportionibus* (Proportion). His compositions fused the style of the Italian ballad and madrigal with the structure of the French motet.

The Fifteenth Century

Belgian music knew its greatest age during the period of Burgundian rule. The influence of the Belgian composers spread throughout Europe, contributing particularly to musical development in France and Italy. The composers of the Franco-Flemish school based their compositions on the equality of all voice parts and joined these parts by means of an imitative, contrapuntal procedure. The structure of this music was extremely refined and complicated, characterized by dissonance, rhythmical contrasts and contrapuntal artifice.

DUFAY AND BINCHOIS

Two of the early leaders of the Franco-Flemish school of music were Guillaume Dufay (c.1400-74) and Gilles Binchois (c.1400-60). Dufay, regarded as the greater of the two, wrote primarily secular music and spent most of his life in Italy. In his compositions he skillfully joined the rather rigid style of the Gothic period with the feeling for melody expressed in the early Florentine school. He developed four-part music, and is credited with the improvement of musical notation. His compositions include masses, motets, magnificats and songs. Binchois excelled in secular songs, for which he

THE MUSIC

The Middle Ages

THE EARLIEST INFORMATION ABOUT music in Belgium is found in Latin writings concerning the sacred and war songs of the ancient Gallic and Belgian tribes. The first extant musical documents, however, date from after the establishment of the Carolingian empire and the foundation of the famous *Scholae Cantorum* by Roman monks in French monasteries. During this time, the most important musical center in Belgium was the monastery of Cambrai.

The first known Belgian composer is the Benedictine monk Hucbald (c.840-c.930), head of the school of music at Saint-Aamand. Although Hucbald wrote hymns and sequences and was charged with the reorganization of the Church music schools in about 893, his fame rests primarily upon his *De Harmonica Institutione* (The Harmonic Institution), one of the earliest treatises on polyphonic music. In this work, he treated the eight modes of church music (based on the ideas of the 5th-century Roman philosopher Boethius) and invented a system of musical notation in which the syllables of the text and the notes were written between a series of horizontal lines.

used French lyrics. He commonly wrote in three parts, and his works were extremely popular during his lifetime.

OKEGHEM AND OTHERS

The second Belgian polyphonic school was led by Jan Okeghem (c.1430-95) and the Dutch composer Jacob Obrecht (see *The Netherlands: The Music*). This school, which spanned the latter half of the 15th century, marks a definite turning point in the evolution of music. Okeghem and Obrecht achieved unity in their compositions by using simple variations on themes rather than merely repeating them, as had been done previously. Okeghem, a pupil of Dufay, worked in the service of the French court in Paris, and wrote primarily music for four voices. His capacity for invention is seen in his mass *Missa Cujusvis Toni*, which could be sung in any of the Church modes. In his fugues, Okeghem used the now-common *stretto* form, in which he "answered" his melody by repeating it at closer intervals than in the original.

Other pupils of Dufay included the elegant and refined secular composer Antoine Busnois (died 1492) and the theorist Johannes Tinctoris (c.1446-1511), who founded the first school of music in Italy and edited the first dictionary of music, *Terminorum Musicae Diffinitorium,* in about 1475.

The Flemish-born Heinrich Isaac (c.1450-1517) was known in Italy as Arrigo Tedesco (Harry the German) because of his simple, beautiful German songs. These light, secular compositions were admirably suited to the atmosphere of the Medici court, where he did most of his work. Isaac also wrote masterly Church music, and demonstrated great skill and ingenuity in the leading of the parts.

The Sixteenth Century

During the 16th century, both sacred and secular composers began to fit their music more closely to the meaning of the literary text. Josquin des Prés (c.1450-1521), a pupil of both Dufay and Okeghem, is often considered the greatest composer of his time. His works mark the transition between the music of the Middle Ages and that of the Renaissance, and he has sometimes been called "the Chaucer of music." Although born in the town of Condé in French Flanders, Des Prés composed in the Franco-Flemish polyphonic style. He developed the methods he inherited from Dufay, Okeghem and Obrecht, bringing to the traditional melodic and contrapuntal styles his own expressive and creative imagination. He made use of the more melodious and harmonic thirds and sixths, rather than the common fifths, octaves and fourths, and has been credited with the invention of the *sharp* in musical notation.

Des Prés is most noted for his

The Triumph of Caesar, *by Peter Paul Rubens. The Baroque flamboyance of the painting is reminiscent of much Belgian music of the late Renaissance period. One of the greatest Belgian composers of this time was Orlando di Lasso (c. 1530-94), also known as Roland de Lassus, whose elaborate musical compositions were characterized by dynamism, impetuosity, dramatic accents and bold modulations.*

great Mass cycles and his work with the French song. His works were printed and widely distributed, and he shaped the development of Belgian music during the first half of the 16th century.

Other leading composers during the early part of the century were Nicolas Gombert (c.1500-56), Jacobus Clemens non Papa (c.1500-56) and Adrian Willaert (c.1480-1562). Gombert contributed to the gradual progression toward the instrumental and vocal fugue, which unified the musical texture by avoiding rests, cadences and other things which might break the unity of the melodic line. The clear and powerful works of Clemens, with their bold modulations, are often compared to those of Palestrina.

The greatest of these three composers was Willaert, who served as chapel master at St. Mark's in Venice for much of his life. His best work was in the form of the madrigal, which took its inspiration from secular poetry and placed the melody in the soprano. He is viewed as the founder of the Venetian school, which dominated Italian music for the next century and a half. Two of his com-

Philippe de Monte (1521-1603), one of the finest Belgian composers of the early Baroque period, wrote some 1200 madrigals in addition to numerous masses, motets and other pieces.

patriots, Jacques Arcadelt (c.1514-75) and Philippe Verdelot (died c.1567), were also influential in the development of the madrigal form, as were Cyprien de Rore (1516-65) and Jakob de Werthe (1535-96).

DE MONTE AND DI LASSO

Philippe de Monte (1521-1603) was one of the most typical composers of the time. He wrote about 1200 madrigals and was one of the first composers to express emotion in his sacred compositions.

The greatest Belgian composer of the latter part of the century was Orlando di Lasso (c.1530-94), also known as Roland de Lassus, who sought to "illustrate the meaning of the variations in the text." Di Lasso was admired and celebrated throughout Europe, and his contemporaries referred to him as the Prince of Music and the Belgian Orpheus. He served Duke Albert V of Bavaria, and his sole duty was to make music. His compositions are characterized by dynamism, impetuosity, dramatic accents and a flair for the comic and picturesque. Di Lasso was a prolific composer—some 2000 works are attributed to him, including music for the 7 penitential psalms, motets, masses, Italian madrigals, French chansons and 7 books of sacred and secular German songs. His virtuosity is well illustrated in his *Magnum Opus*, which includes no less than 500 motets for 2 to 12 voices.

The Seventeenth and Eighteenth Centuries

During the closing years of the 16th century, Belgian music underwent a period of rapid decline, and Belgian musical life during the first half of the 17th century centered about foreign musicians serving at the Spanish court in Brussels. The most original native composer was the organist Henri Dumont (1610-84), whose *Le Motet Français* (The French Motet) was imitated by other Belgian composers of sacred music.

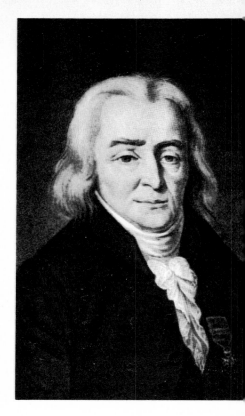

During this time, purely instrumental parts, solos and dialogues between the "small" and the "large" choirs were slowly added to religious compositions.

The most significant composers of the 18th century were André Ernest Modeste Grétry (1741-1813) and François Joseph Gossec, both of whom settled in Paris and were influential in the founding of the *Conservatoire* there. Gossec was extremely popular during his day. He composed the first symphonic pieces for French orchestras and introduced the use of horns and clarinets in the orchestra; his influence on the development of French instrumental music was extremely important. His works include overtures, oratorios, choral and orchestral works and a series of grandiloquent works (including *Fourteenth of July Hymn* and *Tribute to Liberty*) for performance at the elaborate festivals and ceremonies which were so popular in his day.

The charming and delicate works of Grétry contrast with those of Gossec. His extremely melodic compositions include 50 operas, 6 symphonies, quartets, sonatas and a number of graceful ballets. Grétry attempted to follow the inflections of

A. E. M. Grétry (1741-1813), one of the most influential Belgian composers of his time, wrote some 50 popular operas, the best known of which is Richard Cœur de Lion (1784).

the speaking voice in his stage works, and his best-known opera is *Richard Cœur de Lion* (1784).

The Nineteenth and Twentieth Centuries

The 19th century saw the rise of a nationalistic style of music. The teacher and composer Peter Leonard Benoit (1834-1901) led in the revival of Flemish music based upon the folksong. One of his chief followers was Jan Blockx (1851-1912), composer of symphonies, cantatas, operas and songs. Another was the pianist and composer Edgar Tinel (1854-1912), who is known for his sacred music and oratorios.

FRANCK

The most noted 19th-century Belgian composer, however, was César Auguste Franck (1822-90), whose best works are those written for the piano and stringed instruments. In his larger orchestral works, Franck was almost obsessed with chromaticism and his style lacks some of the naturalness and delicacy which characterize his chamber music.

Franck has sometimes been called

François Joseph Gossec (1734-1829) was born in Wallonia, but spent most of his life in Paris. An extremely popular composer, he greatly influenced the development of French orchestral and chamber music.

the founder of the modern French instrumental school, and his unconventional music had a marked influence upon his younger contemporaries. He was an inspired and dedicated teacher, and his students included the original and rhapsodic Guillaume Lekeu (1870-94) and the fresh and extremely talented Joseph Jongen (1873-1953), who based some of the best of his pieces upon Wallonian folklore.

The teacher, critic and composer Paul Gilson (1865-1942), by contrast, was influenced by the sonorous craftsmanship of the orchestrators of the Russian School. One of his most brilliant students is Marcel Poot (1901-   ), director of the Brussels Conservatory, whose works include symphonies, string and piano compositions, opera and ballets. Another noted Belgian composer of this generation is Jean Absil (1893-   ),

a sure craftsman who excels in chamber music.

AFTER WORLD WAR II

The composers who came into prominence after World War II broke sharply with their predecessors. They abandoned folklore as the chief source of inspiration, turning instead to the atonal creations of Stravinsky and Bartók. Camille Schmitt (1908-   ) and Victor Legley (1915-   ) adopted Schönberg's twelve-tone system, while the works of Jean Louël are characterized by their complex polytonality. Norbert Rousseau (1907-   ) is fond of vast proportions and impressive choral constructions, and Gérard Bertouille (1898-   ) has attempted to integrate the modern trends in composition with the traditional forms. One of the most noted modern Belgian composers is the gifted and original David Van de Woestijne (1915-   ), whose works include an orchestral and a violin concerto and compositions for the voice, the harpsichord and stringed instruments.

Belgium today also has a number of outstanding music critics, teachers and performers. The country is the site of many schools, festivals and concert halls, and the Belgian people seem to appreciate both modern and traditional music. While awarding praise to the young composers, the public also flocks to performances of the *Pro Musica Antiqua* society, which is now making an extensive series of recordings.

The composer and teacher Peter Leonard Benoit (1834-1901) spearheaded a late-19th-century movement advocating the rejuvenation of Belgian music through the use of native Flemish and Wallonian folksongs.

THE FILM

ALTHOUGH BELGIUM'S DOMESTIC FILM production is small, it should be remembered that some of the "greats" of the French movie industry are Belgians. Belgium does not lack the artistic talent for a national cinema, but France's highly developed movie industry and extensive studio and laboratory facilities make an economically sound domestic film output impossible.

Feature Films

One of the most noted Belgian-born directors who worked in France was Jacques Feyder (Jacques Frederix, 1888-1948). Some of his silent movies—such as *Thérèse Raquin* (1928) and *Les Nouveaux Messieurs* (The New Gentlemen) 1929—and his sound films—*Le Grand Jeu* (The Great Gamble) 1934, *Pension Mimosas* (1936) and *La Kermesse Héroïque* (Carnival in Flanders) 1937—have become film classics.

The screenwriter Charles Spaak, brother of Belgian Foreign Minister Henri Spaak, has made numerous contributions to the French movie industry. He wrote or collaborated on Feyder's *Thérèse Raquin*, *Les Nouveaux Messieurs* and *La Kermesse Héroïque* and scripted Julien Duvivier's *La Belle Équipe* (They Were Five) 1937, *La Bandera* (1935) and *La Fin du Jour* (The End of the Day) 1939. Jean Renoir produced his greatest movie, *La Grande Illusion* (The Great Illusion) 1931, from a script written by Spaak. There can be no doubt that Spaak was the most significant screenwriter of the French cinema during the years preceding World War II. Since the war, Spaak and André Cayatte have co-authored *Justice est Faite* (Justice Is Done) 1950, *Nous Sommes Tous des Assassins* (We Are All Murderers) 1954, *Le Dossier Noir* (The Bad Record) 1956 and *Le Passage du Rhin* (Tomorrow Is My Turn) 1960.

That excellent and durable star of the French cinema and theater Fernand Gravet in a native of Belgium, as are the actors Jean Servais, Victor Francen, Fernand Ledoux and Madeleine Ozeray. The works of the Belgian-born novelist Georges Simenon are the greatest single source of present-day screen adaptations.

Although a large percentage of the Belgian population shares a common language with France, 55 per cent of the country's people are Flemish and speak a language similar to that spoken in neighboring Holland. Therefore, the producer-director Jan Vanderheyden began national Flemish production in Antwerp in 1934. His films *De Witte* and *Uylenspiegel* showed promise, but he was forced to cease working in the Belgian cinema in 1945 because of his wartime activities with the Nazis.

Since 1945, about 25 Flemish-language feature films and a few French-language films have been made in Belgium. With the exception of *Les Mouettes Meurent au Port* (The Sea Gulls Die in the Harbor), directed by Ivo Michiels and Roland Verhavert, these films are primarily of local interest.

Documentaries

Belgian documentary films are on a much higher level than Belgian feature productions. Documentary film production is subsidized by the Belgian government, which operates an excellent training school for young film-makers, *Institut Technique Supérieur de Cinématographie*.

Henry Storck's best documentaries were *Une Idylle à la Plage* (Idyll on the Beach), *Histoire du Soldat Inconnu* (The Story of the Unknown Soldier), *Images d'Ostende* (Visions of Ostend), *L'Ile de Pâques* (Easter Island) and *La Maison de la Misère* (The House of Misery). Storck has recently made some excellent movies about art, partly in collaboration with Paul Hasaerts, and has tried his hand at feature production with *Le Banquet des Fraudeurs* (The Feast of the Swindlers). Paul Hasaerts also made a picture about Flemish art, *Siècle d'Or* (Golden Age).

Charles Dekeukeleire's exciting *Combat de Boxe* (Boxing Match) 1927, proved his great editing abilities. His *Histoire d'un Détective* (The Story of a Detective) 1929 and *Visions de Lourdes* (Visions of Lourdes) 1932, were followed by *Le Mauvais Œil* (The Evil Eye) 1936, based on a script by the well-known Flemish playwright Herman Teirlinck. *Terres Brûlées* (Scorched Earth) 1935, recorded a trip across Africa and *Au Pays du Scalp* (In the Country of the Scalp) 1938, was one of a series of documentaries Dekeukeleire made during an extended voyage through South America. Some of his later pictures are *L'Atome* (The Atom) 1953, *Trois Villes d'Eau* (Three Spas) 1954 and *Charles-Quint et Son Temps* (Charles V and His Time) 1957.

One of the most prominent younger Belgian directors is Luc de Heusch, who became known through his brutal and harsh *Gestes de Repas* (Account of a Meal). Paul Meyer's *Klinkaart*, based on a novel by the Flemish writer Det Van Aken, portrayed a young girl's first trying day at work in a brick factory still run under outmoded working conditions. André Cauvin, who now lives in Israel, made a number of good documentaries in the Congo, such as *Bongola* and *L'Équateur aux Cent Visages* (The Hundred Faces of the Equator). His *L'Agneau Mystique* (The Mystic Lamb) analyzed certain masterpieces of Flemish painting.

The per capita attendance at movie houses in Belgium is one of the highest in Europe. From 1935 to 1947, annual film festivals were held at Brussels, but in 1948 they were moved to the resort Knokke-le-Zoute.

A frame from Charles Dekeukeleire's fine documentary film In the Land of Till Eulenspiegel, *which was produced in 1949.*

THE NETHERLANDS

A canal in Amsterdam, the largest city in the Netherlands. Although Amsterdam is officially the capital, the center of government and the seat of the sovereign are at The Hague.

LOCATION AND GENERAL FEATURES

THE NETHERLANDS (LITERALLY, "LOW lands") is a country in northwestern Europe about half the size of the state of South Carolina. Known officially as the Kingdom of the Netherlands, it is sometimes also called Holland, the name of a region which today comprises the provinces of North and South Holland.

On the north and west the Netherlands has a coastline on the North Sea; the country is bordered on the south by Belgium and on the east

An aerial view of The Hague, *the administrative seat of the Netherlands government. Around the square lake, the Vijver, in the heart of the city, are grouped the towered parliament buildings. In the center of the court is the* Ridderzaal, *or Hall of Knights, where sessions of the Parliament (Staten-Generaal) are held.*

by the Federal Republic of Germany (West Germany). The Netherlands extends from 50°45′ to 53°52′ north latitude and from 3°20′ to 7°13′ east longitude. Excluding inland waters, it has an area of 12,870 square miles; when these waters are included the total is 15,800 square miles.

Inlets of the sea penetrate deep into the country and estuaries of large rivers such as the Rhine, the Maas and the Scheldt form additional watery areas. The struggle against water and against the sea has been one of the most important factors in Dutch history. Large portions of the country's territory have been reclaimed from the sea by constant effort over many centuries.

In spite of their continual conflict with the sea, or perhaps because of it, the people who came and settled on the marshes of Holland succeeded in creating one of the most vital and viable states in Europe. The Dutch undertook bold voyages that gained for them a colonial empire and profitable commerce that rivaled those of larger and stronger nations. As is the case with other colonial powers, the empire today has been greatly reduced, but the country itself still occupies a position of importance and prestige among nations.

The Netherlands enjoys a geographical situation favorable to communication with near and distant neighbors. Within its boundaries are the mouths of the Rhine and Maas rivers. Thus the country dominates the main outlets to the sea used by a large area of West Germany. There is access to the Mediterranean across Belgium and France, and routes from Scandinavia and northern Germany to Belgium and France pass through Netherlands territory.

England is only 110 miles away across the North Sea. Until modern shipping and air travel developed, this sea was broad enough to offer the Dutch protection, but not so wide as to hinder them from making contacts with peoples living around it. Even in early Roman times (the 2nd to the 5th century A.D.) there were many trade routes across the area and commerce flourished.

The Netherlands has few natural frontiers with its neighbors. Extensive marshy areas in the northeast, which once impeded traffic between the Netherlands and Germany, have been largely reclaimed. Neither are there natural barriers between the Netherlands and Belgium. The Campine heathlands separating North Brabant from the Belgian province of Antwerp are not a real obstacle. Along the coast, the border province of Zeeland is broken up into numerous islands by inlets of the sea, but these waterways serve rather to increase communication than to act as barriers.

ORGANIZATION OF THE STATE

Administrative Divisions

THE NETHERLANDS IS DIVIDED INTO 11 provinces: Drente, Friesland, Gelderland, Groningen, Limburg, North Brabant, North Holland, Overijssel, South Holland, Utrecht and Zeeland. Each province is governed by a Crown Commissioner appointed by the sovereign and by a popularly elected provincial estate, or council.

The basic unit of local administration is the municipality, or commune, of which there are about 1000 in the entire country. Municipalities are governed by Crown-appointed burgomasters (mayors) and popularly elected municipal councils.

The National Government

The Netherlands is a constitutional monarchy; its constitution was drawn up in 1814 and has been revised many times since. The royal family is the house of Orange-Nassau and, unlike neighboring Belgium, a woman may accede to the throne if there are no male heirs. Since 1948, the sovereign has been Queen Juliana.

The sovereign appoints the presidents of the two houses of Parliament, the cabinet ministers, the provincial Crown Commissioners and the municipal burgomasters. He or she is head of the armed forces, conducts foreign relations, signs all bills passed by Parliament and may dissolve Parliament.

There are two bodies which assist the sovereign in executive matters. The first is the Council of State, a permanent advisory body which makes recommendations on administrative problems and on the introduction of legislation. The effective central executive body is the Council of Ministers, or cabinet. It originates most legislation and is responsible to Parliament.

PARLIAMENT

The Parliament, or States-General (*Staten-Generaal*), is made up of a First Chamber consisting of 75 members elected by the provincial councils for six-year terms, and a Second Chamber of 150 members popularly elected for four-year terms. The Second Chamber may propose new bills or amendments to bills in force, while the First Chamber may only approve or reject bills proposed by others—by the sovereign, the cabinet or the Second Chamber.

The sovereign may dissolve Parliament, but should this occur new elections must be held within 40 days. All citizens over 23 years of age are entitled to vote in the Netherlands, and appearance at the polls is compulsory even if the voter casts only a blank ballot.

The Legal System

The judiciary is headed by a 17-member Supreme Court. There are 5 courts of appeal, 23 district courts and 62 canton courts. A three-member Auditing Court has responsibility for reviewing the administration of the country's finances. Canton courts, presided over by a single judge, deal with minor offenses, while the district courts, usually with three judges, handle the more serious cases. Courts of appeal also have three-member panels, and their decisions may be appealed to the Supreme Court.

Judges are appointed for life by the sovereign, and may be removed only by the Supreme Court. The Netherlands does not have trial by jury.

Religion

Although the members of the royal family belong to the Dutch Reformed Church (Calvinist), there is complete freedom of worship in the Netherlands. About 41 per cent of the people belong to the Dutch Reformed Church or other Protestant groups, about 40 per cent are Roman Catholic, and about 19 per cent adhere to the Jewish and other faiths or have no formal religious affiliation.

The Dutch Reformed Church is organized into 1 synod, 11 provincial districts, 54 classes, 158 districts and 1430 parishes. There is a Catholic archbishop at Utrecht, and there are dioceses at 's Hertogenbosch (Bois-le-Duc), Breda, Groningen, Haarlem, Rotterdam and Roermond.

POPULATION: NETHERLANDS	
PROVINCE	**POPULATION**
	(1963)
Drente	324,517
Friesland	487,061
Gelderland	1,339,682
Groningen	485,978
Limburg	928,596
North Brabant	1,575,211
North Holland	2,123,904
Overijssel	835,494
South Holland	2,787,124
Utrecht	708,885
Zeeland	285,448
Ijsselmeer Polders	2,440
TOTAL	11,889,962*

* Includes 5,622 persons without fixed residence.

Education

The literacy rate in the Netherlands is over 99 per cent, and education is compulsory for all children from 6 to 15 years of age. Elementary education is given in municipally administered schools and in private schools. Most of the latter are denominational and receive state subsidies provided they meet state-required standards. After six years of elementary school, the Dutch student can take two more years of primary schooling, or enroll for three or four years of advanced primary education.

Distribution of population

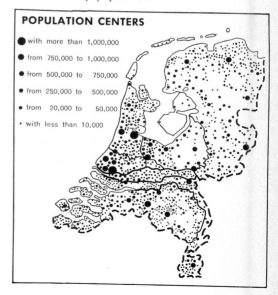

POPULATION CENTERS
- with more than 1,000,000
- from 750,000 to 1,000,000
- from 500,000 to 750,000
- from 250,000 to 500,000
- from 20,000 to 50,000
- with less than 10,000

The Lijnbaan, a lively shopping center in Rotterdam, the capital of the province of South Holland and one of the largest shipping ports in Europe. Of the 11 provinces in the Netherlands, the western provinces of North and South Holland are the most heavily populated and contain the country's three largest cities: Amsterdam, Rotterdam and The Hague.

There are three types of secondary schools. The *hogere burgerschool* (municipal secondary school), which has a five-year course and stresses economics, mathematics and science; the gymnasium which offers a six-year course in classical studies and the humanities, and the lyceum, with a five- or six-year course, which provides a combination of the curricula offered by the other two high schools. In all these schools there is emphasis on the study of the English, German, French and Dutch languages.

There are also advanced technical schools, at the advanced-primary, secondary and college levels. These provide training for work in industry, agriculture and many other fields.

The Netherlands has three state universities: at Leiden (founded in 1575), at Utrecht (1636), and at Groningen (1614). Institutions not administered by the state are the Municipal University of Amsterdam, the Free (Protestant) University of Amsterdam, the Roman Catholic University of Nijmegen, the Technological Institute of Delft, the Technological Institute of Wageningen, the Netherlands School of Economics in Rotterdam and the Roman Catholic Economic Institute in Tilburg.

In addition, and particularly for the benefit of foreign students, the Netherlands has set up international institutes of higher learning, such as the Institute of Social Studies, the Hague Academy of International Law, the Netherlands Institute for Art History and the International Agricultural Center.

Language

The language of the country is officially called Netherlandic; popularly it is known as Hollandsch, or simply Dutch. A Germanic tongue, it is the same in its written form as the Flemish of Belgium, but orally there are a number of regional dialects. The Frisian language is also spoken in the Netherlands, and many Dutch people know one or more foreign languages.

Monetary Units, Weights and Measures

The monetary unit is the guilder, also known as the florin. It is divided into 100 cents, and is valued at 27.6 United States cents. The metric system of weights and measures has been used since 1820.

Status of the Colonial Empire

In 1945, after World War II, Indonesia (the Netherlands East Indies, with the exception of Netherlands New Guinea, now known as West Irian), declared itself independent. Several years of fighting ensued, and in 1949 Indonesian independence was formally recognized. In May 1963, after a period under United Nations administration, West Irian was transferred to Indonesian control, pending self-determination elections scheduled for 1969.

In 1954, internal autonomy was granted to Surinam (Dutch Guiana; 55,140 sq. mi. and 308,000 inhabitants) and the Dutch West Indian territory of the Netherlands Antilles (371 sq. mi. and 188,914 inhabitants).

PHYSICAL GEOGRAPHY

Geological Formation

FROM THE GEOLOGICAL POINT OF view, the territory of the Netherlands is relatively young, most of it being made up of recently deposited alluvial material. The western part of the country was still under the sea in the last (Pliocene) division of the Tertiary period, due to the fact that the rock bed had begun to sink at that time. The quantity of silt brought down by the Rhine and other rivers was so great, however, that some of the land lost by the sinking process was restored.

After the British Isles had been separated from the continental mainland, ocean currents coming from the southwest caused huge amounts of sand to accumulate along the Netherlands coast. A long line of dunes was formed, separating the sea from inland basins into which the rivers flowed. The silt brought down by the rivers mounted up in these inland basins, transforming them slowly into marshlands. The vegetation which grew in these marshes was the basis for substantial deposits of peat.

Still another line of sand dunes was formed later beyond this oldest line, but again the sea penetrated, breaking the sandy barrier at several points and forming new lagoons. The turf and peat carried away by the sea were replaced by extensive deposits of marine clay, especially in the areas of present-day Zeeland and in the north.

The latest line of dunes was formed between the 4th and 9th centuries A.D. This line also was broken up by the sea; some of the dunes remain today as the Frisian Islands, which extend from the province of North Holland north to the shores of Denmark. The five inhabited and four uninhabited islands lying off the provinces of North Holland, Friesland and Groningen are called the West Frisian Islands and belong to the Netherlands. Other islands in the chain belong to Germany and Denmark.

In the eastern Netherlands, during the Quaternary period, the rivers deposited layers of silt upon the deposits of marine clay already lying in the flat valleys. This process created lands of great fertility which, in later years, were protected by man-made dikes.

The northern part of the country was subjected to the great Quaternary glaciers, extensions of which reached the Netherlands from Scandinavia, leaving moraine formations. Moraine substrata exist to the north of a line going from Koevorden to Zwolle and Ijmuiden, and between this line and a more southerly one running from Nijmegen to Haarlem through Utrecht. Other traces of moraine deposists are found in the Gooi and Utrecht hills, in those bordering the Veluwe terrace to the east, in the Daarle and Wierden hills, and in the Twente region. This glacier encroachment also turned the course of the Rhine westward.

Sometime before the Roman occupation (2nd to 5th centuries A.D.), the sea had broken through the protecting dunes to form a long inlet, the Wadden Zee. Further invasions of ocean waters in the 12th and 14th centuries caused the Wadden Zee to overflow and merge with an inland lake known as the Zuider Zee. In 1932, a 20-mile-long dike from Friesland to North Holland was completed, making the Zuider Zee an inland lake once more, with the new name of Ijsselmeer.

Topography

Most of the Netherlands is flat, its rural areas being largely given over to agriculture or pasture land. The highest terrain, only about 1100 feet above sea level, is found in the province of Limburg. Here, bordering the northern Ardennes of Belgium, is a chalk plateau through which swift streams have cut deep valleys.

River terraces made up of silt and pebbles deposited by rivers during the Quaternary period are found in the Campine area of North Brabant and Limburg. Although once covered only by heather or sparse woods, many of these areas have now been made agriculturally productive. Similar terrain exists north of the Maas and the Rhine, but here there are also glacial deposits. In some regions, such as in the provinces of Drente and Groningen, glacial erosion has left great hollows which now contain peat bogs. The valleys of the Maas, the Rhine, the Ijssel, and the coastal areas of Zeeland, Friesland and Groningen consist mainly of flat land made up of alluvial silt and marine clay.

Sandy beaches and dunes line most of the Netherlands coastal areas, including the seaward coasts of the West Frisian Islands. From the tip

The windmill was for centuries the chief means by which excess water was pumped from polders into canals and other drainage outlets. Today, electric plants have replaced most of the windmills, although some are still in use.

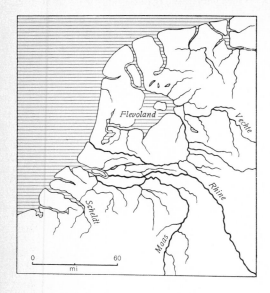

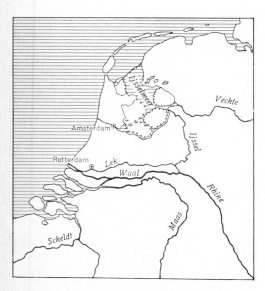

Left, top to bottom: *Maps showing three successive phases in the age-old struggle carried on by the Dutch against the encroachments of the North Sea. The two upper maps show the Low Countries before and after the great deluges of the 12th through 14th centuries. The bottom map shows the results of modern efforts to reclaim the lands lost in previous centuries.*

of North Holland as far south as the Rhine estuary, the coast has few indentations. But in lower South Holland and Zeeland the coastal zone is divided into numerous islands, separated by wide estuaries, such as those of the Eastern Scheldt, the Western Scheldt, the Waal and the Maas.

RECLAIMED LAND

Actually, it is the work of man almost as much as that of natural phenomena that has determined the shape and landscape of the present-day Netherlands. Man has drained submerged areas, built dikes to protect them from further inundation, fertilized the soil reclaimed and planted crops. On more than one occasion, however, the sea has broken through the man-made barriers. The struggle has been fiercest in the provinces of Friesland, North and South Holland and Zeeland.

History records disastrous flooding in the 15th and 16th centuries; after this the Dutch intensified their efforts to build dikes to keep the sea out. As recently as February, 1953, however, the ocean broke through several miles of protecting dikes in Zeeland to submerge the islands of Overflakkee, Schowwen, North and South Beveland and Walcheren. Many hundreds of deaths were caused, and thousands of acres of land were flooded. This catastrophe, plus the proven success of closing off the Ijsselmeer, stimulated plans for constructing dikes to close the gaps between the islands from the Hook of Holland in South Holland to Walcheren in Zeeland.

In addition to the struggle to control ocean waters, the Dutch have had a less dramatic but no less important struggle to prevent flooding of their fields by the rivers flowing through the country. For this, too, dikes and retaining walls, and sometimes the device of changing the course of a river, have been used.

Thus, by its extensive and complex system of dikes, the Netherlands has reclaimed and preserved large areas of land. Some 20 per cent of the country's total territory lies below sea level. Such low-lying land, consisting of fertile fields known as polders, is criss-crossed by ditches which collect excess water that is then pumped out into canals or small rivers and lakes lying above the polder levels. Until the relatively recent installation of electric power stations, windmills, traditionally a distinctive feature of the Dutch landscape, did the pumping, and also supplied power for industry.

Drainage of the waters of Lake Ijsselmeer has been undertaken to reclaim hundreds of thousands of acres. Here huge polders have been and are being created. Parts of the Northeast Polder are already under

cultivation, and towns have been built, the most important being Emmeloord.

Rivers

There are few watercourses belonging entirely to the Netherlands, but some of the most important European rivers run through Dutch territory to the sea. These rivers often flow at elevations above those of the bordering plains and are confined by strong dikes to prevent flooding of the surrounding countryside.

The Maas forms the frontier with Belgium (where it is known as the Meuse) for some 45 miles. When it penetrates Dutch territory it follows a course, first northward and then westward, almost parallel to the Dutch branches of the Rhine, emptying finally into the Hollandsch Diep estuary.

Almost immediately after entering the Netherlands, the Rhine divides into two branches. The southern branch, named the Waal, divides near its mouth into several arms, the main one of which flows into the Hollandsch Diep. The northern branch divides again near Arnhem into the Lower Rhine, which flows westward to the North Sea, and the Ijssel River, which drains into the Ijsselmeer.

The only parts of the Scheldt River that belong to the Netherlands are the Western and Eastern (Wester and Ooster) Scheldt estuaries. Other rivers include the Vechte, which rises in West German territory and crosses the province of Overijssel to flow into the eastern part of the Ijsselmeer; and the Hunse, entirely within the Netherlands, which rises in Drente and flows across Groningen to the Lauwers Zee inlet of the Wadden Zee.

A cross section of one of Holland's polders, land reclaimed through the drainage of lakes and other waterways and maintained through a system of canals, dikes and locks. In recent years a project has been undertaken to drain the waters of the Zuider Zee (Ijsselmeer). Thousands of acres have already been secured and are now under cultivation.

In addition to its rivers, the Netherlands has a large number of canals which serve the many purposes of irrigation, drainage and navigation. The canal network has a total length of 4817 miles.

Climate

Because of the long seacoast and generally level terrain, a maritime climate prevails throughout most of the Netherlands. Westerly winds moderate the cold of winter and alleviate the heat of summer. Temperatures average about 36°F. in winter and rarely rise over 80°F. in summer.

Humidity is high everywhere, and cloudy days are common. Precipitation in the form of small showers occurs throughout the year, but though frequent, these showers are apt to be light. The greatest annual rainfall (30 to 31 inches) occurs on the Veluwe terraces and in the hills of southern Limburg, and the least (24 to 25 inches) on the Zeeland coasts and near the Ijsselmeer. Autumn is the wettest season on the sea coast, but inland the heaviest rainfall occurs during the summer months.

Vegetation and Wildlife

Because the Netherlands has such a dense human population, and because so much of its area is under cultivation or urban development, natural vegetation and wildlife is limited. Grasses are abundant on the lands devoted to pasture, and flowers such as daisies, buttercups and dandelions bloom profusely. There are woods of oak, elm, beech and pine, particularly in Gelderland, offering cover for the few undomesticated animals such as foxes and deer. Sanctuaries have been established to protect the numerous birds, and both the fresh and salt waters are richly endowed with many varieties of fish.

HUMAN GEOGRAPHY

RELICS FOUND IN THE REGION indicate that the Netherlands was inhabited in Paleolithic times. A slightly more advanced civilization developed in the area during the Neolithic period (c.6000 to 3000 B.C.), and after 2000 B.C. Celts from the south and Nordics and Frisians from the north and east migrated to the territory. Germanic Saxons and Franks arrived toward the end of the Roman occupation.

THE PEOPLE TODAY

A mingling of all these peoples took place in the southern areas, now the provinces of Zeeland, North Brabant and Limburg, and in most parts of today's Netherlands. However, in the north, in Friesland, the Frisians preserved their racial characteristics.

Immigration into the Netherlands since the Roman occupation has not been significant, and since medieval times most immigrants have been political or religious fugitives from Flanders, France and, most recently, from Hungary and Indonesia.

The population of the Netherlands was estimated at 2,000,000 in the early 19th century. In 1830, the first formal census reported 2,600,000 people. By 1930 the population had grown to 8,000,000, and by 1963 it had reached an estimated 11,889,962. The increase has been particularly concentrated in the industrialized provinces of North and South Holland, where the population has risen fourfold in the 20th century, and in the provinces of Utrecht and Drente. It has been less spectacular in the more agricultural Zeeland region.

The population growth has been due more to an increase in the birth rate and a decline in the death rate than to immigration. The birth rate today is 21.2 per thousand people and the death rate 7.6 per thousand.

There has never been a great mass emigration from the country. The Dutch colonial possessions, with the exception of South Africa, were exploited commercially rather than fully settled. Most of the Dutch families who left to live more or less permanently in the Dutch East Indies had to return to their motherland when Indonesia became independent. By 1964, however, a few were going back to Indonesia to resume management of Dutch enterprises there.

POPULATION DENSITY

In terms of land area, the Netherlands has the highest population density of any country in the world —934 persons per square mile. (If

Classic view of a tulip field in the outlying district of Haarlem, capital city of the province of North Holland. Market gardening flourishes in the southern part of the provinces of North and South Holland behind the dunes lining the coast of the North Sea. Flower bulbs grown in this area are sold all over the world and are an essential item in the Netherlands economy.

the United States' land area were settled with equal density, the country would have a population of more than 3 billion!). The provinces of North and South Holland, which contain 40 per cent of the country's population, have densities well above the national average. The provinces of Utrecht and Limburg also have more than 934 inhabitants per square mile, while Drente, Overijssel and Gelderland have considerably less.

RURAL SETTLEMENT

The compact form of village prevails in the eastern part of the Netherlands, because when the area was settled natural surroundings were unfavorable for agriculture and land for cultivation had to be developed cooperatively, inch by inch. Woods and pastures were shared by the settlers, another factor which led to their living close together. Such villages, which are quite frequent in Drente, are made up of groups of houses separated by wooded areas. There are also hamlets and a few isolated dwellings, since in recent times some of the former common lands have been granted to individual families for cultivation.

In Limburg and North Brabant, the typical village has a compact center, from which houses and little groups of houses surrounded by several acres of land spread out along the roads in all directions. The villages on the drained and improved lands of the west show evidence of planned rather than haphazard design. This is particularly noticeable in the most recently reclaimed areas.

Cities

Like its neighbor, Belgium, the Netherlands has a long tradition of urban life; trade and industry have flourished since medieval times. Cities and towns are especially numerous in the western part of the country, particularly in the region back of the dunes, where they are somewhat sheltered from the sea but still within easy access to the rich agricultural polder areas. The provincial capitals and some of the other important centers are described briefly below in alphabetical order.

Amsterdam, the Netherlands' capital, is located on the banks of the Ij and Amstel rivers in the province of North Holland. It is the country's largest city and the leading commercial and industrial center. Connected to the North Sea and inland Germany by a series of canals, Amsterdam is one of the busiest ports in Europe. The unique architectural plan of the city—about 100 small islands connected by numerous canals and bridges—has given it the name "the Venice of the North."

The city of Delft, just a few miles south of The Hague in the province of South Holland, has been called a "living masterpiece" of antique craftsmanship and beauty. The tree-shaded canals lined with Gothic and Renaissance houses reflect an old-world way of life lovingly preserved. The city, renowned for its blue china, or delftware, was the birthplace of the great 17th-century painter Jan Vermeer.

AMSTERDAM (pop. 866,830)

Amsterdam, the constitutional capital, is the Netherlands' largest city. Located in North Holland province on the southern bank of the Ij, an inlet of the southwestern Ijsselmeer, Amsterdam has access to the North Sea via the North Sea Canal, to inland areas and West Germany via the Merwede system, and to the Waddenzzee and the North Sea via the North Holland Canal.

The city originated as a fishing hamlet and was chartered in 1300. Its prosperity grew steadily in the 14th and 15th centuries and increased even more after 1648, when the Scheldt River was closed to free navigation, causing Amsterdam's closest rival, the Belgian city of Antwerp,

to decline. Merchants, diamond cutters and other flocked to Amsterdam, and it became the leading trading center of all Europe.

Amsterdam was the capital of the Kingdom of the Netherlands under Louis Bonaparte and became the capital of the modern state in 1814. Actually, however, it is the capital in title only; the business of state is conducted in The Hague, and Amsterdam functions only as the site where governments and monarchs are sworn in.

Amsterdam is divided by canals into a number of islands which are

joined by many bridges. The layout and ancient buildings give it a unique and picturesque appearance, and the city attracts large numbers of tourists each year. Among the many museums are Rembrandt's House, where he lived and worked from 1639-58 and which now houses a collection of his work, and the Rijksmuseum which contains a magnificent collection of paintings by famous Dutch artists, including the world's most valuable collection of Rembrandt's paintings.

The city is the seat of the stock exchange and the headquarters for

Dordrecht, in the province of South Holland, was the most important city in Holland during the Middle Ages. Today it is a thriving inland port and shipbuilding center. The city is situated at the confluence of four large rivers: the Merwede, the Noord, the Oude Maas and the Dordtse. Its busy docks and quays still maintain a distinctly medieval character.

most of the country's banking, insurance, commercial and industrial enterprises. Its most famous industry is diamond cutting, and some of the greatest stones known, such as the Cullinan and Victoria diamonds, were cut here. There are also heavy industries (the manufacture of railroad equipment, power plants and aircraft); shipyards; and plants which produce textiles, clothing, beer and processed foods. There are silver-smith shops on Kalberstraat, and Leidsestraat is a famed shopping thoroughfare.

Ships reach the busy Amsterdam port via the complex canal system. The city is also an important rail junction.

ARNHEM (pop. 127,955)

The capital of Gelderland province, Arnhem is on the right bank of the Lower Rhine River. First mention of the city dates from the 13th century, and Arnhem was chartered in 1233. Although taken by Charles the Bold in the 15th century, by the French in the 17th and by the Prussians in the 19th, Arnhem developed more peacefully than most urban centers of the area until it suffered massive destruction in World War II. Residential suburbs surround the city, and parks and forests nearby are a tourist attraction. The old buildings that suffered bombing damage are being restored.

Arnhem's industries produce steam engines; steel, copper and tin; and fine instruments for use in the physical sciences and mathematics. There are also breweries and leather-tanning establishments.

ASSEN *(pop. 30,825)*

Assen, the capital of Drente province, is located 15 miles south of Groningen. Founded in 1257 at the site of a small convent, it lies in a picturesque wooded area. Nearby are stone monuments from prehistoric times.

Important rail lines from Scandinavia run through Assen, and the city has some light industry, including the manufacture of clothing and brushes. It is also a food-processing center and a market for agricultural products.

EINDHOVEN *(pop. 174,612)*

Chartered in 1232 and located in North Brabant province, Eindhoven remained little more than a village until the 1890s, when an important electrical industry was founded there. Since then, Eindhoven's growth has been spectacular. Much of the city was badly damaged by bombing during World War II.

Because of its relatively recent growth, Eindhoven is chiefly a modern city, with large tracts given over to model houses for industrial workers. Eindhoven is best known for the manufacture of light bulbs, but paper, tobacco products, textiles and radios are also produced, and the city is the site of the country's one automobile factory.

GRONINGEN *(pop. 149,486)*

Groningen is the capital of the province of the same name. Situated in the northeastern part of the country, it has developed in relative isolation from the rest of the Netherlands. Groningen dates from before the 9th century, when Norsemen invaded the region. It flourished as an independent city until 1536, when it was taken by Charles V. It was retaken by Maurice of Nassau in 1594.

An ancient moat still surrounds the center of the city. There is a university dating from 1614, and the Church of St. Martin which was begun in the 13th century and finished in the 15th. Groningen is the marketing center for the livestock and other agricultural produce of the surrounding area. It also has flour, sugar and textile mills, as well as chemical and shipbuilding industries. It is the junction of many important canals and railroads.

HAARLEM *(pop. 169,497)*

Haarlem, the capital of North Holland province, was settled in the 10th century, fortified in the 12th and chartered in 1245. The counts of Holland made it their residence. A Catholic stronghold, Haarlem was besieged during the Protestant Reformation, captured by Charles V in

On their way to a sawmill, logs float down a canal in Middelburg, the capital of Zeeland province. Middelburg is located on Walcheren Island, but a land reclamation program has joined it to the rest of the Netherlands' land mass. The city has maintained its medieval charm and enjoys a lively tourist trade.

1573, and retaken by William of Orange four years later. Its textile industries began to develop in the 17th century when Huguenot refugees from France brought in their skills in the weaving of linens and silks, and in the making of lace.

Haarlem has a 15th-century Great Church (Groote Kerk), and its Frans Hals Museum has a fine collection of paintings, including many by the artist for whom it is named. The city hall dates from the 13th century.

Textiles are still produced in Haarlem, but the main activity is marketing the tulip, hyacinth and other bulbs and horticultural products of the region.

THE HAGUE *(pop. 605,876)*

The Hague has been the administrative center of the Netherlands since 1830. Originally the site of a hunting lodge for the counts of Holland, it developed from little more than a clearing in the woods (the original name, 's Gravenhage, means count's hedge or wood). A castle was built in the mid-13th century, and settlement around it grew rapidly during the 14th and 15th centuries. The Hague became the capital of the Dutch Republic in 1581, and was the site of the first meeting of the *Staten-Generaal* (Parliament) in 1586. The city, nevertheless, was not chartered until the early 19th century, and it was superseded as the official capital by Amsterdam in 1814. Its roles as a diplomatic center and administrative capital continued, however.

The Hague is an elegant city, with broad avenues lined by trees and imposing mansions. In the old quarter near the Royal Palace and around the Green Market, the 13th- and 14th-century streets are narrow and lined with small shops. The residence of the royal family is located in The Hague, as are the national Parliament and Supreme Court buildings. Here, too, are the Royal Museum of Painting (which contains works by Rembrandt) and the Great Church of St. James (15th-16th centuries). Also in The Hague is the Peace Palace which houses the United Nations International Court of Justice.

Although the city's main activities are diplomatic and political, many of the country's major corporations and banks have their headquarters here, and The Hague is an important printing and publishing center.

LEEUWARDEN *(pop. 85,386)*

The capital of Friesland province, Leeuwarden was once a medieval fortress, but its walls have given way to boulevards and parks, and only a moat remains as a reminder of the

A cattle fair in the city of Hoorn, a seaport on the Ijsselmeer in the province of North Holland. Hoorn, a beautiful city noted for its 16th- and 17th-century buildings, is a trading center for cheese and cattle. In the 17th century, the "Golden Age" of Holland, Hoorn was the capital of West Friesland and her sailors and merchants traveled all over the world. The tip of South America was named Cape Horn (Hoorn) in honor of the birthplace of Willem Cornelis Schouten (1580-1625), who was the first to round that continent.

fortress plan. The city's Great Church and chancellery date from the 15th and 16th centuries respectively. The town hall was completed in 1715 and the Frisian Museum in 1781. The latter contains a collection that records the history of the Frisian people. Dairy industries, particularly the production of butter and cheese, predominate, but footwear and various kinds of paint are also manufactured.

LEIDEN *(pop. 98,013)*

Leiden, in South Holland, is famous as the birthplace of Rembrandt; for its resistance to the besieging Spaniards in the 16th century; and as a haven for the Pilgrims before they set sail for America in 1620. Leiden's university was founded in 1575, and in the 17th and 18th centuries it became renowned as a center for the study of Protestant theology, science and medicine.

Economic activities are mainly concerned with processing and marketing the agricultural products of the surrounding area, notably cheeses, but Leiden also has a fine reputation as a printing and publishing center.

MAASTRICHT *(pop. 93,409)*

Maastricht is the capital of Limburg province. Situated on the left bank of the Maas near the Belgian border, it was first settled by the Romans, who crossed the river at this point. Fortified in the early 13th century, Maastricht suffered through the religious wars of the 16th century, being occupied first by the Protestants and then by the Catholics. Its citizens were massacred by the Spaniards in 1579, and the city was repeatedly besieged during various conflicts in the 17th, 18th and 19th centuries. It was occupied by the Germans during World War II.

Parts of the ancient fortifications may still be seen. Among its notable buildings are the oldest church in the Netherlands, the 6th-century Romanesque Cathedral of St. Servatius. Due to its location near sandstone quarries, Maastricht's principal industries produce ceramics, glass and bricks.

MIDDELBURG *(pop. 23,231)*

The capital of Zeeland province, Middelburg is located on Walcheren Island which, due to the construction of dikes and polders, is no longer an island but the seaward extremity of a peninsula. Known since medieval times, when it was an important trading town, Middelburg still boasts a

13th-century abbey, but its Gothic town hall was badly damaged by bombing during World War II. Tourism is actively promoted, and residents add to their city's picturesque atmosphere by wearing traditional costumes. Middelburg has sawmills and is a center for the marketing of dairy products.

ROTTERDAM *(pop. 730,963)*

Rotterdam is the capital of South Holland, the second-largest city of the Netherlands, and one of the most active ports in all Europe. Lying on the New (Niewe) Maas about 15 miles inland, it is connected to the North Sea by canal. It is the meeting point of waterways leading to Belgium, France, Switzerland and West Germany, as well as to all the important centers in the Netherlands.

Rotterdam began around 1260 as a fishing village, although some of its early citizens also grew flax on the outskirts. It was chartered in 1340 and fortified soon thereafter. Its importance as a trade center grew, receiving a setback under Napoleon, but reviving again after 1830. The center of the city was demolished by World War II bombings, but the

Leiden, in the province of South Holland, is one of the great cultural centers of the Netherlands and Europe. It is renowned as the birthplace of Rembrandt, the greatest Dutch painter, and for its fine university, founded in the 16th century.

Utilization of the soil

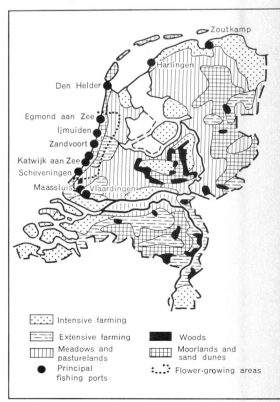

Intensive farming
Extensive farming
Meadows and pasturelands
● Principal fishing ports
■ Woods
Moorlands and sand dunes
Flower-growing areas

15th-century Church of St. Lawrence remains. The Boymans Museum has a fine collection of Dutch and early Flemish paintings.

Trade is the leading economic activity, along with related industries, such as shipbuilding. There are ware-housing facilities for coal, grain and lumber, and sizeable petroleum refineries, the raw materials for which are imported. There are also chemical industries, distilleries, sugar refineries and leather-tanning establishments.

's HERTOGENBOSCH *(pop. 75,091)*

The capital of North Brabant province, 's Hertogenbosch is situated on the Zuid-Willemsvaart Canal. It was chartered in 1184 by Duke Henry I of Brabant and, until 1876, was a fortified town. Its Cathedral of St. John dates from the 15th century. The city's industries are mostly light manufacturing establishments producing footwear, tires and tobacco products.

UTRECHT *(pop. 261,043)*

Utrecht, capital of the province of the same name, is an ancient city, originally settled by the Romans. Established as a bishopric by St. Willibrord near the end of the 7th century, it was also a thriving commercial center by the 9th century. The religious and mercantile interests, however, began to quarrel over control of the city. The quarrels exploded into actual combat in the 1480s, and broke out again from time to time until Charles V bought out the bishops' rights to temporal rule in 1527. The Treaty of Utrecht, which marked the end of the War of the Spanish Succession, was signed here in 1713.

Utrecht's Gothic Cathedral of St. Martin (14th century) has a tower over 300 feet tall. The Church of St. Catherine dates from 1524. The University of Utrecht, founded in 1636, is world-famous and attended annually by over 6000 students. The Royal Mint of the Netherlands is located in the city.

Although Utrecht is largely a residential city and a cultural center, it has some heavy industries, including the making of cement, and some light

industries (bicycle manufacture, and gold and silver processing) and is the site of an annual International Industries Fair. It also markets the agricultural produce of the surrounding area.

ZWOLLE *(pop. 56,779)*

The capital of Overijssel province, Zwolle lies on the Ijssel River. It has several 15th-century structures, among them a gateway, the Church of St. Martin and the Church of Our Lady. Canals through the city follow the routes of ancient fortifying walls.

Zwolle is a rail and highway junction and a market center for the surrounding agricultural region. There are also shipyards and ironworks.

ECONOMIC GEOGRAPHY

THE ECONOMY OF THE NETHERLANDS depends chiefly on industry and trade, but the country's agriculture is also highly developed and productive. There was a marked expansion of the Dutch economy about the middle of the 19th century. This came about partially because of the opening of the Suez Canal, which shortened the route to the Dutch East Indies.

Also important was the fact that at this time the Ruhr region of Germany was making great advances as an industrial area; thus the estuaries of the branches of the Rhine on the Netherlands coast became even more important as outlets for German products. To provide easier access to the sea, the Dutch improved their river ports and built larger canals. Today no other country in Europe handles a higher volume of foreign trade in proportion to its population.

Agriculture

Although agricultural production has increased steadily because of mechanization and improved methods, today only about 11 per cent of the working population are farmers. Wheat, grown mainly in the south, is the leading grain crop (603,062 metric tons in 1962), followed by rye, oats and barley. Enormous quantities of sugar beets (almost 3,000,000

The Friday Cheese Market is one of the most unusual sights in the city of Alkmaar, a leading cheese center in the province of North Holland. Every Friday, from late April through September, cheese is bought and sold the way it has been done for centuries. Unloaded from trucks or barges, the cheeses (from 4 to 14 lbs. each) are loaded onto barrows. Then a "work guild" takes over; veems, men in white uniforms with colored straw hats, hoist the cheeses over their shoulders after they are sold and bring them to the weighing houses. There the cheeses are weighed on 300-year-old scales of the same color as the veems' *hats.*

Location of major industries

tons in 1962) and potatoes (about 2,500,000 tons) are grown, as well as flax and seed crops.

HORTICULTURE

As early as the Middle Ages the Dutch observed that the soil along the coast just inside the dunes was suitable for growing vegetables and flowers. South of The Hague, in numerous scientifically managed hothouses, tomatoes, cucumbers and lettuce, as well as other vegetables and many varieties of flowers, are grown. These hothouses are heated, and the expanses of glass and the numerous chimneys of the furnaces give the landscape an industrial rather than an agricultural aspect. Many vegetables are also grown outdoors, and there are numerous orchards of fruit trees.

A notable specialty is the growing of flower bulbs, particularly those of tulips and hyacinths, which are exported all over the world. This activity is pursued in many parts of the country, with the greatest concentration in and around Aalsmeer, south of Amsterdam, and further west between Haarlem and Leiden.

LIVESTOCK

About 50 per cent of the agricultural land, both in polders and elsewhere, is given over to pastures and fodder crops to support large herds of dairy cattle. The quality of the stock has been raised to a high level through careful breeding, and the dairy industry makes an important contribution to the Dutch economy.

Cheesemaking, formerly a cottage industry, is now carried on in modern processing plants. Dutch cheeses are known throughout the world, especially those coming from Edam, Gouda and Alkmaar. Alkmaar is also a cheese-marketing center. Total cheese production amounted to 223,000 tons in 1962. In the same year, the Dutch dairy industry produced over 7,000,000 tons of milk, 434,915 tons of condensed milk and 101,520 tons of butter.

The raising of pigs and sheep is also an important activity, but even more so is the raising of poultry, an enterprise that markets some 38 billion eggs a year.

Fisheries

Fishing adds both to the domestic food supply and, when exported, to the country's revenue. There are 2500 vessels in the Dutch fishing fleet and the annual catch is over 200,000 tons, the major proportion of which is herring. The Dutch are credited with discovering how to smoke herring in order to preserve them. Vlaardingen is the principal center for this industry. Oysters, mussels and various fresh-water fish are also caught. The chief fishing ports are Ijmuiden in North Holland, and Vlaardingen and Scheveningen in South Holland.

Industry

About 42 per cent of the working population of the Netherlands is engaged in industry, which produces an abundance of various products. There are two general types of industries: those, such as food processing, which use local raw materials and export significant quantities of the end products; and those which import raw materials, process them and export the finished or semifinished goods. The latter industries

Modern oil refineries in Pernis, near Rotterdam. Both domestic and imported petroleum are processed in Pernis and then transported by pipelines via Rotterdam to the Rhine area of West Germany.

This streamlined thoroughfare connects the cities of Rotterdam and Arnhem. All the larger cities and towns in the Netherlands are linked by modern road systems whose solidity belies the marshy soil upon which they are built.

are located mainly in or near the great port cities.

Textiles are produced chiefly at Overijssel, Brabant, Breda, Nijmegen and Arnhem, and in sufficient quantities to satisfy the demand at home and leave enough to account for about 10 per cent of industrial exports. At Pernis, near Rotterdam, are oil refineries and facilities for making a number of synthetic products.

The metals industry accounts for over 30 per cent of the country's exports. Using imported materials exclusively, this industry turns out pig iron, steel, tin plate, wire, cast-iron pipe and a number of copper, lead, and aluminum products. Engineering plants produce steam and internal combustion engines and other machinery, as well as structural parts for bridges, oil refineries and factories. In the electrical engineering field, centered mainly around Eindhoven, products range from minute transistors to complete power plants.

Shipbuilding is a traditional activity of this seafaring nation, and there are shipyards at Rotterdam, Amsterdam, Schiedam and Flushing, plus a number of smaller yards where boats and barges for inland waterway travel are made. Recently, however, international competition has cut into the Netherlands shipbuilding industry, as reflected by the fact that only 53 sea-going vessels were under construction in January 1963, as against 101 in January 1962.

Mining

Coal, petroleum, salt and clay are the country's only natural resources. Most coal comes from the Netherlands States Mines' operations in Limburg, and there are smaller deposits in Brabant and Gelderland, which are worked both publicly and privately. The annual production is about 12 million tons. Coke for export is produced from the coal of two of the state mines. Crude oil output amounts to over 12 million barrels per year; the domestic product is refined at the Pernis refineries, along with imported petroleum. A pipeline runs between Rotterdam and the West German Rhine area.

Salt, processed both for table and industrial use, is found in the eastern and northeastern parts of the country. Clay is available in many areas, and is used to make bricks both for building and road-paving purposes.

Transportation

About half the goods coming to and leaving the Netherlands travels by the inland waterways. Many imports and goods for export move along the canal system connected with the Rhine and Maas rivers, and there are large canals leading to the sea. Products for internal markets are also carried on the water routes. The total length of navigable rivers and canals is 4817 miles.

The most important waterway is the Rhine-Waal river system between West Germany and Rotterdam, which also connects with Amsterdam. The

Mineral resources and related industries

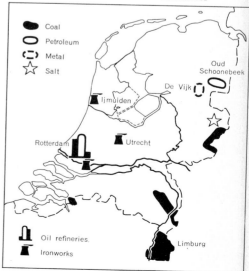

Maas, which has been canalized, links Limburg to the rest of the country. The northern region lacks large canals, but there is a network of smaller ones centered on Groningen.

The Netherlands merchant fleet is among the largest in the world, and had a gross registered tonnage of 5,037,000 in 1963. Also in that year, there were 1525 ships—57 passenger liners, 426 ocean-going freighters, 921 coastal vessels and 121 tankers.

The Koninklijke Luchvaart Maatschappij (K.L.M. Royal Dutch Airlines) provides regular service to 74 foreign countries. It is one of the largest commercial airlines in the world.

Since so much cargo travels by water, the railroad system provides mostly passenger service over its 2020-mile length, about half of which is electrified. There is a total of almost 3000 miles of roads in the country, many of them being thoroughfares connecting the major cities.

Tourism

The Netherlands' picturesque countryside, historic buildings, convenient location and well-developed transit facilities attract large numbers of visitors to the nation each year. Amsterdam is probably the most frequently visited spot, but many other cities and regions also have thriving tourist industries.

Foreign Trade

In 1947, the Benelux Treaty established a customs union (the agreements for which had been signed in 1944) among Belgium, the Netherlands and Luxembourg. The treaty did away with import duties on goods sold by one of these countries in either of the others. The Benelux countries are also members of the European Economic Community, along with France, Italy and West Germany.

In recent years the Netherlands has had a slightly unfavorable balance of trade. The largest proportion of Netherlands trade—about 50 per cent—is with the Common Market, but active trade is also carried on with the United States and the United Kingdom and with African and Asian countries.

Volendam, a peaceful fishing village on the Ijsselmeer in North Holland province, attracts numerous tourists each year. The inhabitants still dress in costumes which were in fashion 300 years ago and earn their living by giving visitors a glimpse of what life was like in Holland in bygone days.

Modern Dutch women from the town of Roosendaal wear traditional costumes to celebrate an annual fete. The costumes —peaked bonnets with up-tilted flaps, aproned skirts and coral beads—commemorate the colors in the Dutch flag, red, white and blue.

THE DUTCH CHARACTER

"NATURE HAS GIVEN US NOTHING. She has refused us all her gifts. All this you look upon today is but the fruit of our own work, our own zeal, our own industry." Thus wrote the Dutch poet Jan Frederik Helmers, speaking proudly and passionately of his native land. Another Dutch poet, Jan Wybenga, wrote: "When the tide turned it left us with dead symbols that urge us to fight on; broken mills and towers, squares and villages, all swept off by the waves. Then, on the brink of the skyline, a man and a woman pass by, and in the still beauty of this sight a new life will begin."

Here, encompassed within a few poetical sentences, lies the essence, the foundation, of the Dutch character: patience and fortitude, hope and ambition, and the willingness to begin over and over again until those hopes and ambitions are permanently realized. Few peoples have so often seen their hopes and ambitions fulfilled only to have the fruits of their efforts, time and again, stolen or destroyed—either by invaders from the south and east, or by the ever-menacing sea to the north and west.

Every nation, in the course of its history, has to fight for its political existence; few, however, are forced to fight for their geographical existence as well. The Dutch, however, hemmed in between the great European powers on one side and the encroaching North Sea on the other, have been forced to do both—and have accomplished both with eminent and continuing success.

The Roman scholar Pliny the Elder, after a journey to the northern Netherlands in the 1st century A.D., remarked that, "You cannot tell whether it is land or water." Centuries later the mighty Napoleon, viewing this corner of Europe with wholly unwarranted contempt, said that Holland is nothing but *terre d'alluvion de fleuves français* ("silt from French rivers")—he apparently considered the Rhine a French river!

The people who settled this precariously situated land, however, saw and envisioned far more than either the dubious Pliny or the chauvinistic Napoleon. Taking this unlikely land as their own, they set to work with unsurpassed industry and tenacity to create from the sunken lands and "French silt" a country and a nation that were to win the admiration and respect of the world. They not only maintained the lands of their ancestors but managed, amazingly, to win back two-fifths of their country from the sea.

It is no mere coincidence that the motto of the Dutch royal family is *Je maintiendrai*—"I will hold on!"

A SEAFARING NATION

Water is the fundamental, the unchangeable element in the life of the Dutch. Nowhere is this more clearly

In celebration of "Fisherman's Day," a flotilla of herring boats enters the port of Scheveningen, the largest fishing village in the Netherlands. Scheveningen is a seaside suburb of The Hague (only two miles away). Its sandy beaches and lively night life have made the sprawling village a well-known resort area.

reflected than in their many idiomatic expressions and similes, which so often have direct reference to this seafaring life. "To keep your head above water" means to maintain your courage in the face of adversity. "To lose your rudder" means, aptly, to get drunk. "Do not pull a drowned cow out of the canal" parallels the American expression "let sleeping dogs lie." Thus, as can be seen, the Dutch, despite their constant and often tragic struggle with the sea, have never lost their sense of humor in regard to it—a sense of humor that, indeed, forms an essential part of their hardy and admirable character.

Side by side with this sense of humor one finds in the Dutch character a practicality that may, on occasion, give way to an excessive realism or even a certain parsimony

and meanness. But no one is more aware or more critical of such qualities than the Dutch themselves. They are, above all, a people with their feet firmly planted on the ground—perhaps because this ground has so often been washed away from under their feet.

CUSTOMS AND TRADITIONS

Children and the Family

HOLLAND HAS BEEN CALLED THE "country of prolific families," although today there are perhaps fewer children, proportionally, than in former times. But it is still not uncommon for a Dutch family to have a dozen children, or even more. In Holland, as elsewhere, far more people are born each year than die.

Although the old proverb "In Holland you don't die" is a bit of an exaggeration, statistics show that the annual birth rate is nearly three times as great as the yearly death rate (21.2 births as against only 7.6 deaths per 1000 population).

MOLDING THE CHARACTER

The children are really the central interest of family life as they are of Dutch society as a whole. Yet, on the surface at least, there seems to be a contradiction here; for while Dutch children are undoubtedly healthy, well nourished and allowed to play outdoors as much as possible, in a way they also seem to be neglected. They are left very much to themselves, even in towns where the street is their only playground. Often they are dressed carelessly, their hair is untidy, their face and hands often bruised and scratched.

The reason for this apparent neglect is the Dutch tendency to bring up children naturally and with few restrictions. Dutch mothers like to expound their theories on education (there is much talk on this subject, even if it is not always clear what teaching methods they really mean.) It is significant that in Holland the modern educational methods of Montessori, Froebel and Decroli, to name a few, have met with full official approval, and the authorities there welcome new ideas and experiments in education. Every Dutch family has to pay the *schoolgeld,* a school tax which varies according to the means of the family and the number of school-age children.

In the traditionally proper and decorous atmosphere of the family, where words like *deftig* (respectable, decorous, dignified) and *gezellig* (comfortable, warm, satisfactory) play an important part in family parlance, the children unconsciously absorb the educational principles through which their character is formed.

Much stress is laid on personal independence, responsibility and self-discipline. For New Year, or on other occasions, children are often given a sum of money which they will have to pay back later with interest out of other small gifts they have received or money they have earned for performing special tasks. Thus, they learn to look after their own money.

Dutch children grow up healthy and well fed with abundant milk, butter, chocolate, cheese and vegetables; they enjoy great freedom indoors and outdoors, they have plenty of room in gardens and on playgrounds for every kind of game. They learn to skate, to swim, to row and to sail on the lakes and canals. Since a great number of boatmen are obliged to live with their families on the lakes and the canals, special schools have been created, which are easily accessible from the canals, and the boatmen's children can attend.

BIRTH AND INFANCY

Even before he or she is born, a child is already the object of everyone's attention. *Hansje in de kelder* ("Johnny in the cellar") is the toast to the unborn baby, a toast drunk at parties in honor of the expectant mother.

It is the custom to make constant allusion to the "little nest" at an engagement dinner, to swallows building their nest under the eaves or to storks building on chimneys. There is also constant allusion to the *mujsies* (mice). When the happy event finally occurs, it is the custom to send sweets together with the announcement of the birth to friends and relations. These sweets are also called *mujsies.*

A tulip field in the region of Noordwijck, the chief bulb-growing area in the Netherlands. Among the most exciting events to take place in Noordwijck is the annual Tulip Rally, usually held in late April or May. Hundreds of automobiles are fancifully decorated with tulips, creating a fantastic procession of brilliant colors.

and white lace on the door of the room where a baby is born. If it is a boy the pink shows through the lace, but if it is a girl, a white paper is inserted under the lace so that no pink can be seen. In the district of Haarlem, instead of the board a small lace cushion is pinned up, pink for a boy and white for a girl.

These quaint customs were not always merely symbolic. In the past it was a gentle warning to all, even to magistrates and policemen, not to enter, for even the knocker and the doorbell were wrapped in straw to assure silence so that mother and child could rest without disturbance.

ST. NICHOLAS AND CHRISTMAS

The children's most important festival is that of St. Nicholas (Santa Claus), celebrated on December 6— a day when children, within limits, may do as they like. At school, practical jokes are allowed and the children give orders to the teachers.

St. Nicholas is traditionally accompanied by *Zwarte Pie* (Black Peter), who follows his master on foot. St. Nicholas himself, mounted on a white horse, wears a plumed cap and a cloak and rides along the streets, across the squares and even—so the children are told—over the rooftops.

But it is Black Peter who brings the presents. The owner of a workshop or a factory will dress up as Black Peter or St. Nicholas and give the presents to the children of his employees—an occasion that provides much fun for all concerned. The children are also given the traditional sweets, mostly baked in the form of well-known characters or animals. They often have the initials of each child displayed in marzipan.

The figure of St. Nicholas is perhaps more important to children than Christmas itself, for Christmas is a rather solemn family festival celebrated around the Christmas tree, where the father reads the story of the Nativity out of the Bible. At New Year's, after receiving their gifts of money, the children accompany their parents on family visits to exchange presents and wishes of good

In Holland great importance is attached to the role of the godparents. They are chosen after the seventh month of the mother's pregnancy. This is no mere formality, for, especially among peasants, the duty of a godparent is taken seriously. If the parents die, the godparents are expected to undertake the education of a child. The godparents of the eldest child are usually its grandparents on the father's side; those of the second child and those born thereafter are chosen by the mother from among relatives or friends.

It is an old custom for a baby to be blessed by its father and mother in the room where it was born; it is then presented to relations and to its brothers and sisters. The latter are told that the mother brought the baby home "in a boat," or, perhaps, that she found it "under a cabbage leaf."

Many such customs are now gradually disappearing or newer customs are taking their place. But there are still parts of Holland where the old tradition prevails of putting up a notice board covered with pink silk luck. The traditional *oliebolen* (a kind of fried apple) is served and everyone partakes with hearty appetite.

Attachment to the Royal Family

The Dutch like to make a festival out of the simplest anniversary, even that of a mere acquaintance. Behind every kitchen door hangs a calendar showing dates of birthdays and other anniversaries.

Above all, the Dutch, even the Catholics (who are less attached to the royal house than are the Protestants), celebrate the birthday of the Queen. On this occasion all the streets are beflagged, royal banners are flown, and floral decorations in orange, the color of the house of Orange-Nassau, are seen everywhere. Sometimes an orange tree, or an evergreen instead (the climate of the Netherlands is not always suitable to citrus fruits!), is planted in the center of a square.

Attachment to the royal family is a true expression of the Dutch spirit. An example is the *Prinsjedag* (Prince's Day) on which the royal family visit The Hague, where they are welcomed by an enthusiastic population. This occurs on the third Tuesday of September. On this day the Queen opens parliament in royal splendor. Amid historical pageantry, surrounded by standards and uniforms, she rides in a golden coach along the streets of the city up to the silk canopy at the entrance of the Hall of Knights, where the solemn session takes place.

It is also the custom for the first herring catch of the season to be

The windmill is the most characteristic feature of the Dutch landscape. Of oriental origin, it is believed to have been introduced into Holland by Crusaders returning from the East. The importance of the windmill in keeping the land safe from inundation by the North Sea gave it a very special place in Dutch life. Today windmills still dot the countryside, but many of them are obsolete, having been replaced by electrical pumping and power stations.

presented to the Queen. It is brought in a cart ornately decorated with the national colors—white, red and blue. The Queen then takes a herring in the traditional way: holding it between finger and thumb and daintily dropping it into her open mouth.

School Customs and Traditions

Dutch youth and their schools, whether public or private, all have one thing in common: an atmosphere of individual freedom, self-sufficiency and responsibility, and a deliberate lack of strict supervision.

In addition to their regular studies, the children learn gardening, collect shells, beetles and butterflies, and make nature albums; they may also learn how to cultivate vegetables or grain, potatoes, beetroot, wheat or rice. In many schools animals, such as mice or other rodents, are kept. Nature studies—in keeping with the Dutch love of nature and the outdoors—are given great emphasis. This love of life in all its forms stays with the Dutch throughout their lives, from childhood to university and beyond.

There is virtually no illiteracy in Holland. Parents who do not send their children to school risk a prison sentence.

There are many opportunities for specialization in secondary schools, ranging from technical studies to housekeeping or gardening. One example of Dutch secondary education is the language school near Utrecht, which is administered by the students themselves and subdivided into groups of fifty, each group studying one language. At the same time, every student can have technical or vocational training.

UNIVERSITIES

The three largest universities date back hundreds of years. Leiden dates from 1575, Groningen from 1616 and Utrecht from 1626. All three are state universities. Other universities belong to municipalities or to religious bodies.

The University of Leiden, one of the most famous in Europe, was founded by William the Silent in gratitude for the lifting of the Spanish siege. He offered the city the choice of having all its taxes cancelled or of having a university; the citizens wisely chose the latter. On the anniversary of the day when the siege was lifted, white bread and herrings are distributed among the people. Until the second half of the 19th century, the students were required to speak Latin amongst themselves, and to this day Leiden has a special reputation for language studies. Members of the Dutch royal family are educated there.

About 80 per cent of the university students are unable to pay for the high cost of their education and have to work to earn the difference.

STUDENT CORPS

A notable sociability develops among students who join a student corps. There is the Roman Catholic *Het corps* and the Protestant *Studenten-societeit*.

Student corps are often, however, quite snobbish. To become a member, a student has to be presented by a sponsor and pay a monthly fee of forty florins. For this reason the corps are largely the preserve of rich students. The new member has his hair shorn, after which he undergoes a three-week trial. If successful, he may then belong to any of the literary, dramatic, social or other miscellaneous groups. Each group has its own table in the corps hall, and students of all groups meet there for debates or merely to drink and smoke together. Professors (*heer*, as they are addressed) do not take part lest they should suffer loss of prestige.

Equipped with umbrella and shopping bag, a young girl and her brother ride down a street in Amsterdam. It is said that Holland is the country of bicycles. People of every age and occupation, during all kinds of weather, ride their bikes through the narrow streets and bustling thoroughfares.

The eight-horsed, golden carriage of the Queen stops in front of the Hall of Knights in The Hague to inaugurate one of the Netherlands' most colorful festivals, Prinsjedag *(Prince's Day). On* Prinsjedag, *the third Tuesday in September, the Queen, surrounded by uniformed cavalry, flags and all manner of splendid pageantry, officially opens the parliamentary sessions.*

Wearing ribbons as emblems of their new dignity, the newly elected *praeses collegii*, the chief of the *Het corps* of Leiden (at Utrecht he is called the rector) and the five members of the *collegium* (in Utrecht, the *senaat*) are presented to the *Rector Magnificus*.

The freshmen, besides their haircut, are known by their *muts* (caps) and by the *laag bordje* (collars) they wear around their necks. They, the *groenenvers* (freshmen, "greenhorns"), have to recite humorous rhymes praising the older students and expressing their own "abysmal nothingness."

Members of Catholic corps visit schools and hospitals, but their most enthusiastic celebrations occur during the feast of St. Nicholas, on the *dies natalis,* or foundation day (at Leiden only), and at their graduation festival.

On St. Nicholas' day (Dec. 6) there is a procession in which a student rides (in false beard) on a carriage drawn by plumed horses with two Moorish outriders. On Feb. 8, the *dies natalis,* after the Rector's opening speech and a speech by a student, professors and students attend banquets, which end with a serenade in honor of the Rector.

When a student comes to take his *doctoral,* there is the *promotie-diner* with the inevitable group photograph, followed by a noisy *maskerata.* The new "doctor" rides in a carriage with a guard of honor consisting of two *paranimfen,* usually his best friends. The coach with the coachman and the liveried flunkeys, wearing the faculty's colors, drives up and down the streets, while around it the students shout, laugh and sing uproariously.

Titles and Nicknames

The word *heer* (Sir), which is the appellation due to a professor has been mentioned above. The Dutch attach much importance to titles and forms of address. In this way they specify social ranks which they consider sacrosanct. Although class differences have tended to be less rigid in recent years, there are still rigidly outlined social boudaries which few Dutchman will ever cross. Rare is the Dutchman who will associate on intimate terms with one whom he considers his inferior—even if the person below him is the richer. There is a strong feeling of deference towards social superiors.

In everyday speech a woman is addressed as "miss" (even though married) if she is considered inferior because of her position or occupation, and vice versa, she is addressed as *mevrouw* (Mrs.) if she is judged an equal. *Freule* is the title of the unmarried girl who belongs to the nobility. The workman, the shopkeeper or the laborer is addressed according to his occupation, but

Two men wheel a fancifully decorated organ through the streets of Amsterdam. Behind a facade of wooden sculpture and painted panels, pipes and drums are hidden. The sound of the Amsterdam organ is unique—an appealing blend of a jazz band, a symphony orchestra and a church organ. Place a dubbeltje *(10-cent piece) in the collection box and anything from a waltz to the latest song hit or a classical selection will be played.*

never as *heer,* The "well learned" *heer* is a professor; the "noble and competent" *heer* is the lawyer. A member of Parliament is addressed as "most noble and revered," a pastor as *zeer geleerde* (very learned) or *orweel ewerwaarde* (most venerable). The farmer is only "esteemed." A letter is signed with a *hoogachtend* (high regard).

When you greet a person it is not polite enough to say "good day," but you must say at least "a good day to you."

LOVE AND COURTSHIP

The love of a Dutchman is not without *deftigkeit* (dignity, decorum), a quality of cool reserve which has put its mark on nearly every aspect

of life in Holland. "They have not enough warmth to fall in love," wrote an English ambassador in the 19th century. But perhaps it is more just to say that the Dutch attach a great deal of importance to propriety and appearances, and that this, combined with a natural timidity even when they are sentimental, gives rise to the general impression that the Dutchman is a nice enough, but rather cool, fellow.

The term "lover," with all the connotations it carries in English and other languages, is non-existent in Dutch phraseology. When a Dutchman says *minnaar,* he is using an idiomatic expression. When for "I love you" he says *ik min u,* he is speaking not seriously, but in fun.

A love scene in public is infinitely more subdued than its counterparts in Paris. The most typical picture, and one much more characteristic of the Dutch, is that of a young couple riding side by side on their bicycles with, perhaps, the boy's arm casually (certainly not tightly) around the girl's shoulder.

In Dutch society, the men maintain a double attitude toward women. On the one hand, women are completely independent in social life and have equal rights with men; but, on the other hand, the centuries-old puritan influence is still reflected in strict adherence to traditional forms of behavior within the family.

To be a woman is to be, above all, a truly feminine housewife; the professions and non-domestic interests always take a second place.

The Dutch ideal of beauty is traditionally rather florid and voluptuous, but recently foreign influences, particularly in the fields of fashion and cosmetics, have become increasingly marked. The women of Friesland, golden haired and fresh-complexioned as they are, are supposed to be especially beautiful. The clothing they wear is, traditionally, less fashionable than solid. Lipstick and smoking in public (though pipes, until recently, were occasionally smoked by women in some parts of the country) are considered to be in extremely bad taste. For example, in Groningen a girl from a good family would never think of applying for a job overdressed or wearing lipstick.

Dutch girls get married rather late as a rule, and there is generally a long engagement; a distinction is made between a *vaste* and a *losse verkering,* that is to say a "fixed" or a "loose" engagement. Divorce is not uncommon, but it usually occurs —when it occurs at all—only after ten or fifteen years of married life. In marriage, mutual independence— within limits—is respected. Nevertheless, it is considered imperative in Holland for a man to have a large family if he wants to fulfill his social responsibility. Paradoxically, however, it is also in Holland that clubs of bachelors and old maids flourish and have innumerable meetings.

ENGAGEMENT AND MARRIAGE

There are many old Dutch customs regarding the social institutions of engagement and marriage. Some of these, of course, have been forgotten and others are fast disappearing—like the old Batavian custom in which the bride was given two oxen, a richly harnessed horse, a sword, a shield and a javelin; or another more recent custom in which the wife was "bought" for gold, which was given to her in a carved wooden box or tied neatly in a handkerchief. If the girl untied the knot or opened the box it meant acceptance. Thus, if she did not accept, she would never know just how much gold was being offered.

It is still the custom in certain old fishing villages and on the *polders* (farms) for the sexes to sit separately, not only in church but, until quite recently, on the beaches too. Even in the streets, an engaged couple is rarely seen walking together. When the young Zeelander sees a girl milking a cow he waits until the pail is full, then steps forward and offers to carry it. Her refusal or acceptance of his offer are symbolic of her feelings toward him. Another custom is for the suitor to come to the orchard gate of the girl's home when her parents are at church; he then asks to be allowed to smoke, and if permission is given by the girl, it is again symbolic of her acceptance.

In North Holland, there is an old proverb which says, "The lover fears the poker." Its meaning is that, when the suitor visits the girl's home for the first time, he has to watch for a "sign." If he is offered a chair, it means that he is welcome, but if the girl touches the poker at the fireplace, it means that the boy is summarily rejected as a possible future husband.

There was a time when the only way to avoid military conscription in Holland was to get married. Hence the indirect question often asked by the young man of his hoped-for bride: "Must I draw a number?" (that is, in the conscription lottery, or draft). Many a military career depended on the answer.

At Volendam a young couple, not yet engaged but about to be, will sit under the church bell which is later rung to announce their engagement. At Zwolle, a farming district, it is the custom to pay farmhands six weeks salary in advance on St. Martin's day, for there is a market on that day when boys are given a chance to win the hands of the farmers' daughters.

Old customs regulating the rela-

The serenity and loveliness of this canal in the city of Delft are expressive of the Dutch way of life. The people, serious, straightforward and practical, for centuries have had to struggle to keep their land from being inundated by the sea. But throughout their travails they have nonetheless cherished the beauty and the simple pleasures of nature. Their homes, always filled with flowers and plants, their love of walking and cycling, their picturesque buildings and bridges all reflect a deepfelt regard for visual and natural delights.

tionship between an engaged couple are still respected in the country; for example, a boy must always ask the permission of the girl's parents to visit his fiancée.

Between the day of the official engagement (at the town hall) and the wedding, there is a period of three weeks, the *ondertrouw,* during which the couple are officially known as *bruidegom* (bridegroom) and *bruid* (bride). During this time the *bruidegom* gives a flower to his *bruid* every morning.

After the *ondertrouw,* when the engagement has become public, friends visit the families of the young couple to offer congratulations. It is then the custom to act out comedies or burlesques, written by one of the friends, in which humorous and often biting allusion is made to the past life of the betrothed couple. At one time these were very long, some having been known to last from eight o'clock in the evening to six o'clock in the morning. This is also the only time when a certain liquor, called the *bruidstranen* (bride's tears), is drunk.

The wedding day itself is celebrated with great solemnity. Long marriage processions can often be seen consisting entirely of barges floating along the picturesque canals, every craft richly hung with colorful decorations. Even the windmills are gaily decorated for a wedding.

In Holland the periwinkle is the nuptial flower; hence the expression "to tie the periwinkle," meaning the floral decorations at the wedding feast. The betrothed are dressed in their traditional clothes. The wedding takes place in church if the couple are Catholics; in church or the town hall if they are Protestants. The wedding ring is worn on the fourth finger of the left hand by Roman Catholics and on the same finger of the right hand by Protestants.

At the wedding banquet the bride wears a special hairdress made of paper flowers in many colors. Inside it a cross is hidden, symbolic of the tribulations that inevitably accompany the joys of married life.

VILLAGE LIFE

IT IS A SAD BUT TRUE FACT THAT many of these venerable customs are gradually disappearing. For instance, what now appears to the tourist as the national dress of the whole country is more often than not a mere local survival of once-nationwide traditions—traditions that are, indeed, often kept up merely for the sake of the tourist.

This is true, for example, in Roman Catholic Volendam and in Protestant Marken. Volendam is especially famous for the old-fashioned Hotel Spaander, built entirely of timber and furnished with Delft porcelain; each room is furnished in a typical Dutch style, with a supply of Delft porcelain, dainty Dutch majolica fireplaces, stoves, *pipenreks* (pipe racks), teapots together with their *theemuts* (tea-cosies) and oil lamps.

Here in Volendam and in Marken, too, the tourists arrive with guides furnished by the local travel agency in *strombooten* (motorboats) to drink tea in old fishing villages where one can still see the tarred huts with the day's washing hanging on the line. But, like so much else, these villages, in fact the entire Ijsselmeer, are undergoing a radical change as the surrounding region is being transformed into polders.

TRADITIONAL DRESS

Women in Volendam wear black petticoats with bodices, colored aprons, coral necklaces round their necks and beaked lace caps. It was here that the men's baggy pants, their Sunday waistcoats with silver buttons and heavy silver chains originated. This purely local costume has erroneously been taken for the Dutch

A young child from Marken in the province of North Holland. In Marken, as in the neighboring town of Volendam, the people often wear traditional dress. The baggy trousers and blue smocks worn by the men of Marken are famous, as are the flowered bodices (inspired by costumes of the East Indies) and cardboard-stiff bonnets worn by the women.

Young couples promenade during a folk-dance festival in Marken. The girls are wearing the traditional Dutch clogs. These wooden shoes, which have become a national symbol of Holland, were adroitly conceived to withstand the country's moist and marshy soil. The men's clogs, called hogelklompen, *are heavier than those of the women or children, called* tripklompen.

national costume. This "national costume" is nowadays worn more for the sake of tourists. Equally genuine traditional clothes, often markedly different in appearance, can be found in many other districts.

At Giethorn, not far from Staphurst, the center of the polder area, the traditional costume is enhanced by a traditional landscape. But the well known picture of the heavy *treckshuits* (barges) loaded with merchandise and people, towed by a heavy draft horse with a boy walking ahead and blowing a trumpet, has now almost wholly disappeared.

Although there are no more *treckshuits*, countless *stoomboten* and *ponters* (light rafts) move along the canals, packed with anything from milk cans to cheese, and it is a strange sight, where the waterlevel is above the ground, to see these craft floating as if above the fields. In Amsterdam one can hear the constant sound of trumpets—the signal the rafts give before turning a corner.

Giethorn, too, is built on a maze of waterways. The gabled houses among the large shady trees are connected by graceful, high-arched bridges. The only road runs along the main canal.

The entrance to every farm is through a *plankje*, a turnstile painted in vivid colors. If it stands crosswise, it indicates that no one is home. Formerly it was the custom to put up a notice with *Te huis* or *Niet huis* to indicate that the owners were in or out. Outside in the meadows the famous black and white Dutch cows are grazing peacefully. They are said to yield up to five thousand quarts of milk annually. From March to November they are at pasture in all kinds of weather, however harsh, grazing on the rich grass of the polders. Sometimes one can see cows wearing special coats, often brightly colored, to protect them from the rain.

At Urk, formerly an island in the Zuider Zee and now transformed into a village of the *Noordoostpolder*, the women wear stiff, pale-blue bodices lined with kidskin. The men wear the characteristic baggy black pants, black shirts, clogs and a belt with large silver buttons.

At Spakenburg, the *kraplak* is the typical wear for women; it is a cloaklike mantle of printed cotton, which is thrown back over the shoulders so that it gives the women a rather rigid, squarish appearance. It is set off by a close-fitting headpiece decorated with lace.

THE GOLD AND SILVER OF ZEELAND

In Holland, a man's religion can be discerned from the clothes he wears. You can tell a Roman Catholic woman by her wide, three-cornered bonnet, while the Protestant woman's headdress is close fitting with the corners rounded. With men it is the color that counts, generally bright colors for Catholics and dark ones for Protestants. The *borstrokken* (long-sleeved waistcoats) are worn with a belt and large silver buttons. The silver handle of a knife usually sticks out of their pockets (and from boys' pockets too). In some places the buttons on the necks of their striped shirts are of gold or silver.

There is a passion for gold and silver on the island of Zeeland and a story is told of an island where horseshoes were made of silver until one day, in punishment for so much vanity, the island sank into the sea.

Above: *Fishermen take time out from the day's activities. In their exaggeratedly baggy pants, striped shirts, short jackets and jaunty hats they carry on Dutch traditions of dress and occupation.*

Below: *In their pointed bonnets, aproned skirts and wooden clogs, these girls from Volendam take off on a wild merry-go-round ride at a local amusement center.*

Zeeland is the most rigidly conservative part of Holland and the Sunday "blue laws" are strictly observed there. No entertainment, no work, not even bicycling are allowed.

It is told how on a Sunday in 1953 there was a serious danger of floods; nevertheless the farmers refused to lift a finger in defense of their homes. All they did was to gather on the dikes and sing hymns.

Old farmers still wear gold earrings and the women's traditional headdresses may still be seen, though many are now kept in museums. (There is such a museum in Middelburg, capital of the district.) It is also here, in Middelburg, that the bell in the belfry of the famous abbey is endearingly referred to as *Lange Jan* (Long John) while the clock of the town hall tower is called *Folle Babet* (Mad Babette), because, being "mad," it races against time trying to outdo Long John and is always five minutes ahead of it.

In Zeeland, the women wear white linen bonnets on weekdays and similar bonnets daintily trimed with lace on Sundays, just as they did more than a hundred years ago. Not much has changed since. The same rich ornament is worn around the head to hold the headdress in place, with the two jewelled ends showing over the temples. When a girl of Zeeland gets married, she has to reverse this *naal* on her wedding day.

The women in Zeeland also wear gold earrings, brooches and stone or coral necklaces with gold clasps. The face of a Zeeland woman is thus richly framed, and the jewels are passed on from mother to daughter. So are silver shoe buttons, silver clasps for handbags and large ornamented scissors—all are lovingly passed down from generation to generation.

Typical of the Zeeland dress is the long full skirt with a silk apron for Sunday, and the *beuk en kleuren,* the pointed bodice, made of silk and trimmed with lace and ribbons. Above it and under the mantle a richly embroidered shawl is wrapped across the bosom.

GOLD HELMETS AND TIARAS

In the old days Frisian traditional dress was magnificent; today it is more simple and is worn only on Sundays. There is a full apron, a wide lace collar, an embroidered handbag and the famous headdress, the *oorijzer* (ear-iron), which can now be seen in very few villages. It consists of a close-fitting headwear of gold or silver from which precious stones dangle on the temples. Formerly, wherever Dutch women assembled, at festivals or celebrations, ornate helmets glittered everywhere. Later, they became tight-fitting metal caps under which the hair was shorn (it was said to cause the hair to fall out). However, modern Dutch girls rebelled against this medieval torture.

There was a time when the women of Friesland might not be seen in public with uncovered head. As they rode to church or to a public function in a beautifully decorated open carriage, their glittering *oorijzers* could be seen with the lace held down by the *naals* or by a diadem covering the back of the head. A hundred years ago such a headdress cost a very large sum; today it is a museum-piece.

In Dutch Brabant, which is predominantly Roman Catholic, a headdress made of two parts is worn. It is a full-bottomed linen bonnet falling over the shoulders and covered by a plaited and embroidered baroque *poffer*. In winter, black pelerines (fur capes) edged with red are worn and nineteen or more petticoats (nobody has ever quite succeeded in counting them all).

Scheveningen, Ijmuiden and Vlaardingen are the most important herring fishing towns. Herring fishing brings in a yearly revenue of hundreds of thousands of florins. The fishing season lasts from May to autumn, when the flotillas return from their fishing expeditions off the coasts. Then freshly painted *haringbuis* (barrels) await their arrival neatly ranged along the wharf. The whole village is down in the harbor; the women who have been patiently making nets await their husbands' return and the children run about in great excitement to welcome their fathers.

Dutch Clogs

Dutch clogs, which are still worn everywhere throughout Holland, are known the world over and from them many customs and idioms have derived. It can happen, for instance, that a man rowing along a canal will throw a clog with the toll money inside it across to the keeper, who will then return it in similar fashion to the owner (empty, of course). A Dutchman wanting to express his consternation over some disturbing event will ruefully exclaim "My clogs are broken!"

In Holland, if the ground is not sandy it is swampy, and water runs and oozes everywhere. Clogs are the best possible footwear under such conditions. In North Brabant or in Veluwe the farmer carves his heavy clogs (the *hogelklompen*) for himself and a somewhat lighter type (the *tripklompen*) for his wife and children.

Wherever traditional clothes are still worn, children wear the same as their parents. On the island of Marken, small girls and boys, up to five years old, wear clogs, skirts and long hair under similar caps, so that one can hardly tell a girl from a boy.

Dutch Pipes

In the 17th-century the inhabitants of Gouda were taught how to make clay pipes by English soldiers in the service of Prince Maurice of Nassau. These pipes, like Delft pottery, have become known as one of Holland's most typical products. In Maastricht, which was once the Roman colony of *Trajectum ad Mosam* (The Bridge on the Maas), pipe

In honor of a special holiday, the market square of Middelburg, capital of Zeeland, is filled with brightly colored canvas booths. Vendors sell sweets, toys and handicrafts while a band plays music in the circular tent in the center of the square.

Cheeses are weighed in during the traditional Friday Cheese Market which takes place in Alkmaar, during the months of April through September. The men who handle the cheeses wear straw hats decorated with colored ribbons. Teams of men (each team wearing its own colored ribbon) compete to see which can haul more cheese.

and tobacco (imported from America) are the objects of special festivities. A long procession of burghers, including women in traditional dress, and headed by the mayor, march across the town smoking long pipes. The procession ends in the central square, where a lively entertainment follows. This, like the Maastricht Carnival, reflects the influence of Germany, which lies only a few miles away across the border.

The long Gouda pipes are made in many forms; some are almost two feet long, others mere cigarette holders; some are called "mysteries," because when smoked a surprise design becomes visible on the originally white bowl of the pipe. At one time these "mystery" pipes were given free to rich and poor alike at public meetings. They were kept in specially numbered racks, the *pipenrek*. This *pipenrek* was an important piece of furniture and every public building, even theaters, had them. Even today many private houses contain these old *pipenreks,* each holding a rich collection of pipes. In Gouda there is a pipe museum where the most beautiful pipes and *pipenreks* of the past are preserved.

THE JOY OF SKATING

IN WINTER THE YOUNG SWAINS FROM The Hague, from Amsterdam and other towns large and small skate along the frozen waterways leading to Gouda in order to buy a pipe for their girls. They then carry them home, taking great care not to drop them.

Dutchmen are prudent when they skate. There is a proverb, "Do not go on the ice the first day it bears." As a matter of facts, skating days are not too numerous except in Friesland, where the winter is generally colder and the lakes and waterways are very often frozen through to the beginning of spring.

The Dutch become really enthusiastic the moment they put on their skates, usually simple blades strapped to their shoes or even, as with the peasant, to clogs which have specially fashioned soles. Skating is even more popular than cycling in Holland, which is probably the only country in the world where schoolchildren are given special skating holidays each year.

It is in Friesland that the famous "eleven cities tour" is held along a route starting from Leukwaarden and passing through eleven towns and villages and across a glittering plain where, in the background, the dark outlines of windmills loom.

The skaters start off at six in the morning and have to be back before midnight. Besides this long-distance

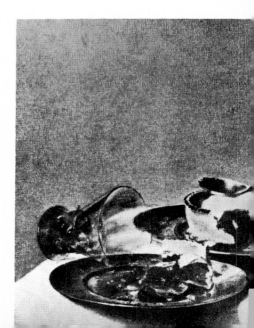

skating, which is a genuine test of physical endurance, there is also a competition for the best time. The winner of this event, like the famous Jaap Eden, is considered a national hero and is honored during the following celebrations when the popular *skotsetrje* is danced.

This is when the Dutch really burst into gaiety, helped by *skiedam*, the national drink; then there is *ad vokaat*, a mixture of cognac and egg, and countless *boreeltjes* (glasses) of *jenever* (juniper), brandy, or other national liquors, which according to the national saying should be taken *een glassje iedere tag* (only one glass daily), for they are extremely potent. To this they will perhaps add a bite of *unitsmijter* (fried eggs) and a slice of ham or beef on a thick piece of bread. Nevertheless, there is a humorous Dutch proverb warning against too much drink: *"Als de wijn is in de man, dan is de wisheid in de kan"* (When wine is in the man, wisdom is in the can).

TULIPOMANIA

THE TOWN OF AALSMEER IS SITUATED at the center of one of the great tulip-producing regions of Holland. Its river is the Singel, and along it and its canals mountains of flowers are seen floating on barges. At Aalsmeer these barges are unloaded with much care, and the flowers are sorted, labeled and classified.

There is a "flower exchange" at Aalsmeer, where only cut flowers are sold. The customers sit around in a sort of vast amphitheater, chatting amiably as business goes on. There is an electric indicator that shows advances and declines in the prices. Whenever a buyer is interested he pushes a button and the hand stops on the indicator; he may then make his purchase, and once again the indicator begins to move. Flowers are transported by airplanes every afternoon in all directions, while Amsterdam and other towns are supplied by special flower trains.

From April to September there is a permanent huge flower show in Amsterdam, where the hothouses alone cover an area of many acres. Then, on the first Saturday of September, there is the final show with fantastically decorated flower carts.

Those who wish to see "onions in bloom" can find them in the triangle between Haarlem, Leiden and Noordwijk. Here, too, are the two famous Keukenhof nature parks, Lissa and Linnaenshof (so named after the great botanist and tulip-grower Linnaeus). This area attracts native Dutch tulip fanciers and tourists alike.

Along every road children can be seen offering flowers of all colors and varieties. The people return home carrying huge bunches.

Today the exaggerations of the 17th century (which were the golden years in Holland) have disappeared. The great flower culture was started when an Austrian ambassador brought tulip bulbs to Europe from Turkey. Their culture was introduced to Holland by the botanist Clusius. There followed what can only be called a *tulipomania*. Rich landowners started to cultivate bulbs on the sandy soils of their estates, behind the dunes of the North Sea. They all did well. More and more new species were created and exclusive possession of a particular rare species was worth

Painting of a peasant woman, by the Dutch artist Jozef Israels (1824-1911). Although it is commonly supposed that most of the people in the Netherlands are either farmers or fishermen, in fact only 11 per cent of the population is employed in these fields. About 42 per cent of the working force is engaged in industry, primarily processing.

a fortune. In a flower catalogue, dating from 1637, a rare bulb is listed at the price of 4230 florins. In the archives of Alkmaar and Haarlem, one can read of staggering bargains; houses, carriage and pair, thoroughbred horses were given in exchange for a few rare tulip bulbs. The list is endless; one finds items like two carts loaded with wheat, four with barley, four fatted cattle, twelve sheep, two measures of wine, four barrels of beer, two thousand pounds of butter, one thousand pounds of cheese, a complete man's suit and a silver goblet—all in exchange for bulbs. A brewer gave his brewery for one special bulb, which he then destroyed in fury when he discovered that it was not an exclusive species. A sailor ate some bulbs, mistaking them for common onions, and then found he had eaten something worth thousands of florins.

This folly grew to such extremes that there was a regular tulip exchange with rampant speculations and numerous frauds; shares were issued implying quantities of tulip bulbs which not all the gardens of Holland could have grown. Finally, the government was obliged to put an end to it all by a decree which

The remnants of a night's feasting are suggestively captured in Still Life *by the Dutch painter Willem Claesz Heda (1594-c.1681). Dutch food is noted for being wholesome, tasty and hearty. In the Dutch diet* boterham *(bread and butter), herring and milk are the main staples, along with such national dishes as* erwtensoep, *a thick pea soup cooked with bits of sausage or pig's knuckles, and* hutspot, *a pork and vegetable stew that dates back to the Spanish invasion.*

caused many people to end their days in debtors' prison.

In World War II, during the German occupation, tulips once again became the flowers of children, who in the famished winter of 1944 were kept alive on tulip bulbs. The bulbs are edible, provided the slightly toxic center is removed.

Today the lovely tulip display around Haarlem is more humble. Flowers are cut before they are in full bloom. Bulbs are dried and treated to thrive in almost any climate. They bring Holland an annual revenue of more than 90 million florins.

WINDMILLS

ONE CAN STILL FIND ETCHINGS THAT show 17th-century New York, then called New Amsterdam, with the familiar outline of windmills in the background. The pioneers from the Netherlands could not have put a more telling signature to their pictures, for it is not often that the characteristic and most picturesque symbol of a country also stands for its greatest necessity.

It is not, of course, as if the Dutch were the only people who have put the wind to practical use. The first trace of windmills can be found in 1299 in the Orient, in Persia and Arabia, where their true origins are lost in misty legends. Judging by the date, it was probably the Crusaders, bearers of so much good and evil, who brought the windmill back to Holland.

However that may be, the oldest mill that can be seen today is in Ede, in Gelderland, where it was put up by the Emperor Charles V in the mid-16th century. Although the windmill may have come from the Orient, its builders, specialists and perfectors throughout history have been Dutchmen, the best known of whom was the 16th-century engineer Cornelius Corneliszoon.

Lovers of tradition may well regret the windmill's passing, for in Holland as elsewhere diesel engines and motors of every kind have taken the place of the picturesque old windmills, as, for example, in the province of Zaan, where out of a former thousand windmills only a dozen now stand. In the entire country there are now only about a thousand left.

If one looks at a map where windmills are marked, one can see that they are more numerous where the land is below sea level—in Friesland, for example, where their familiar silhouettes on the skyline still strike the eyes.

But these winged giants are still at work; they pump water to drain the land for the new polders in Friesland, in North and South Holland and in Zeeland. In other parts of the country, *korenmolens* (corn mills) can be seen at work virtually everywhere; the sweeps (the "wings" of the mills) turn to saw timber, to clean rice, to press oil seeds or to mix colors, like the ones painters like Rùysdael and Seghers used. They make drugs and grind spice, egg shells, tobacco and cocoa.

Today the sails of windmills are constructed according to an aeronautical formula; they revolve mounted on the wind shaft at the top of the building, fixed crosswise. They are rectangular in shape, made up of small removable blades, like shutters, hinged in the sail frames. These can move to catch the slightest breath of wind; and, if that is not sufficent, they are spread with sail-cloth, which partly or totally covers the frames.

The mill, too, can revolve round a main shaft; in fact the polder mill is really derived from the old *postmolden* (post-mill) modeled on the oriental pattern, pivoting on a massive upright pole on which the whole construction rests.

The motion of the sails is transmitted by cogwheels to the internal machinery, which works millstones, pumps, saws, or does whatever is required.

Then there is the *standermolen,* an open mill with outside props. This is the oldest existing type, generally an upright, rectangular structure, with a steep roof; the entire millhopper is supported from the ground. The *wipmolden* is a picturesque smaller type, typical of South Holland, and it is also an open mill resting on outside props.

The miller generally lives in the basement of his mill. His home is like a dwarf's house in a fairy tale. With its windows and doors brightly painted and its gay curtains, the tiny house squats under the weight of the tall building it seems to be carrying.

The 17th-century Waag, *or weighhouse, in the city of Nijmegen near the German border. Founded on the site of the ancient Roman settlement of Noviomagus, Nijmegen became a flourishing trading center during the Middle Ages, and was a member of the Hanseatic League. Today it remains an important inland shipping center.*

If there is no habitation in the basement, it serves as a storehouse for whatever is being produced. In a windmill every motion is vertical, the power emanating from the wings being transmitted downwards, either to the basement itself or to an adjacent storeroom. It is fed with raw material from the top, and the final product, whether grain, timber, or whatever it is, ends up in the basement.

Among the many types of windmills is the *bovenkruier*, where the entire mill top revolves so that the position of the sails is set by the wind itself according to its direction. A variety of the *bovenkruier* is the *beltmolen* (a mill standing on a heap of cinders); then there is the *zeldenrust* (seldom at rest), which, as its name implies, is always working.

Windmills are mostly built of bricks or stones, and, in the polder area, of timber. They still have traditionally gay colors; the wooden parts are painted in clear tones, often green or white, while the *wipmolens* in Leiden are rusty brown. The oldest mill roofs are decorated with what are called *makelaars,* a front carved with acorn patterns. Sometimes they are tarred.

The main axis on which the wings turn are often decorated with a star painted gold or red, sometimes blue or white. These ornaments are found less and less; the *makelaars* are disappearing, as are the "carved beards" which formerly used to protrude from the bottom of the axis hole.

If on a windy day the miller has unfurled all his sails and the mill is turning empty, people say: *malen met blote benen* (to grind with bare feet). There are many more such expressions *daar bij die molen* (about the mill).

But the true language of the mill is the language the sails themselves speak. They are an open book to the expert Dutch eye. They tell all there is to know about those who live there. The mill is in working order if the sails rest at right angles, vertically and horizontally, but when they stand athwart, with the sails furled, there is some special reason for their immobility. Perhaps some machinery is being repaired, or, if it is a polder mill, it can mean a protest against an insufficient water supply. There is little a mill cannot say with its sails: that it is in need of labor, that it can take no grain at the moment, that it is asking for the "mill doctor" because it is *krepele* (broken down), or even that it has a calf for sale.

The wings can speak of joy and of sorrow. When somebody has died in the family, they stand athwart just beyond the position of the quarters. If it is the miller himself who has died, the blades and the sails are dismantled for three whole days. When they begin to work again, mourning will continue for a year and seven weeks more, but all this time when at rest, the mill will be turned to face the miller's house. If the miller's wife dies, the blades (but not the sail-cloth) are removed from only three wings for three days. If a son dies, thirteen of the blades are taken out. Nine are removed for a brother and three for a cousin. If a funeral procession passes, the wings stand still in honor of the dead.

There is the festive position to celebrate a birth or a marriage. Then the wings stream with ribbons. There is a great display for feasts such as Pentecost or, even more elaborate, for a wedding. Then the wings are interlaced with the sails, hearts dangle from them, wreaths, stars, Cupid's arrows and a cage (which symbolizes the state of matrimony). Trumpeting angels look down from the top.

As a feature of the landscape, the windmill suggests power. It is a landmark of the greatest importance in this gentle, horizontal, often monotonous countryside. The eye rests on the familiar and much beloved shape, which always dominates, whether it be standing in a polder or near a village. From a distance its form seems delicate and fragile, but as one approaches it, it reveals its imposing massiveness.

FOOD AND DRINK

THE DUTCH ARE TRADITIONALLY frugal. Because of their many herds of cattle, one would think they ate a

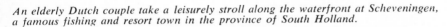

An elderly Dutch couple take a leisurely stroll along the waterfront at Scheveningen, a famous fishing and resort town in the province of South Holland.

An aerial view of the great dike stretching for some 20 miles between the provinces of Friesland and North Holland, separating the great basin of the Ijsselmeer from the North Sea. This dike, part of a mammoth engineering project which is changing the geographical face of modern Holland, was constructed to facilitate the draining of the Ijsselmeer and make possible the reclamation of hundreds of thousands of acres of land.

great deal of meat; but this is not so. Their cattle breeding is based chiefly on the dairy cow, not on beef-cattle. Even the greatest part of the butter and cheese they produce goes for export, while the Dutchman himself often (though by no means always) has margarine or peanut butter with his bread.

This famous bread and butter, *boterham*, is their main nourishment. Its tradition goes far back. Even Rembrandt lunched off bread and butter with cheese and herring. The *koffietafel* they have at noon, with either coffe or tea, is mostly composed of cheese or ham or sausage sandwiches, eaten by most people at their workplace or in their office. At eleven o'clock in the morning a cup of coffee is taken; in the afternoon, a cup of tea. In the evening comes the only warm meal, with either *uitsmeter* or a *haringhek-*

kerssteeg (herring sandwich). There are "tons of herrings and rivers of milk." Perhaps this was the picture in his mind's eye when Sadi de Gorter wrote: "Together with the Rhine, the Maas and the Scheldt, milk is one of the great rivers which flows across the land of the Dutch." Milk and herrings are their favorite food, and as the proverb says, *haring in 't land, dokter aan de kant* (with herring in the house, the doctor is out of it).

Among their national dishes there is the *kalbspolet*, with rice, green peas and lettuce; they also frequently partake of cod served with boiled potatoes. Besides local specialties, there is the popular *erwtensoep*, a soup of dry peas cooked for hours, together with bacon, cured salami and pig's feet, and seasoned with onion, celery and leeks. The other well-known national dish, the *hutspot*, dates from 1575 when, coming out of starving Leiden,

a boy found a dish of pork and vegetable stew still cooking, left behind by the departed Spaniards. To this day the *hutspot* is cooked until it becomes a mash.

Dutch Cheeses

It was by "royal privilege" that, in the year 1571, the now-famous cheese market was instituted in the quaint town of Alkmaar. Ever since that date, every Friday morning (by noon the market is over) from every farm, dairy or village, all kinds of dairy products flood the Alkmaar market.

The uninitiated foreigner may think that there is only one type of Dutch cheese, but the connoisseur knows the difference between the round yellow Edam (which has a red skin for export) and the cylindrical Edam, which has a higher fat content, or the Leiden cream cheese, seasoned with fennel, which is sold at Alkmaar and especially at Edam.

In the market town of Alkmaar (there is a market, of course, in every Dutch town) there is an old church and a new church (*Oude e Nieuwe kerk*), the *Stadhuis* (town hall) and the *Waagenbouw* (or simply *Waag*), which was originally a 15th-century chapel and was transformed into an official cheese-weighing house eleven years after the market was set up.

The ground on which the cheeses are heaped in neat pyramids is strewn with straw. The men who carry the cheeses wear traditional costumes: a white suit and a straw hat with colored ribbons—red, green, blue or yellow—indicate the companies for which they work. The ribbons dangling from wide brims flutter in the breeze. Ever since 1604 these men have formed a closed corporation, the posts being passed down from father to son.

Even with American tourists in shorts, or Germans loaded with cameras milling about in the square handling the cheeses, the picture remains much the same as it was centuries ago. Whenever a bargain is struck, the carriers load the cheese on handbarrows which have bent shafts and leather straps that are passed over the shoulder. The cheese is then weighed, stamped with ink and rolled with the utmost skill onto rafts moored in the canal. From there it is shipped to the large cities and exported to waiting customers in every part of the world.

The Royal Palace of Amsterdam was completed in 1648. A great architectural feat (16,000 piles had to be sunk into the ground to support the weight), the Palace was designed by Jacob van Campen and Daniel Stalpaert in a style clearly reminiscent of Italian Classicism. Under the influence of the Protestant Reformation, many of the structures built in Holland during the 17th century returned to Classical architectural traditions to counteract what were considered the excesses of the Baroque "Catholic" school.

A 16th-century engraving showing the historic city of Groningen in the northern Netherlands. Founded before the 9th century, Groningen figured importantly in Dutch history during the Middle Ages (especially at the time of the Crusades) and during the bitter struggle against Spain in the 16th century.

INTRODUCTION

THE NATION KNOWN OFFICIALLY AS the Kingdom of the Netherlands and popularly as Holland had had a relatively short existence as a separate entity. Prior to the late 16th century the term "the Netherlands" referred to a considerably larger area, including not only the territory of the modern kingdom but also that of the present-day states of Belgium and Luxembourg. At that time a schism, predominantly religious in inspiration, occurred, dividing the area into southern and northern sections. The south remained, as it had been since the 1st century B.C., under foreign domination; the north—Holland—fought for and won its independence.

Until the time of the great schism, the Netherlands was such a homogenous area that it would be both difficult and meaningless to treat separately the history of its northern and southern parts. The major political, social and economic developments of the entire region have been dealt with in the article *Belgium: The History,* and the reader is referred to that article for a discussion of the early stages of Holland's growth. However, although the major developments prior to the late 16th century held true for the north as well as the south, there were from the earliest times several distinctions between the two regions. These distinctions have continued to influence the development of the north and south since their separation.

First of all, the south is hemmed in between the two chief European powers: Germany and France. It is of great strategic importance to both these powers, and has invariably been caught up in the frequent wars between them. The north, on the other hand, borders Germany but not France, and its strategic importance is comparatively less. In time of war, if the French want to move into the Netherlands area they must begin in the south, and the retaliation of Germany or some other interested major power has almost always checked them before the north has become a battlefield.

The south, with its fertile land and abundance of communications, encourages human settlement; it has been populous from the beginning of recorded history. The north, more exposed to the invading sea, was not

William I of Orange (1533-84), founder of the Dutch republic, attempted to liberate and unify the entire Netherlands region (including modern Belgium, Luxembourg and Holland) during the late 16th century. Religious and linguistic differences, however, coupled with political and military problems, forced William to settle for the independence of the northern provinces (the modern Netherlands). The southern provinces (Belgium and Luxembourg) remained under foreign (chiefly Spanish) domination. William was called "the Silent" because of his habit of concealing his true thoughts behind a façade of pleasant but noncommittal language.

acting in cooperation with their fellow citizens. A further impetus to unity came from the fact that in the north there has always been only one major linguistic group; in the south there have been two, and this has created a serious barrier to communication and understanding between the inhabitants of the southern region.

By the 1500s the unity of the north was certainly far from complete, but yet it was sufficient, together with the protection from total invasion that the area's geographical situation afforded, to encourage a sense of national identity and a desire to protect it. The immediate impulse to political freedom may have been a matter of religion, but the basis for independence had been solidly established well before the religious crisis erupted.

THE STRUGGLE FOR INDEPENDENCE

AS WAS EXPLAINED IN BELGIUM: THE History, the League of Arras and the Union of Utrecht formed in 1579 marked a definite break between the northern and southern provinces, but they did not establish permanent boundaries between the two regions. Considerable territory which had first been included in the Union of Utrecht was subsequently won back by the Spaniards. This was due in part to the diplomatic and military genius of the Spanish governor, Alessandro Farnese. It was also brought about by the initial weakness, both political and military, of the northern provinces.

William I of Orange was always more popular in the north than in the south. He was given his epithet—the Silent—because of his habit of concealing his true thoughts behind pleasant but meaningless phrases. He was enough a man of the north to be trusted there; in the south he was suspect and misunderstood.

William realized his limitations as a national leader, and in an attempt to hold the Union of Utrecht together and to procure French support against the Spanish menace he tried to make Francis, duke of Anjou and brother of King Henry III, nominal ruler of the rebel provinces. Actual political control, however, was reserved for the central legislative assembly, the estates general.

This maneuver was utterly unsuccessful. French military aid was not

easily won for human habitation. The familiar saying "God created the world, but the Dutch created Holland" is not without validity.

The north is advantageously situated for commerce, but until comparatively recent times, when flooding could be brought under a fair degree of control, the hazards of living there were so great that the population was sparse. For many centuries cities were smaller than in the south and industrialization was less widespread. As a result, the social turmoil experienced in the south as workers

fought aristocrats for additional privileges, was felt much more mildly in the north.

Finally, in the interest of survival, the people of the north had to act together against the menace of incursions from the sea. This forged greater bonds of unity than developed in the south, where physical safety left the people free to court prosperity, and where prosperity encouraged competition. Although many of the northerners did become prosperous, their influence could never be taken for granted; they grew used to great enough to be decisive and Francis, a Catholic, was unacceptable in the strongly Calvinistic areas. The duke, chafing under the restraints on his power, attempted to take Antwerp by force in 1583, and his defeat so discredited him that he had to withdraw to France.

In spite of the duke's official position, the leadership of the north never left William's hands. It was under his authority that the estates general, on July 26, 1581, issued a stirring declaration of independence. In bold and clear language this document set forth the principle that a sovereign must fulfill certain obligations to his people; in failing to do so, Philip II of Spain had forfeited his right to rule the Netherlands.

Philip was well aware of where the real northern power lay, and he was convinced that if William could be eliminated he might recapture all the lost territories. To this end he put a high price on William's life, and after many unsuccessful attempts, an assassin managed to kill him in 1584. The north, however, showed no inclination to capitulate after his death.

THE ORGANIZATION OF THE GOVERNMENT

The core of the independent region of the Netherlands was the so-called United Provinces—Holland, Zeeland, Utrecht, Gelderland, Overijssel, Friesland and Groningen. They were bound together for defensive, financial and other limited purposes in a loose federation. Almost a decade passed before the monarchy gave way to a republican form of government.

Local authority remained strong in the United Provinces. Members of the estates general were chosen by provinces, and the decisions of this body had to be unanimous. Thus the individual provinces could block any actions they disapproved.

Executive power was in the hands of stadholders. These were originally representatives of feudal lords, later provincial governors. Over the course of several centuries most of the stadholderships in the north devolved on members of the House of Orange, and the leader of this family came to be something of a national executive. Such was the status of William of Orange and, after his death, of his son, Maurice of Nassau. Maurice, however, was only 17 years old in 1584, and for the next few years the United Provinces were governed in his name by older men, the most prominent of whom was Johan van Olderbarneveldt of the province of Holland.

THE EARL OF LEICESTER

The position of the north at the time of William's death was precarious. Farnese's forces continued to advance; there was little question of Dutch military inferiority. More troops had to be procured, and after the experience with the duke of Anjou, it was decided to seek support not from Catholic France but from Protestant England. Although Queen Elizabeth I refused to commit her nation to a large-scale involvement in the struggle over the Netherlands, in 1585 she sent one of her favorites, the Earl of Leicester, to act as governor-general of the United Provinces.

Leicester's troops provided badly needed manpower, but the Earl himself was a failure as a military strategist and he took his role as civilian ruler far more seriously than either Elizabeth or the Dutch estates general intended. He was recalled in 1587, having done little for the northern cause.

THE CHECKING OF SPANISH ADVANCES

By 1585 Farnese had retaken all the Netherlands except the United Provinces and the northern sections of Flanders and Brabant. Had not the Spanish been diverted at this point by wars on other fronts, it is likely that the northern provinces also would soon have been reconquered. As things worked out, however, the few Spanish advances after 1585 were only temporary. By 1594, with the government of the United Provinces in the hands of Maurice of Nassau and his cousin William Louis, stadholder of Friesland, the position of the north had much improved.

The north was further strengthened in 1596 by the conclusion of a triple alliance with France and England against Spain. The agreement was not a long-lasting one; in 1598 France made peace with Spain and in 1604 England followed suit. By 1609 both the Spaniards and the Dutch were war-weary and they agreed to a 12-year truce.

The Early Seventeenth Century

The early part of the 17th century was a time of material prosperity. Dutch commerce increased tremendously, and the founding of the Dutch East India Company in 1602 presaged the opening of a vast and lucrative colonial empire.

POLITICAL AND RELIGIOUS QUARRELS

The peace of these years was marred by what began as a religious conflict between orthodox Calvinists and a group of dissidents known as the Arminians, who believed that the official church doctrine should be modified on several points. The quarrel soon took on political overtones. Maurice and the advocates of strong central authority supported the orthodox view, while those who wanted power to remain with the provinces sided with the Arminians.

The provincial leaders effectively hampered the working of the government, and in 1618 Maurice countered with a show of armed strength. Opposition leaders were removed from office, and a national synod of the church upheld the orthodox position, silencing the Arminians. One of the major casualties of the conflict was Olderbarneveldt, whose support of the Arminian faction cost him his life.

Maurice of Nassau (1567-1625), son of William the Silent, continued his father's work by maintaining the independence of the United Provinces (established in 1579) against the Spanish. A brilliant military commander and strategist, he successfully countered Spanish efforts to regain supremacy, defeating the Spaniards in a number of important battles on Dutch territory during the late 16th and early 17th centuries.

—the Stuarts—to the English throne. To assure his control of his own country, he strengthened his hold on the Dutch government by arresting dissident leaders in the province of Holland, but he died of smallpox in November 1650 before he could put his militaristic foreign policy into effect.

THE PEAK OF DUTCH POWER

WILLIAM III OF ORANGE WAS BORN A week after his father's death, and for 22 years, until he took control, the new nation was without a central executive. The provinces took advantage of this situation to strengthen their position vis-à-vis the central government. Among the provincial leaders was the very able Jan de Witt of Holland, who was the guiding force in Dutch domestic and foreign policy until William III took over.

Throughout the first half of the century the Dutch had continued to expand their commerce and their colonial empire. In addition to their possessions in the East and West Indies they held New Amsterdam (later New York) on the North American continent. By 1650 the Dutch fleet was twice the size of the English and French fleets combined and Amsterdam was the richest city in Europe.

WARS WITH ENGLAND

Such gains inevitably led to rivalry with England, the other major commercial power of the time. The English navy began to interfere with Dutch shipping, and in 1651 England passed the Navigation Act, aimed at curtailing Dutch trade. In the first British-Dutch sea war, which raged from 1652 to 1654, neither side was able to score a decisive victory. The British were in a slightly superior position in 1654, and the terms of settlement were unfavorable to the Dutch. De Witt, on behalf of the province of Holland, also concluded a secret agreement with Cromwell's republic pledging the exclusion of the House of Orange from the stadholdership. This agreement was re-

PEACE WITH SPAIN

When the truce with Spain expired in 1621, hostilities resumed; the conflict became part of the Thirty Years' War, which involved most of Europe. By 1648 Spain, exhausted, had to recognize the independence of the United Provinces and to cede to them the northern sections of Brabant and Flanders. The terms of settlement were contained in the Treaty of Munster, part of the Peace of Westphalia. Thus the conflict between the Spanish and Dutch, which had begun in the late 1570s, was finally ended. This long series of battles is sometimes known as the Eighty Years' War.

Maurice of Nassau had died in 1625 and was succeeded by his brother Frederick Henry. The latter was succeeded in 1647 by his son William II, who had married the daughter of the deposed King Charles I of England. William was not content with the Treaty of Munster but in 1650 entered into a secret agreement with France to resume the war against Spain, with the goal of partitioning the southern provinces and also of restoring his wife's family

Naval Battle in the Waters of Haarlem, *by the Dutch artist Hendrik Vroon. The naval battle of Haarlem, fought between Dutch and Spanish forces in 1573, presaged the rise of Dutch naval power in the 17th century. By 1650, the Dutch fleet was twice the size of the English and French fleets combined. Although England ultimately became supreme on the seas, Dutch seapower enabled Holland to acquire a vast and far-flung colonial empire.*

The Gothic Dom Tower in Utrecht, an historic city in the central Netherlands. The famed Treaty of Utrecht (actually a series of treaties signed at Utrecht between 1712 and 1715) ended the War of the Spanish Succession, which had embroiled much of Europe in bloody struggle since 1701. The treaty, which was of great importance for the future course of European history, provided the Netherlands with few political or territorial advantages, and was a harbinger of the decline of Dutch power in the 18th century.

placed when Charles II was restored to the English throne.

In 1665 war resumed, and the Dutch were now supported by the French. They scored a major victory in destroying the British fleet in the Medway. The British then signed the Treaty of Breda, under which the Dutch ceded New Amsterdam to England, in exchange for the Dutch Antilles and for Surinam in South America.

The Rule of William III

In 1672 hostilities broke out again; this time Louis XIV of France sided with England. The English attacked by sea, the French by land, and while the Dutch were able to stand off the former, the latter made alarming advances. Popular dissatisfaction with De Witt's regime grew, and in July he and his supporters were forced to accept William III as stadholder and captain-general for life. Shortly thereafter De Witt and his brother died at the hands of a mob for their alleged crimes against the republic.

William was faced with a grave military situation; the city of Amsterdam could only be saved from capture by the French by opening the dikes and creating a water barrier between the city and the French army. This William did and it was a brilliant move, but subsequently he did not distinguish himself militarily. He was, however, a shrewd diplomat. By 1673 he had made alliances with the Austrian Empire, Spain, Brandenburg and Denmark. This support caused England to abandon France and Louis XIV, finding himself alone in the war, decided to withdraw his forces.

William was linked to the restored English royal family through his marriage to King Charles II's niece, Mary. He tried to use these ties to get England to join his campaigns against France, but his plan was unsuccessful. In 1678 the conflict which had begun in 1672 was formally ended by the settlement of Nijmegen, in which the Dutch neither gained nor lost anything of importance.

THE WAR OF THE GRAND ALLIANCE

In the years that followed, Louis XIV continued to be watched with suspicion, not only by William but by all the major European leaders. Various alliances were formed and re-formed against him. In September 1688, Louis invaded Cologne and the Palatinate, touching off the complex series of military engagements which came to be known collectively as the War of the Grand Alliance.

Later in the same year, William III made a move which had nothing directly to do with the French king but which greatly influenced the course of the war. Charles II of England had now been succeeded by his brother James II, whose autocratic policies and staunch Catholicism soon alienated large segments of the English population. Though William was James' son-in-law, he gave favorable attention to the foes of the monarch when they asked him to come to England and help their cause. He landed on the British coast in December, 1688, at the head of a sizeable army and marched on London. James fled the country. Parliament ruled that he had abdicated, and conferred the English crown jointly on William and his wife Mary. After his coronation William lost little time involving England, which had hitherto remained neutral, in the continental war against Louis XIV.

In spite of the forces lined up against him, Louis XIV more than held his own in the war for several years. Until 1691 William's participation was limited because he was occupied with putting down a rebellion in Ireland, which had remained loyal to James II. After the Irish fighting was halted, William became active on the Continent. Although he was not outstanding as a military commander, his involvement of England in the war on a large scale undoubtedly was crucial in turning the tide against Louis.

Under the Treaty of Ryswyk which ended the war in 1697, William won French recognition of his status as King of England and valuable commercial concessions for Holland. In addition, the Dutch were given the right to garrison a number of towns in the southern provinces; these were to serve as barrier fortresses against any future French attack by land.

THE EFFECTS OF WILLIAM'S DEATH

William III died in 1702. He and Mary were childless, and thus the House of Orange did not provide a successor to the English throne. William's lack of a direct heir also weakened the position of his family in Holland. During his lifetime William had accomplished a great deal, both for Europe as a whole and for

The late 16th-century town hall in the city of Franeker in Friesland province of the northern Netherlands. Friesland joined with the other Netherlands provinces in the Union of Utrecht (1579). But the province continued to elect its own stadholders, and thus maintained a partial independence until 1747, when its stadholder, William IV of Orange, became sole stadholder of all the United Provinces. The people of Friesland speak Frisian, a dialect that is related to, but also has great differences from, the Dutch language.

his native country. But Holland, though it had become a major European power under William's leadership, had serious internal weaknesses, and these began to manifest themselves soon after his death.

THE EIGHTEENTH CENTURY

IF THE 17TH CENTURY WAS ONE OF eminence for the Dutch republic the 18th century was one of decline. There were a number of reasons for this. First of all, the resources of the government had been overtaxed by the wars of the preceding century. Additional measures to raise revenue were needed, but the people opposed them. They were understandably weary of war. There was no imminent danger from without, nor were there compelling financial reasons for engaging in campaigns of conquest. The Dutch people were exceedingly prosperous, and after more than a century of struggle they wanted to be free to enjoy their prosperity. They were not willing to supply funds to maintain a large army and even the navy, which had so often been the nation's salvation in the past, was allowed to decay.

Another reason for the decline was the fact that after William III's death there was no effective national leadership. Five of the seven provinces refused to recognize William III's designated heir, a cousin, John William Friso. For 45 years the republic was without a national stadholder. On the two previous occasions when a similar situation had occurred, provincial strongmen like Olderbarneveldt and De Witt had provided adequate leadership; this time no figure of comparable abilities appeared. Provincial governments assumed more and more authority and the estates general, since it was under provincial control, could not act effectively. Corruption and inefficiency were widespread.

Dutch weakness was evident as early as 1715, when the nation could obtain no advantages in the Treaty of Utrecht which ended the War of the Spanish Succession. There were no actual losses, and indeed the right to garrison barrier fortresses was reaffirmed when the Austrian Habsburgs took over the southern provinces. Nonetheless, acute observers could not help contrast Dutch authority in 1715 with what it had been in William III's day.

The town hall of Groningen, capital of the province of the same name, in the northeastern Netherlands. The building was begun in the Classical style in 1787 and finished, with an admixture of French and Italian influences, in 1810. The eclectic result, an architecturally harmonious creation, mirrors the diverse influences that played upon Dutch culture after the establishment of political independence in the 16th and 17th centuries.

THE WAR OF THE AUSTRIAN SUCCESSION

The policy of such leaders as the republic had was to avoid foreign entanglements. It was a wise enough plan, but it could not he maintained, for the Dutch were no longer in a position to act on their own—they could only respond to the moves of other European powers. Thus they were forced to enter the War of the Austrian Succession (1740-48), siding with England and Austria against France. Economic decline began to set in during these years, and national leadership was all but nonexistent. In 1747, French forces marched into the Dutch territories in Flanders south of the Scheldt.

As before, when the nation was in peril, the people looked to the House of Orange. John William Friso had died and his son, William IV, was made stadholder of all the Dutch provinces and captain- and admiralgeneral. These offices were soon declared hereditary in his family. This William, however, lacked the stature of his predecessors. Yet the war was safely ended, though not through his doing. He died in 1751.

Since William's offices were now hereditary, his death did not leave the nation without a stadholder. However, William V was a minor and the nation was ruled by a regency until 1766, during which time the central government was further weakened, as were the armed services. Had there not been a determined effort to preserve neutrality throughout the Seven Years' War (1756-63) it is likely that the nation would have been overrun.

The Breakup of the Republic

William V, once he came to power, proved to be something less than his country's salvation. He was a weak and vacillating man dominated by his wife, the daughter of Frederick William II of Prussia.

During his long reign the republic steadily deteriorated. The final breakup came as a result first of the American, then of the French Revolution. The Dutch were naturally sympathetic to the American colonists, and although William V tried to maintain an official neutrality the British were increasingly displeased by the clandestine support the Americans were given by the Dutch. A war ensued,

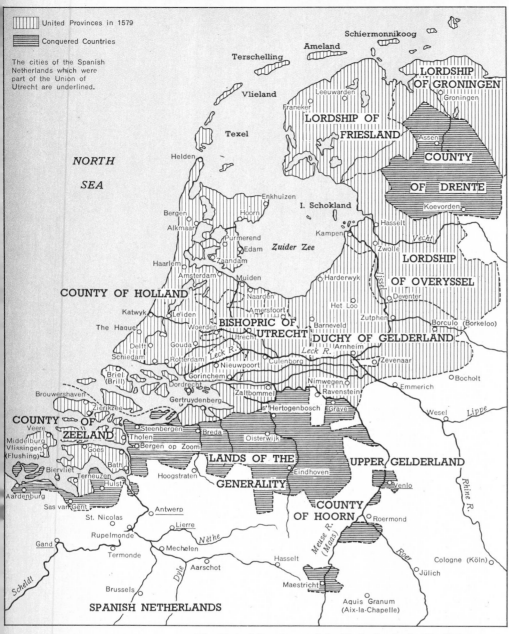

The United Provinces of the Netherlands in the 18th century.

the revolutionary cause had aroused considerable sympathy among opponents of the House of Orange. William V and his wife could not count on foreign support this time; all Europe was in retreat before the French. As the invading armies advanced, William saw no alternative but to flee to England, which he did in 1795. After he left, the Dutch signed a treaty with the French under which they were allowed to retain nominal independence but were required to support a French army on their soil, pay a sizeable subsidy, and surrender their part of Flanders.

The Patriots, renamed the Unionists, came to power, and the Batavian Republic was proclaimed. Reforms were instituted, modeling the new government on that of revolutionary France. Such attempts to set up a popular democracy with a strong centralized government were resisted by the traditional forces, which formed the Federalist party. After several years of turmoil, during which radical democrats, moderate democrats and conservatives vied for power, a moderate regime was finally established.

THE NAPOLEONIC ERA

This regime controlled the country until 1801, when Napoleon began to take a great interest in the Batavian Republic. He wanted to bring the Dutch government more closely under his control and to extract additional revenues from it. To these ends he forced a new constitution on the country, cutting the power of the central government and restoring considerable authority to the provinces. In 1806 he decided to do away with the republican organization of the country altogether and make his brother, Louis, king. Forced to choose between accepting Louis or suffering annexation, the Dutch reluctantly elected the former. In June, 1806, the Kingdom of Holland was proclaimed.

Although Louis was forced upon them, the Dutch found little to quarrel with in his behavior. Far from being a mere mouthpiece for his brother, he exhibited a sincere concern for the welfare of his new subjects. Napoleon at this time was trying to bring England to heel by imposing the Continental System, a strict prohibition against the import of British goods anywhere in Europe. The Dutch, whose economy was based on trade, were the worst violators of this prohibition, and Napoleon wanted his brother to bring them

which shattered the prestige of the Dutch navy and temporarily cost the republic all its overseas possessions.

THE PATRIOTS

William V's lack of success promoted the growth of a strong opposition party, the Patriots, which blamed him and his followers for all the setbacks the republic had suffered. Civil war seemed imminent, and in 1787 William withdrew to his country estate, allowing the Patriots to gain control of the nation.

At this point his wife, Wilhelmina,

appealed to her father for support. Frederick William obligingly sent an army to the Netherlands. There was hardly a struggle; in less than a month the country was in Prussian hands. William V was restored to his so-called power and many of the Patriots fled the country. They regrouped in France, from whence they were to return a few years later with the revolutionary armies.

French Domination

Well before French armies crossed the Dutch borders in December 1794, into line. Louis' attempts to do so were at best half-hearted, and his exasperated brother removed him from the throne in 1810, and the short-lived kingdom was integrated into Napoleon's empire.

THE KINGDOM DURING THE NINETEENTH CENTURY

THE DIRECT RULE OF NAPOLEON WAS at first accepted by the Dutch, who looked with favor on his financial and governmental reforms. Two things, however, were definitely not liked—the strict enforcement of the Continental System and the conscription of large numbers of troops for the imperial army. These measures soon cost Napoleon his popularity, and when he was defeated at Leipzig in 1813 the Orangists were able to take control of the country.

William VI, son of William V who had died in exile, was summoned home; he made a triumphal entry into Amsterdam in December and was given the title of sovereign prince. In the same month a constitution (Grondwet) was drawn up, repudiating the old republican form of government and establishing a monarchy. Executive authority was considerably stronger than it had been under the republic, but the provinces were allowed to retain many of their traditional privileges.

Union with Belgium

The constitution soon had to be revised, for it was decided at the Congress of Vienna in 1815 that the new kingdom should include the southern as well as the northern provinces of the Netherlands. William (now King William I of the Netherlands) and the others who promoted this plan argued that north and south together could constitute a state strong enough to check any future French expansion in this strategic area.

In terms of European power politics their argument was valid enough, but they seem to have given little consideration to the internal stability of the enlarged state. Neither the Dutch nor the Belgians were consulted on the matter; they suddenly had to accept each other as fellow countrymen, and this was very difficult for both to do. North and south had been separated for more than 200 years. Although the religious differences which had impelled the separation were no longer a matter

for warfare, bitterness and suspicion remained strong. Intense economic rivalry had grown up; dissimilar administrative systems had developed; customs and tastes varied sharply. There really was no point of unity except the artificial, political one.

Under such conditions the welding of north and south into a stable and integrated nation would have been an almost impossible task for anyone. And King William I was not an ideal person for the job. He had a strong personality and definite ideas on how his kingdom should be organized. His choice of government personnel, his economic policies and his attempted religious and educational reforms were generally accepted in the north but aroused strong southern opposition. William's capacity for compromise was limited, and by 1828 the southern leaders had resolved their

own considerable differences and had united against him.

As tensions mounted and riots began to break out in the cities, William did make one serious attempt at conciliation. His oldest son enjoyed great personal popularity, and William sent him to Brussels to talk to the southern leaders and try to persuade them to put an end to the unrest. The report the Prince of Orange brought back to the north was not a favorable one: antagonism was so strong that the least the southern leaders would accept was administrative separation of the two sections of the kingdom. This William could not countenance. In September 1830 he sent the Dutch army to Brussels.

Bitter street fighting raged for four days. Other southern cities sent troops to help the Brussels patriots, and on Sept. 27 the Dutch army was ordered

Michel Andriaanszoon de Ruyter (1607-76), one of the greatest Dutch admirals, was a key figure in the mid-17th-century wars with England that were to determine the course of European maritime history. He inflicted heavy losses on British shipping during a bold raid up the Thames in 1667. This induced the British to sign the Treaty of Breda, which seemed favorable to the Dutch at the time but ultimately proved far more beneficial to England. By the terms of this treaty, the Dutch were given control of Surinam (Dutch Guiana) in South America, while the English received permanent possession of the North American colonies of New York, New Jersey and Delaware, which they had seized from the Dutch in 1664.

to withdraw. This marked the actual, though not the official, second break between north and south.

THE TERMS OF SEPARATION

Belgium proclaimed its independence in October 1830, but this declaration was meaningless until it was recognized by the major European powers. Naturally enough, William exerted his influence to block recognition. After much complicated negotiation, it was decided by the major powers that Belgian independence would be acceptable if the new nation agreed to a number of conditions and was willing to make certain concessions. Some of these concessions, embodied in the Eighteen Articles drawn up in London, were designed to appease Holland.

The Belgians were not happy with the Eighteen Articles but accepted them; William, also unhappy with them, did not give his assent. He sent his army back to the south in September 1831 and this time scored an easy victory. France promptly intervened on the side of the Belgians, and French troops halted William's advance. England, which did not want to see the southern provinces in French hands, pressured France to

withdraw its troops and called a conference to reconsider the terms of Belgian independence.

What emerged from this conference was the Treaty of London (Nov. 15, 1831), which contained six additional stipulations for Belgian independence. The new concessions Belgium was required to make benefited the Dutch, but William was still dissatisfied. Particularly unacceptable to him was the partition of Luxembourg, which, though not formally a part of the Kingdom of the Netherlands, had been under his personal rule. Under the Treaty of London he had to cede over half of the grand duchy to Belgium.

So displeased was William with the treaty that he refused to withdraw his troops from Antwerp until 1832, and then only because of combined British and French pressure. He finally accepted the Treaty of London in 1838, and the formal agreement between Holland and Belgium was signed the following year.

Constitutional Reform

William's decision to affirm the separation of north and south was partly made in deference to Dutch

public opinion. The people were dissatisfied with the unsettled conditions and wished to devote their energies to domestic affairs, which in the crisis with Belgium had been seriously neglected. What they had in mind, however, was little more to William's liking than the Treaty of London had been.

The constitution of the kingdom was by no means a liberal one. Monarchical authority was strong, and the first pressures for revision were in this area. In 1840 William was forced to make his ministers responsible to the estates general rather than to himself and to agree to measures which weakened his control over the nation's finances. He was not happy with these concessions, nor was he pleased by popular resentment of his proposed marriage to the Countess d'Oultremont, a Belgian Catholic. On October 7, 1840, he abdicated in favor of his eldest son and retired to his country estate.

THE REIGN OF WILLIAM II

His son, who reigned as William II, was more moderate in his views, though far from a liberal. Pressures for reform continued during his reign. Popular revolutions broke out in many parts of Europe in 1848, and to prevent their spreading to Dutch soil William II created a committee to revise the constitution. This committee, headed by the liberal leader Jan Rudolf Thorbecke (1798-1872) instituted changes which gave the lower chamber of the estates general the right to initiate legislation and to approve annual budgets; allowed the upper chamber to be elected by the provincial estates rather than to be appointed by the king as formerly; and assured all citizens of full civil rights. The franchise, which had been very restricted under the original constitution, was extended, though not significantly; the right to vote remained based on property qualifications.

William II died in 1849 and was succeeded by his son, William III. The revised constitution, though it contained more reforms than the monarch wished and less than the liberals desired, proved to be workable during William III's long reign. The only serious conflict between the monarch and the lower chamber of the legislature occurred in 1866. When the issue was taken to the electorate, the vote proved indecisive and both sides recognized the necessity of compromising their differences.

The main square of the city of Utrecht in 1795, showing, in the center of the square, one of the so-called "trees of liberty" which were planted to symbolize the French Jacobin ideals of "liberty, equality, fraternity." During this period, France controlled the fate of the Netherlands, and the short-lived Batavian Republic, modeled after the government of revolutionary France, was established on Dutch soil.

Social Problems

Domestic problems, of which the Dutch had many in the latter half of the 19th century, centered more on social conflicts than on monarchical versus legislative power. One of the issues which plagued the country, as it did neighboring Belgium, was the organization of the educational system. In 1857, a law was passed which provided for schools in which no one religion was taught. These so-called "neutral" schools received government subsidies, whereas denominational schools did not.

Objections to this system led to what seemed on the surface a strange political union—the anti-Revolutionary party was formed, composed of both strict Calvinists and members of the growing Roman Catholic population. These groups had been at odds for centuries, but in their desire to give their children religious education they found common cause. In 1889 a new education law was passed which granted subsidies for both "neutral" and denominational schools. The issue was permanently settled in 1917 by a constitutional amendment which required the government to provide equal support for both types of school.

LABOR LEGISLATION

The most serious problems of the late 19th century developed as a result of industrialization. Holland did not have a sizeable urban working class until the 1860s, when heavy industries began to develop rapidly. As was the case in most other countries which were industrialized during this period, the existing laws were not adequate to protect the rights of the workers and prevent their being exploited. In 1872, a constitutional prohibition of trade unions was repealed and a number of unions soon sprang up. The year 1874 saw the passage of a child labor law, and in 1899 a similar law went into effect regulating the working hours and conditions for women and adolescents. It was not until the early 20th century, however, that comprehensive labor legislation was obtained.

Political leadership in the social field was first in the hands of the Social Democratic League, formed in 1881. The programs of this organization were radical and extra-legal methods were often advocated. A more moderate group formed the Social Democratic Labor Party in 1894; this party initially propounded

Jan Rudolf Thorbecke (1798-1872), the leading Dutch statesman of the 19th century, served three times as premier of the newly established Kingdom of the Netherlands (which came into being after the final demise of the republic during the chaotic days of the Napoleonic era). Thorbecke instituted numerous social, legal and religious reforms in the Netherlands, and was known throughout Europe as one of the great liberal reformers of his time.

orthodox Marxism, but soon turned its attention to working for parliamentary reforms within the existing governmental system.

As the 19th century progressed, there was increased agitation to broaden the franchise. The reforms of the constitution of 1848 were inadequate in this area: restrictions were such that in 1850 only about 13 per cent of the males aged 25 and over could vote. There was considerable pressure against electoral reform, and the situation was not improved at all until 1887, when a compromise law was enacted. This substantially increased the number of eligible voters, but suffrage still remained far from universal.

FOREIGN AFFAIRS

When the northern and southern sections of the Netherlands broke apart in 1579, the mutual antagonisms were intense and became, if anything, more intense with the passage of time. After the second separation, which also aroused much bitter feeling on both sides, this pattern was not repeated. There was no sudden coming together, but a number of minor agreements reached in the latter half of the 19th century signified a growing rapprochement.

One thing that served to bring the two nations closer together was their common desire to maintain neutrality in European conflicts. Belgium's neutrality had been internationally guaranteed under the Treaty of London; Dutch neutrality was a matter of choice, but it was no less assiduously pursued. There was no formal deviation from this policy during the late 19th century, though Dutch sympathies when their erstwhile countrymen, the Boers, were fighting the British in South Africa, were quite apparent. The Dutch government offered its services to negotiate a peace settlement, and when the Boer leader, Paul Kruger, finally had to flee South Africa, he was warmly welcomed in the Netherlands.

THE TWENTIETH CENTURY

THE PRINCIPAL DEVELOPMENT ON THE domestic front during the first decade of the 20th century was the passage of a large body of labor legislation. This was accomplished only after widespread agitation; a series of strikes were called, the most severe of which was staged in 1903 by railroad workers. Strong government action was needed to bring it to an end. But the workers obtained at least their major goals: working hours were shortened, safety measures were required in dangerous industries, and sickness and accident compensation were provided.

Along with the rest of Europe, Holland turned more and more of its attention to the international scene during the first decade of the 20th century. As war seemed increasingly likely, it was decided that the best guarantee of neutrality was strong defense. Accordingly, both the eastern frontier with Germany and the North Sea coast, vulnerable to English attack, were fortified.

The physical preservation of neutrality was a difficult enough task, but the political maintenance of this position also posed problems. There remained considerable antagonism toward England because of the Boer War, and conversely there were strong natural ties with Germany. The Dutch royal family was of German ancestry, and many of its members had married into German princely families. The German Rhine area had been industrialized in the mid-19th century and Holland was a natural outlet for the exportation of its products; this economic interdependency encouraged friendship and cooperation between the two nations.

In 1908, when the Netherlands became party to a German declaration pledging to defend the territorial integrity of all nations bordering the North Sea it seemed briefly that the Dutch would, after all, choose sides in the coming conflict. This proved not to be the case. In spite of all the difficulties inherent in their neutral position the Dutch maintained it.

World War I

Germany quickly overran Belgium at the beginning of World War I, but no attempt was made to invade Holland. This did not come from an abstract respect for Dutch neutrality but rather from a desire to keep open an area along the North Sea through which badly needed supplies could be brought inland. England did not try to control the area either, realizing that such an attempt would bring German intervention and risk the possibility of Germany's getting control of the entire North Sea coast of Europe.

With both sides operating under these self-imposed restraints, the Dutch found it difficult, but not impossible, to keep aloof from the conflict. They could not avoid being adversely affected by the war—their shipping was seriously curtailed and food supplies ran quite low, but they successfully averted both property destruction and loss of life. The sincerity of their neutrality was evidenced by the acceptance of thousands of refugees from Belgium after the Germans occupied that country and their granting of asylum to Kaiser Wilhelm after Germany lost the war.

Between the World Wars

One beneficial effect of World War I on Holland was that the upheaval stimulated a long overdue extension of the franchise. Under the leadership of Cort van der Linden (1846-1935), the Liberals were able to pass a law granting the vote to all men over the age of 25. This law went into effect in 1917, and two years later women were also given voting rights.

The extension of the franchise promoted the formation of numerous political parties—there were 37 of them by 1929. The multi-party system gave rise to a certain degree of governmental instability, since no party could win a clear-cut majority of the votes. However, the Catholics formed a coalition with two Calvinist parties which proved to be fairly workable; there were only three prime ministers and eight cabinets in the years between the two world wars. In 1918 J. M. Ruys de Beerenbrouck became the first Catholic prime minister in Dutch history. The strongest figure in the coalition, however, was the Calvinist Hendrik Colijn.

ECONOMIC DIFFICULTIES

In many respects the interbellum years were difficult ones for Holland. After two years of apparent prosperity, the country was plagued by depression and widespread unemployment. The government managed to put the country's finances back on a stable footing by 1925, but four years later the world-wide depression set in. Discontent with economic conditions and government measures to correct them gave rise to extremist parties— the Nationalist Socialists (N.S.B.) on the right and the Communists (C.P.N.) on the left. Both parties made sizeable gains in the 1935 elections, but two years later, due largely to a marked improvement in the economy, their strength declined. The Social Democratic party had also grown during these years, and in 1939 two of its leaders were appointed to cabinet posts.

The only bright spot in the Dutch economy during the 1930s was the colonial empire. This included, in the East Indies, Sumatra, Java, Celebes, most of Borneo, western New Guinea and a number of small islands; in the West Indies were the Netherlands Antilles and Surinam (Dutch Guiana). The government-owned industry and agriculture in the East Indies proved especially profitable.

No problems arose concerning the monarchy during the interbellum period. William III had died in 1890, and after an eight-year regency by his wife, Emma, his daughter, Wilhelmina, ascended the throne. She ruled for 50 years and was popular throughout her reign.

FOREIGN AFFAIRS

In terms of foreign policy, the 1930s marked the awakening of interest in international economic cooperation. In 1930 Holland joined Belgium and the Scandinavian countries in the Oslo Pact, which called for mutual consultation and consent on proposed tariff increases. Two years later Holland, Belgium and

A modern housing development, a sign of present-day Dutch prosperity, rises behind a tidy row of boathouses on a canal near Amsterdam. The construction of networks of canals to reclaim land from the sea and facilitate commerce was intensified in the Netherlands during the second half of the 19th century.

Luxembourg concluded the Ouchy Convention, their first attempt to work out common tariff policies. The experiment failed, due to objections from the United States and England, who stood to lose valuable trade concessions if the Ouchy Convention went into effect. It was nonetheless important in that it evidenced a drawing together of the Low Countries.

Throughout the interbellum period the Dutch continued to assert their neutrality. They joined the League of Nations and, as had been the case prior to World War I, made The Hague available as a site for conferences to discuss international problems. As early as 1936, when Germany had once more become a menace, they started to rearm, though this proved a strain on the still shaky economy.

In a last desperate attempt to stave off the war, the sovereigns of Holland and Belgium sent a telegram to the heads of the major European powers offering their services, in whatever capacity was desired, to help maintain peace. The telegram was sent on Nov. 30, 1939. Less than six months later both nations were under German occupation.

World War II

On May 10, 1940, German land forces crossed the Dutch border. They had heavy air support and were also aided by parachutists who were dropped behind Dutch lines. The effect was that of a steamroller; North Brabant fell immediately, the Dutch air force was destroyed, and on May 13 Queen Wilhelmina and the cabinet embarked for England. Rotterdam, all but defenseless, was heavily bombed the following day and the bulk of the Dutch army surrendered; forces in Zeeland held out until May 17.

In the beginning the German regime was fairly moderate, but even in the first year of the occupation such actions as censoring the press, suppressing the socialist parties, interning political and cultural leaders at Buchenwald and discriminating

THE HOUSE OF ORANGE-NASSAU

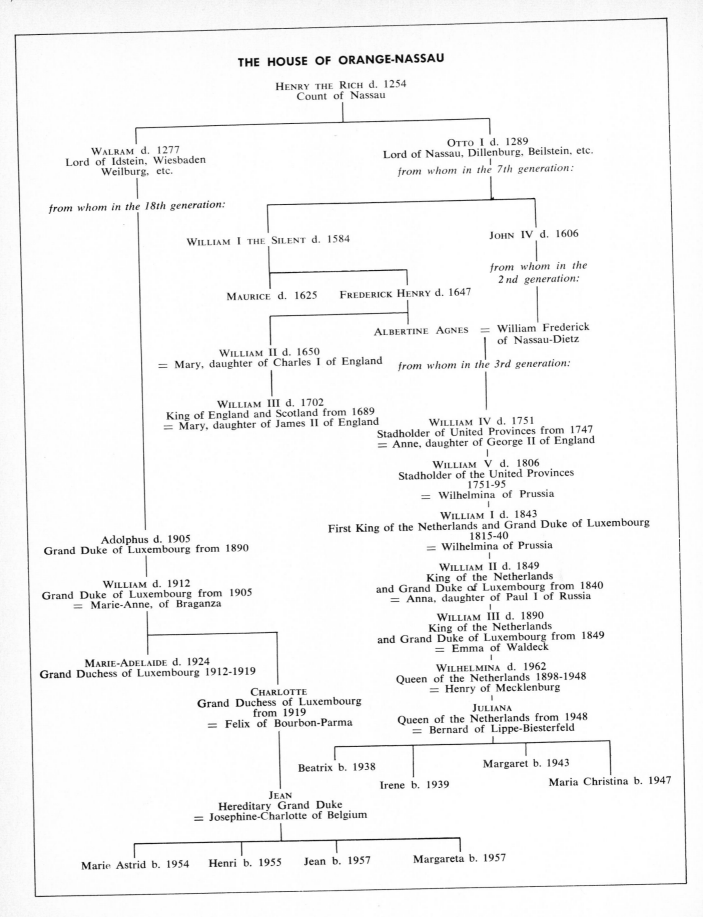

HENRY THE RICH d. 1254
Count of Nassau

WALRAM d. 1277
Lord of Idstein, Wiesbaden
Weilburg, etc.

OTTO I d. 1289
Lord of Nassau, Dillenburg, Beilstein, etc.

from whom in the 7th generation:

from whom in the 18th generation:

WILLIAM I THE SILENT d. 1584

JOHN IV d. 1606

*from whom in the
2 nd generation:*

MAURICE d. 1625   FREDERICK HENRY d. 1647

ALBERTINE AGNES = William Frederick
of Nassau-Dietz

WILLIAM II d. 1650
= Mary, daughter of Charles I of England

from whom in the 3rd generation:

WILLIAM III d. 1702
King of England and Scotland from 1689
= Mary, daughter of James II of England

WILLIAM IV d. 1751
Stadholder of United Provinces from 1747
= Anne, daughter of George II of England

WILLIAM V d. 1806
Stadholder of the United Provinces
1751-95
= Wilhelmina of Prussia

WILLIAM I d. 1843
First King of the Netherlands and Grand Duke of Luxembourg
1815-40
= Wilhelmina of Prussia

Adolphus d. 1905
Grand Duke of Luxembourg from 1890

WILLIAM II d. 1849
King of the Netherlands
and Grand Duke of Luxembourg from 1840
= Anna, daughter of Paul I of Russia

WILLIAM d. 1912
Grand Duke of Luxembourg from 1905
= Marie-Anne, of Braganza

WILLIAM III d. 1890
King of the Netherlands
and Grand Duke of Luxembourg from 1849
= Emma of Waldeck

WILHELMINA d. 1962
Queen of the Netherlands 1898-1948
= Henry of Mecklenburg

MARIE-ADELAIDE d. 1924
Grand Duchess of Luxembourg 1912-1919

CHARLOTTE
Grand Duchess of Luxembourg
from 1919
= Felix of Bourbon-Parma

JULIANA
Queen of the Netherlands from 1948
= Bernard of Lippe-Biesterfeld

Beatrix b. 1938

Irene b. 1939

Margaret b. 1943

Maria Christina b. 1947

JEAN
Hereditary Grand Duke
= Josephine-Charlotte of Belgium

Marie Astrid b. 1954   Henri b. 1955   Jean b. 1957   Margareta b. 1957 against Jews gave warning of what was to come. After the Germans failed to win their hoped-for early victory in Europe, oppressive measures were stepped up.

THE RESISTANCE MOVEMENT

Before the end of 1942, the resistance movement was small and not very active; a few clandestine anti-German newspapers were published, and strikes were called to protest the deportation of Jews. But as Germany's position deteriorated on all fronts and its regime in Holland grew harsher, more and more Dutchmen joined the resistance forces. In April 1943, when the Germans announced their intention of deporting thousands of men to Germany to serve as laborers, a spontaneous series of strikes erupted throughout the country. The Germans quickly and brutally put down this rebellion, but in so doing they only strengthened the determination of the resistance fighters and drove more citizens to join their cause. Queen Wilhelmina, from London, gave them moral encouragement.

When the Allied European offensive began in the summer of 1944, the prospects for liberation brightened. In September North Brabant and Limburg were freed, and the Dutch government in London ordered a general railway strike to hinder the movement of German troops and supplies to the front. This order was successfully carried out, but the Germans nonetheless managed to halt the Allied offensive at Arnhem.

Then ensued what was, for the Dutch, undoubtedly the worst winter of the war. To open up a path through the German lines, the Allies needed to knock out a number of dikes from the air and flood certain areas; inaccurate bombing caused severe civilian casualties. The Germans were determined to maintain their position, and their suppression of any resistance on the part of the Dutch population grew more and more brutal. To make matters worse, fuel supplies had been exhausted and there was a grave food shortage.

The Allies advanced again early in 1945 and liberated the eastern and northern areas of the country. But the Germans stubbornly held on in the west, threatening to flood large areas and to let the population starve to death. They finally surrendered on May 5, but not until they had destroyed the harbors of Rotterdam and Amsterdam.

Queen Wilhelmina (1880-1962) served as queen of the Netherlands from 1898 to 1948 (her mother having served as regent during the period 1890-1898). A wise and benevolent monarch, Wilhelmina was much admired and beloved during her 50-year reign. Of her own accord, she abdicated in favor of her daughter, Juliana (1909-   ), in 1948.

The Postwar Period

The problems of reconstruction after five years of Nazi occupation were tremendous. Some 250,000 people had lost their lives during the war, much of the laboriously reclaimed land was flooded, industry was in ruins, and there was a grave housing shortage. The government set out to accomplish the difficult task of rebuilding the economy and within ten years succeeded in restoring the nation to a high level of prosperity.

One of the postwar government's most successful undertakings has been a vast land reclamation project. Many thousands of acres have been made arable, and more are constantly being added. An important phase of the land reclamation program is the establishment of an adequate flood-control system. The need for this was dramatically demonstrated in 1953 when sea waters surged over large areas of Zeeland, causing almost 1800 deaths and much property damage.

Politically, the postwar period has been a time of stability. From 1948 to 1958 the government was headed by the Labor party leader, Willem Drees (1886-   ), who showed himself to be an able statesman. In 1959 he was succeeded as prime minister by Dr. J. E. de Quay, a member of the Catholic party. Queen Wilhelmina abdicated in 1948 in favor of her daughter, Juliana.

THE END OF THE COLONIAL EMPIRE

Shortly after the close of World War II, native leaders in the East Indies colonies began agitating strongly for their independence. There was sporadic fighting between Dutch and native troops until 1949, when a settlement was worked out creating the new nation of Indonesia from all the former Dutch colonies except New Guinea. This new nation entered into a voluntary association with Holland, but there were continual quarrels and the association was dissolved in 1954.

One of the chief points of contention was control of Dutch New Guinea, which Indonesia continued

to claim after the 1949 agreement. In 1962 a plan was accepted whereby the disputed territory was placed under United Nations control until May 1, 1963, after which it came under Indonesian administration. The agreement calls for a plebiscite to be held by 1969 to determine what sort of political future the native New Guineans want for themselves.

Although the Dutch lost their East Indian colonies, they have maintained amicable relations with Surinam and the Netherlands Antilles in the West Indies. In 1954 these two former colonies were made equal partners with Holland in the Kingdom of the Netherlands. They were granted complete internal autonomy and a voice in the affairs of the Kingdom through representation in the Dutch government at The Hague.

FOREIGN POLICY

After World War II the Dutch abandoned their policy of neutrality. They have continued to work for international peace through the

United Nations, but also joined the Brussels Pact (1948) and the North Atlantic Treaty Organization (1949).

Along with Belgium, the Netherlands has been active in the movement for European federation. The first step in this policy was the agreement to form a customs union with Belgium and Luxembourg. This Benelux Union was promulgated in September 1944, revised in 1947, and came into operation early in 1948. It calls for the abolition of tariffs among the three countries and the standardization of tariffs on goods imported from abroad. Because of the differing economic conditions within the three countries the Benelux Union has faced many problems, but most of them have been overcome.

The success of the Benelux experiment was instrumental in the formation of the Coal and Steel Community, Common Market and Euratom (European Atomic Energy Commission). Holland, along with the other Benelux countries, has been a charter member of these and other organizations set up to bring about closer cooperation among European nations.

FUNDAMENTAL DATES

1579 The Union of Utrecht and the League of Arras separate the northern and southern provinces of the Netherlands.

1602 The Dutch East India Company is founded, marking the beginning of the Dutch colonial empire.

1648 The Dutch republic's independence from Spain is confirmed by the Treaty of Munster.

1652 Commercial rivalry with England leads to the first of a series of sea wars with that nation.

1689 The Dutch leader, William III of Orange, becomes king of England.

1702 William III's death leaves Holland without a national leader and a period of decline ensues.

1747 The House of Orange is reinstated.

1795 Holland becomes a vassal state of France.

1806 Holland is made a kingdom under Napoleon's brother Louis.

1810 The kingdom is abolished and Holland comes under the direct rule of Napoleon.

1813 The Orangists take control of Holland and set up the Kingdom of the Netherlands.

1815 Holland and Belgium are united under King William I.

1839 The final agreement for the separation of Holland and Belgium is signed.

1848 The Dutch constitution is revised to make the government more democratic.

1914-18 The Dutch retain their neutrality throughout World War I.

1940-45 Holland is under German occupation during World War II.

1944 The first agreement for the Benelux Union is signed in London.

1948 The Benelux Union goes into operation.

1949 A number of colonies in the East Indies are granted independence and united as the new nation of Indonesia.

1954 The West Indies colonies of Surinam (Dutch Guiana) and the Netherlands Antilles are given partnership status in the Kingdom of the Netherlands.

1963 The last of the East Indian colonies is abolished as Indonesia assumes administrative control of Dutch New Guinea.

This imposing bronze monument, standing near the harbor of Rotterdam, commemorates the destruction of the city by the Nazis during World War II. The actual bombardment of Rotterdam on May 14, 1940, took place several hours after the city had officially surrendered. The sculpture is the work of Ossip Zadkine.

The castle of Loevenstein, situated near the confluence of the Maas and Waal rivers, was constructed in the 14th century. Its extremely simple and uncluttered lines are characteristic of much Dutch architecture.

INTRODUCTION

THE SAYING "GOD MADE THE WORLD, but the Dutch made the Netherlands" is not entirely unfounded. Throughout history, the people of the Netherlands have drained their lakes and fens, filled in their swamps and heaped up miles of protective dikes to keep their country from being covered by the sea. The arts and architecture of this "man-made" land bear the marks of this age-old struggle against nature in their awareness of the preciousness of space.

Until the Netherlands gained political independence in 1648 (Treaty of Westphalia), the arts of Belgium and the Netherlands generally developed along parallel lines. Therefore, for the sake of convenience, early artistic development in the Low Countries has been treated in detail in *Belgium: The Fine Arts*. In addition, the population of the Netherlands during the Middle Ages was more sparse than that of Belgium, and the constant struggle with the sea did not encourage artistic development. Particularly since independence, Dutch artistic expression has focused primarily upon painting, and the Netherlands has produced such artistic giants as Bosch, Rembrandt, Vermeer and Van Gogh.

EARLY HISTORY (12 B.C.-1100 B.C.)

THE EARLIEST KNOWN INHABITANTS of the Netherlands were several Germanic tribes (including the Franks, Saxons and Frisians), who lived on high mounds of earth to escape the tides and erosions of the sea. These people made their living by farming and buried their dead in enormous beehive-shaped graves. A few of these graves remain in the Drente region,

Right: *A courtyard enclosed by the walls of the 14th-century Utrecht Cathedral. The Cathedral is particularly famous for its 338-foot-high Dom Tower—which has been called "the tower of the church that is missing," for the adjacent nave was destroyed by a hurricane in 1674 and was never rebuilt.*

but all other traces of the art of these Germanic tribes have been destroyed by dampness.

In about 12 B.C., the Romans invaded the Netherlands. They set up a few trading posts, laid out a few roads and collected what taxes they could; but the flat, wind-swept and foggy land did not encourage any real settlement. Therefore, the Roman culture made little impact upon Dutch art, and with the withdrawal of Roman law and order in the 3rd century, the people of the Netherlands grouped themselves about small defensive strongholds.

A series of Frankish invasions culminated in the inclusion of the Netherlands in the empire of Charlemagne, who inaugurated a new method of land conservation in the country during his reign. The traditional plateaus built up above the water level were replaced by a series of earthen walls (dikes) along the waterfront; these freed the land behind them for living space. The construction and maintenance of these dikes was executed by a system of compulsory labor.

After the death of Charlemagne in 814, a series of raids by marauders from Scandinavia created another period of chaos and fear. Communities were broken up and a feudal system gradually arose. For many centuries thereafter, the northern part of the Netherlands was dominated by the Kingdom of Germany, while the southern part and most of Belgium came under French domination. Allegiances were confused in the fringe areas, but the weakness of both the French and the German kings resulted, in fact, in government by local overlords. Cooperation among the various feudal principalities was necessitated by the importance of maintaining the dikes, and rivals became brothers during the storms.

THE GOTHIC PERIOD

MOST DUTCH ART EXECUTED PRIOR to the 12th century was destroyed by the damp climate and successive invasions. Although the Gothic period (12th to 16th centuries) marks the beginning of the evolution of a truly Netherlandish artistic tradition, few examples of Dutch Gothic art remain due to the iconoclastic zeal of the 17th-century Dutch Protestants.

Gothic Architecture

The clay soil of the Netherlands provided the bricks commonly used for various types of religious and secular buildings throughout the centuries, while the size of Dutch buildings has been limited by the lack of a firm rock bed. Thus, the most common, type of structure in the Netherlands is a low, red brick building with a timber roof pitched steeply against the rain and snow. The unending struggle against the sea absorbed much of the attention and energy of the Netherlandish people and discouraged the development of a decorative flair comparable to that seen in Belgian architecture. In contrast, Dutch churches and houses are characterized by a barnlike simplicity and practicality.

During the 13th century, while the Netherlands was still subject to the German kings, architecture was dominated by the so-called Rhineland Gothic style—a variation of French Gothic. One of the best examples of this style is the lovely Hall of Knights, or Ridderzaal (1280), which stands in the middle of a large courtyard in The Hague (see at left). This courtyard forms the core of The Hague's parliamentary buildings, and the throne room of the Ridderzaal are used today for joint sessions of Parliament.

The Hall is magnificently roofed with 59-foot-long beams, and French influence is reflected in the two slim, asymmetrical towers which flank its façade. The decorative themes, particularly the circular motifs of the rose window over the central doorway, have a Romanesque simplicity which contrasts with the elaborateness of most European Gothic architecture.

RELIGIOUS ARCHITECTURE

The 13th-century Oude Kerk (Old Church) which stands in the historic southern city of Delft is a comparatively large structure for Holland. Its beautiful bell tower leans uncomfortably westward, like the Tower of Pisa, and the great bell is therefore rung only on the most auspicious occasions for fear that either the tower or the bell might be damaged. The church has a straightforward simplicity typical of the period; its barnlike interior has a

The Ridderzaal, or Hall of Knights, in The Hague is one of the finest examples of the 13th-century architectural style known as Rhineland-Gothic. The famous throne room within the building is still used for sessions of the Dutch Parliament.

Portrait of Eleonora of Mantua, by Frans Pourbus the Younger (1569-1622). The Pourbus family, also including Frans the Elder (1545-81) and Pieter (1523-84), were among the best-known Dutch court painters of the 16th and 17th centuries.

single nave and a square apse.

Dutch church buildings in the 14th century continued to be devoid of the ornamentation found in other European countries. Square or octagonal towers and steep wooden roofs with conspicuously narrow supporting pillars were common. The cathedrals of Haarlem, Utrecht and Dordrecht, which date from this period, were simplified versions of the French-inspired Belgian churches.

The inland city of Utrecht could support heavier structures than the marshy coastal regions, and the Dom-toren tower of the Utrecht Cathedral is therefore higher and more imposing than most (338 ft.). This tower, familiarly called "the Dom," was designed by Jan ten Doem and built between 1321 and 1382. Its vertical lines are accented by relief sculptures and the arrangement of different colors of brick and stone. The tower rises in stages from a square base to an octagonal crest and has 365 steps—one for each day of the year. It contains seven fine 16th-century chimes and a 42-bell carillon which dates from the 17th century. The

Dom is known as "the tower of the church that is missing," for the nave collapsed in a hurricane in 1674 and was never rebuilt.

St. John's Cathedral in the city of 'sHertogenbosch in Brabant is undoubtedly the grandest cathedral in Holland (see page 179). Situated in a traditional seat of Catholicism, St. John's was erected during the 15th century on the site of a church which had been destroyed by fire in 1240.

The nave is surprisingly high for a Dutch structure (110 ft.), and is flanked by a regal march of 150 columns. This cathedral is probably the most highly ornamented of all Dutch buildings. Its exterior is covered by hundreds of small carved gargoyles and angels, and it took a full century to complete.

SECULAR ARCHITECTURE

The Dutch town gates, fortified castles and rows of small homes which date from the Gothic period have a truly indigenous character.

This 14th-century massive stone gate, known as the Kornmarktspoort, stands guard at one of the entrances to the town of Kampen in the province of Overijssel. The influence of Gothic architecture is seen in its slanting, shingled spires.

Right: *The interior of the Cathedral of St. John in 's Hertogenbosch. St. John's is considered the finest Gothic cathedral in Holland. Begun in the 15th century, it took 100 years to complete. It is noted for its splended proportions and rich ornamentation. The Cathedral's exquisite nave is approached through a corridor flanked by 150 columns.*

The 14th-century castle of Loevenstein, situated at the confluence of the Maas and Waal rivers, is a fine example of the severely simple domestic building tradition (see page 174). It is precisely symmetrical, with square towers flanking the main building block, and small and unembellished window openings. The protective moat reflects the beautifully textured brick.

The practical Dutchmen soon learned to exploit the incessant winds from the sea, and the windmill is the best-known type of Dutch secular architecture. The first windmills, probably imported from the Near East in the 10th century, were used for grinding corn. By the 15th century, the Dutch had learned to use the force of the wind to pump the water from their farms and over the dikes. The windmills are commonly constructed of wood or brick in varying shapes.

Gothic Sculpture

The 16th century saw the emergence of a new architectural form, the elaborately decorated gables which topped the guild and market halls and private houses of Holland. These gables became extremely popular, and their use soon spread to Germany and England.

Through a series of skillful marital alliances, the French rulers succeeded in uniting the Low Countries with Burgundy. During the Burgundian period French art became extremely influential in the Netherlands. The cultural center of the Low Countries was established at Bruges (in northwest Belgium) during the rule of Philip the Good (1419-67). Philip's court lured artists from every province to this lively seaport.

CLAUS SLUTER

One of the artists drawn to Philip's court was Claus Sluter (born c.1400), who is considered the most outstanding sculptor of the late Gothic period. Sluter left his native Haarlem at an early age to produce art for Philip in Belgium and at the Dijon court in France. His talents were therefore influenced by French sculpture, and

the bulk of his work remains at Dijon.

Sluter's realistic style may be seen in the impressive statues of Moses and five prophets grouped around a well at the Abbey of Champmol (Dijon). The faces of these figures have the vigorous, almost exaggerated expressions found in the later Gothic naturalistic style, and the contorted draperies and gestures have a savage energy characteristic of the final evolution of the Gothic sculptural tradition. This highly emotional realism became the dominant influence in Dutch sculpture, and a school of Sluter's followers was established at Hal, near Amsterdam. Un-

fortunately, however, most Dutch Gothic sculpture was destroyed during the later Protestant rebellion.

Gothic Painting

Several important painters, including Dierik Bouts and Gerard David, were born in Holland but went to Belgium as young men and spent their working years there. They are discussed in *Belgium: The Fine Arts.* The first major Dutch artist to resist the lure to the south was Albert van Ouwater (Fl. c.1430-60), founder of the Haarlem School. A relationship between his work and that of Dierik Bouts has been cited and his realism bears a similarity to that of

Van Eyck (see *Belgium: The Fine Arts*). Only one of Ouwater's works, the panel *The Raising of Lazarus* (Kaiser Friedrich Museum, Berlin), is now extant. This panel, painted between 1450 and 1460, is an early example of the anecdotal painting which became so popular in Holland. On one side of the tomb the saints pray as Christ bids Lazarus to rise; on the other side, the official dignitaries express their disgust at the odor of death by holding their garments to their noses.

GEERTGEN TOT SINT JANS

The little-known "Dutch primitive" Geertgen tot Sint Jans (c.1465-95) was a very original and influential painter in his time, but his life was short and only about 15 of his works remain. His curious name indicates his position as official artist for the Commandery of the Knights of St. John at Haarlem—a post of considerable prestige.

Geertgen's use of light, particularly in his landscapes, places him on a par with his Belgian contemporary Hugo van der Goes. In his works he avoided the common and jarring division into foreground, middleground and background, and his figures are statuesque and precisely outlined. One of his finest paintings is *St. John in the Wilderness* (Kaiser Friedrich Museum, Berlin).

BOSCH

At the end of the 15th century, a strange and powerfully original painter appeared in the Netherlands. This painter, Hieronymus Bosch (1450-1516), has been called the greatest master of fantasy who ever lived.

Bosch's subject matter is so startling and original that his form is frequently overlooked. His subjects were often drawn from popular woodcuts and devotional prints depicting familiar Christian legends, but he so transformed them with his vivid imagination that they bear little resemblance to the traditional presentations. Bosch was especially interested in horror scenes which contrasted visions of Hell and Paradise. His depictions of the Passion of Christ are focused more upon the hatred and mockery of the mob than upon the sufferings of Christ. When portraying a saint lost in contemplation, Bosch takes pains to point out the devils which assail goodness, and while an angel appears to St. John in the sky, a monster lurks behind a rock nearby. His monsters are all the more frightening because they are based upon familiar plants, animals and household objects.

Bosch's ability to express emotions through distortion and caricature may be seen in such works as *Christ Crowned with Thorns* (see at left), but even his more conventional paintings—such as *Adoration of the Kings* (The Prado, Madrid)—display his inventiveness. Rather than concentrating on the Madonna and Child, Bosch concerns himself in this work with the multitude of details in the vicinity; attention is focused on a man climbing a tree, a battle raging in the middle distance and the fantastic architecture in the background.

But Bosch's use of the fantastic and the grotesque should not blind the observer to his technical merits as a painter. He was a skillful landscapist, and his "high horizon" technique (which left room for many figures and much activity) influenced the works of the Belgian landscapist Patinir. Bosch also handled

Left: *A detail of the painting* Christ Crowned With Thorns, *by Hieronymus Bosch (1450-1516).*

Opposite Right: *A section of* The Temptation of St. Anthony, *also by Bosch. Bosch was a unique figure among Flemish painters and is considered one of the three greatest artists in Dutch history. His works reveal an unsurpassed genius for fantasy and grotesquerie. He was a brilliant colorist and his paintings display a liveliness and exactitude of brush work coupled with an extremely skillful sense of composition.*

Cornelis Engelbrechtsen (1468-1533). The heavy, oily technique and swirling lines of Engelbrechtsen's hard and needlessly complicated religious pictures were influential among his contemporaries.

LEYDEN

In his short lifetime, the astonishingly gifted painter and engraver Lucas van Leyden (c.1494-1533) achieved an impressive reputation. When he was only 15 years old he executed the famous engraving *Mohammed and the Monk*, which demonstrates his imagination and gift for observation. His successive engravings also showed his genius, but the impact of his paintings is lessened by his crude colors and conventional lighting. The varying quality and intent of Lucas' art reflects the see-sawing, transitional character of Dutch art in the 16th century. Although he executed many original works, paintings such as *The Last Judgment* (see at left) illustrate Van Leyden's failure to assimilate the Italian influences.

VAN SCOREL

The able portrait painter Jan van Scorel (1495-1562) enjoyed tremendous prestige in his time. One of his early teachers was the Italian-inspired Jan Gossaert, and the knowledge of the geography and sculpture of the Mediterranean which he acquired during his travels to Germany, Italy and the Holy Land was reflected in his drawings.

Van Scorel is best known for his cosmopolitan portraits; his experiences in the world seem to have made him an excellent observer of character. He does not dwell upon unessential details such as a bit of lace collar or a vase of flowers in the background, and many of his portraits, such as *Portrait of a Schoolboy* (see at right), have flat backgrounds. *St. Mary Magdalen* (Rijksmuseum, Amsterdam) is a magnificent study of a figure in a landscape. In this work, Scorel used light and shade to establish a certain rapport between the woman and the landscape.

color with the utmost skill and refinement, and his later works are filled with bright figures on white backgrounds. His enamel-like colors and crisp, sure lines added effectiveness to his symbolic interpretations of mythology. Bosch's works were much admired by the orthodox Philip II of Spain and some of his finest paintings, including *The Garden of Earthly Delights, Adoration of the Kings, The Temptation of St. Anthony* (see page 181), *The Hay Wain* and *The Mocking of Christ* are to be found in Madrid.

Sixteenth-Century Painting

At the turn of the 16th century, the influence of the Italian Renaissance belatedly entered Dutch art. By this time, the rebirth of Classicism and the humanistic ideals of Renaissance art had already evolved into Italian Mannerism. In the Netherlands, the new Italian style was awkwardly assimilated; the haphazard coupling of Classical themes and traditional Dutch forms resulted in a deterioration of the quality of painting. Despite its failings, however, this awkward transitional period laid the foundations for the 17th-century "Golden Age" of Dutch art.

Among the first to explore the new ideas from Italy were the conservative Jan Joest van Calcar (d. 1519) and Jan Moseart (c.1475-1556) and the bolder and less successful

HEEMSKERCK AND MOR

Jan van Scorel had two exceptional pupils. The first of these was the religious painter Maarten van Heemskerck (1498-1574), who more than any other Dutch 16th-century artist popularized the dramatic, muscular movement and bold lighting found in the paintings of Michelangelo. *Christ Crowned with Thorns* (Museum of Fine Arts, Ghent, 1532) is an excellent example of the artist's original use of the Italian style.

Anthonis Mor (c.1512-76), also called Anthony More, was another of Van Scorel's pupils. In Italy, Mor was influenced by the tight-packed portraits of Bronzino and adapted his restrained line and composition. Unlike Bronzino, Mor limited his palette to a few variations of browns and grays. He became the official portrait painter at the court of Philip II in Spain and was later called to England to paint a portrait of Philip's future wife, Queen Mary. One fine example of Mor's portraiture is the *Portrait of Lady Gresham* (see page 191).

THE SEVENTEENTH CENTURY

THE PROTESTANT DUTCH WON THEIR independence from Spanish domination in 1648, and the 17th century was a period of unparalleled growth. The country's economic prosperity was due in large measure to its geographic position, which greatly favored the development of maritime enterprises. Dutch merchants grew prosperous, the bold explorations of Dutch seamen soon made the Netherlands one of the foremost colonial powers and a general spirit of self-reliance, progress and liberty characterized what is known as the Golden Age of Dutch art.

THE GUILDS

During the 17th century, the social structure in the Netherlands was centered on the middle class, which held the wealth and therefore the power of the country. The processes of business, management and labor were strictly controlled by a variety of guilds. The guild system began early in the Middle Ages and by the 17th century it dominated the life of the common man, for it was necessary to belong to the appropriate guild in order to work at a craft.

In order to gain entrance to the guild, a boy began as an apprentice to a master, living in the master's house and learning the basic materials and processes involved in his chosen craft. When he had demonstrated sufficient control of his medium, the apprentice was sent out as a journeyman to polish his craft under other masters. Finally he presented himself, his work and his recommendations before the guild for admission. As with the present-day unions, the guild endeavored to supply its members with commissions and to see that they were paid. Guild members also inspected each other's work

Portrait of a Schoolboy by Jan van Scorel (1495-1562). Van Scorel was one of the Dutch painters who successfully combined the Dutch inclination for keen, realistic observation with the monumental and full-blown quality of the Italian High Renaissance. A seasoned traveler, familiar with Italy, Germany and Palestine, Van Scorel revealed his cosmopolitan spirit through his keenly analytical studies of character.

regularly to see that a certain standard was maintained. This excellent system produced generations of consistently fine Dutch craftsmen whose work was respected throughout Europe.

Seventeenth-Century Architecture

The restrained and practical style of Dutch 17th-century architecture contrasted with the decorative and often frivolous Baroque architecture found throughout the rest of Europe. The conservative tradition of Dutch building on the one hand, and the Catholic nature of the Baroque movement on the other. made the style unacceptable to the Protestant inhabitants of the Netherlands. Indeed, the fervent Calvinism of the Dutch had already led to the destruction of much Dutch Gothic art and the conversion of Gothic churches to Protestant use. Instead of the exuberant Baroque, Dutch architecture of the 17th century experienced a new Classicism, which was seen in the works of Hendric de Keyser (1567-1621) and Jacob van Campen (1595-1657).

The conservative Keyser, founder of the Amsterdam school of architecture, is famed for the Noderkerk (North Church) in Amsterdam. He was the first Dutch architect to change church design to meet the requirements of the Protestant religion. In the Noderkerk, the sanctuary in the apse was eliminated and the basic plan was reduced to a great common hall which contained no architectural barrier between people and priest.

The noted Royal Palace in Amsterdam (see page 156), built in 1648 by Jacob van Campen and Daniel Stalpaert, was obviously imitative of Italian Classicism. It was so large that some 16,000 piles were sunk into the ground to support its weight. Van Campen also designed the Mauritshuis (The Hague) and several other Classical houses. He declared that he was reviving *l'architecture ancienne* ("the ancient architecture").

The 17th century saw the appointment of the first national dike-master, Andries Vierlingh. In the next generation, Jan Adriaenszoon Leeghwater (1575-1650) worked out a scheme to drain the huge Haarlem-mer Meer (Haarlem Lake) which required the use of 160 windmills. Although Leeghwater was responsible for the creation of many *polders* (large areas of land wrested from the sea by means of dikes, draining and filling), the Haarlem Lake was not completely drained until the 19th century, when steam power was used.

The continuing prosperity resulted in many new secular buildings being erected, and the commonly preferred architectural style contained charm, if not great innovation. Decorative gables crested the flat façades of Dutch houses, and the lines of elaborate red brick structures which stretched along the busy canals lent a certain quaintness to the appearance of Dutch towns and cities.

Seventeenth-Century Sculpture

The puritanical Protestant attitude toward art placed severe limitations upon 17th-century Dutch sculptors, forcing them to turn to secular subjects. Thus sculpture lost the religious stimulus which had carried the arts through the Middle Ages, and the principal works of the period consisted of second-rate tombstones for leading citizens and bas-reliefs illustrating significant battles in the struggle for independence. Traditional Gothic styles mingled awkwardly with Protestant-inspired severity as though the stone medium was not sufficiently pliable to adapt to the new age.

Seventeenth-Century Painting

Seventeenth-century painting, unlike sculpture, was stimulated to a new brilliance by political and economic changes. The 15th and 16th centuries had witnessed the influx of Italian ideas and the development of a secular art, particularly in the field of portraiture. The 17th century saw the evolution of the group portrait, which often depicted the members of a society or a civic organization. Artistic development reflected the tastes of the middle-class Dutch buyer of art, who differed sharply from the wealthy aristocrats who patronized the arts in Belgium. Landscapes, genre paintings and portraits became the most popular art forms in Holland.

Detail from The Night Watch *(1642), the most famous painting of Rembrandt van Rijn (1606-69). It has been discovered that the painting had been erroneously titled, for a careful cleaning has wiped away all the 'night' atmosphere and has shown that the scene was conceived as taking place in the daytime.*

Laughing Cavalier, by Frans Hals (c.1580-1666), one of the greatest and most popular 17th-century Dutch artists. Hals was a master at capturing the momentary facial expressions which revealed the inner nature of his subject. His facility and speed of painting were astounding, and he influenced many fine young painters to emulate his spontaneous and free-flowing naturalism.

HALS

The wealthy burghers called for a realistic record of the moment, and one of the greatest spokesmen for 17th-century Dutch values was the portrait painter Frans Hals (c.1580-1666). His first resounding success was the group portrait *The Feast of the Guild of Arquebusiers of St. George* (see at right), which he painted in 1616 soon after he set up his workshop in Haarlem. Hals individualized each figure in his portraits with marvelous dexterity.

In the group portrait *The Archers of St. Adrian* (Frans Hals Museum) 1623, the bold patterns of dark and light colors and the contrasting textures of silk scarves and stiff ruffs form a loosely woven unity. By limiting his palette to tones of black and brown accented with an occasional dash of color, Hals could work at an astonishing speed—is was said that he could turn out a portrait in an hour. This technique made it possible for him to capture fleeting expressions in his individual portraits (see above), and his style became more relaxed as he matured. The *Witch of Haarlem* (Kaiser Friederich Museum, Berlin) 1628, displays his virtuosity. A single flick of the brush is made to represent a smile, a fold of material or a cast shadow. The spontaneity of Frans Hals became the rage and his school at Haarlem produced some exceptional popular realists, including Adriaen Brouwer (see *Belgium: The Fine Arts*), Henrick Pot, the genre painters Adriaen and Isaac van Ostade and Judith Leyster. Hals' paintings and technique enjoyed a renewed popularity in the 19th century, when they inspired the works of the early French Impressionist Édouard Manet and the American John Singer Sargent.

Other well-known portraitists of the time included such conscientious but unoriginal realists as Bartolomeus van der Helst, Michiel van Mierevelt and Jan van Ravensteyn.

REMBRANDT

Rembrandt van Rijn (1606-69) is considered the greatest of all Dutch painters. His life was a series of extremes—joy and sorrow, triumph and rejection, wealth and poverty—and it is necessary to sketch the significant course of his personal development to understand the vast scope of his mature artistic output.

Rembrandt, the fifth child of a miller, developed his talents rapidly. Before he was 20 he had opened a studio in his home town of Leiden, and a few years later (1631) moved to busy and wealthy Amsterdam. His early portraits were conventional, but his skillful draftsmanship and unsurpassed use of color and line won him immediate renown.

Rembrandt's clear definitions of spatial arrangement and the placement of figures classed him as a true innovator. One of his best-known paintings is *Professor Tulp's Anatomy Lesson* (The Hague) 1632, which has been reproduced for doctors' offices throughout the western world. This painstakingly realistic group portrait, painted for the guild room of the Amsterdam surgeons, unites the various figures through their singleness of purpose. The total result is dramatic and impressive.

In 1634, Rembrandt married Saskia van Uylenborch. His years of family happiness are recorded in a number of magnificent portraits. In many of these Saskia is dressed in the gorgeous costumes which her rich and successful husband was fond of collecting. The Dresden Gallery contains a remarkably tender *Double Portrait* of the artist and his wife.

In 1642, the year of Saskia's death, Rembrandt painted his most famous and possibly, today, his most valuable, single work, which is now in the Rijksmuseum, Amsterdam. This was mistakenly given the name *Night Watch* many years after it was painted, when accumulated layers of darkened varnish had given it the appearance of a night scene. Recent careful cleaning, however, has revealed the original light effects. This painting, which marks the turning point in Rembrandt's career, shifted from conventional portraiture toward a more profound and original expression. Commissioned by the members of the shooting company of Captain Banning Cocq, it was meant to be another of the group portraits so popular in Holland. Rembrandt's work, however, ranged over a far broader field than his patrons had anticipated. The crowded composition contains a complex play of spaces and movements reinforced by the thrusts of rifles and halberds. Light falls brightly and naturally in some areas, but glows in others with no apparent source. Rembrandt ignored the accepted hierarchy among the members of the group; some insignificant people were given prominence, while more important ones were slighted. Rembrandt invented his own costumes and even had the audacity to throw in a few characters who were not members of the group. In fact, it was as though the artist had staged the event entirely to suit his own artistic intentions. His artistic liberties produced a very unfavorable reaction among his contemporaries, and his popularity waned.

REMBRANDT'S LATER WORK

The paintings which he produced during the 1640s show that Rembrandt's attitude toward art had undergone a noticeable change. His portraits were less precise and objective, and he began probing far beneath the surface of things to present profound psychological interpretations of character.

By 1656, Rembrandt's popularity had fallen so low that he was declared bankrupt. It became necessary for him to sell most of his possessions, including a fine art collection. Lawsuits and a steady decline in commissions resulted in the confiscation of the remainder of his property, and he spent the last years of his life in abject poverty.

Some critics believe that these material conditions spurred an artistic development which would otherwise have come more slowly, for the poverty-stricken Rembrandt's drawings and etchings became increasingly daring and unconventional. The early differences between his realistic and religious works tended to disappear, and scrupulous realism gave way to a search for an inner truth. One of Rembrandt's greatest achievements during his later years is his *Self Portrait* (National Gallery of Art, Washington D.C.). So profoundly has the artist explored this image of his own features that he seems to bare his soul to the spectator. The famous *Aristotle Contemplating the Bust of Homer* (1653) was purchased by the Metropolitan Museum of Art (New York) in 1961 for the record-breaking price of $2,300,000.

Rembrandt's many pupils included the biblical painters Govert Flinck, Ferdinand Bol and Aert van Gelder, who set his biblical figures in theatrical, oriental settings. Another of his pupils, Nicolaes Maes, is noted for his genre paintings, while the works of Carel Fabritius show an exquisite technique and a refined use of color comparable to that of his master.

LANDSCAPE PAINTING

Rembrandt was one of the few Dutch painters of the period who did not specialize in a single type of painting. A number of Dutch artists achieved expression of exceptional merit in the field of landscape painting, and their works found a ready market among the wealthy burghers.

There were divisions of specialization even within landscape painting. Philips de Koninck (1619-88), Jan van Goyen (1596-1656), Hercules Seghers (c.1690-c.1743) and Jacob van Ruisdael (1628-82), for example, depicted the flat Dutch landscape—topping their low, distant horizons with high-piled clouds. De Koninck arranged his compositions with restraint and sensitivity, while Goyen used only grays and pale yellows in his many paintings of the Dutch canals. Segher's paintings have a romantic quality which recalls Rembrandt's landscapes.

The Feast of the Guild of Arquebusiers, *painted in 1616 by Frans Hals (c.1580-1666), reveals the artist's extraordinary gift for characterization, a gift that was to make him the most popular portrait painter of the Dutch burgher class.*

In contrast to the subtlety and sense of unity which characterizes the works of these painters, the works of the famous Van Ruisdael generally depict scenes of untamed nature. He was particularly interested in watery vistas and flat farmlands, which he illuminated by dramatic shafts of light piercing billowing storm clouds (see page 194). He confined himself to browns, grays and pale yellows, and frequently painted stormy seascapes. His´ landscapes did not generally include figures, and what few there were were usually the work of others. Ruisdael's pupil Meindert Hobbema (1638-1709) is best known for his *Avenue of Middelharnis* (National Gallery, London).

Other landscapists chose other subjects; Aert van der Neer painted delicate, pale moonlit scenes, while Willem van de Velde the Elder, Jan van de Cappelle and Willem van de Velde the Younger painted ships and stormy seas. Albert Cuyp and Paulus Potter often included animals in their landscapes. The cities provided the subject matter for the work of Jan van der Heyden and Gerrit Berckheyde, and Emmanuel de Witte and Gerard Houckegeest are known for their impersonal and stark depictions of the bare interiors of Protestant churches. The painters Jan Both, Nicolaes Berghem and Karel du Jardin spent time in Italy, and their pastoral scenes are illuminated by the golden sunlight typical of that country.

Genre Painting

The Belgian artist Jan van Eyck's precise observation of the minutiae of daily life, especially in interior settings, was the source of an entire

body of realistic genre painting. This highly popular form, almost always associated with the Dutch, depicted both burghers and peasants in their moments of leisure.

Each painter also had his own specialty within genre painting. Gerard Terborch (1617-81), for instance, was a master of textures. In his little scenes and portraits, silks, satins, velvets and furs seem remarkably real (see page 208). Like Terborch, Jan Steen (1626-79) and Gabriel Metsu (c.1629-67) depicted the activities of members of the higher social classes, while Adriaen van Ostade and Cornelis Bega painted scenes of peasant life. Ostade's works were simpler and more moving than Bega's, and it appears that Bega exploited the picturesqueness of rustic life largely because there was a good market for it.

The two most significant Dutch genre painters are Pieter de Hooch (1629-c.1677) and Jan Vermeer (1632-75). De Hooch is famous for his paintings of elegant Dutch drawing rooms. He placed his figures in complex arrangements of rooms as though populating a doll's house, depicting them busily engaged in household chores (see *The Linen Closet*, page 192). In his works, De Hooch used fine variations of light to create a carefully controlled over-all pattern.

VERMEER

The quiet and refined art of Jan Vermeer van Delft (1632-75) is considered the culmination of all Dutch genre painting and he, Bosch and Rembrandt are considered the three giants in Dutch painting. Vermeer spent his entire life in Delft, a busy commercial center near Rotterdam. In 1653 he married and became a master painter in the St. Luke's guild in that city. Throughout his life, Vermeer remained at the house of his father. His father's position as an art dealer undoubtedly exposed the young Vermeer to a far wider range of

The glowing warmth of the colors and the soft luminosity of the play of light identifies this painting, Athena, *as the work of Rembrandt van Rijn (1606-69), the greatest painter in Dutch history. A prodigious artist, Rembrandt produced some 500-600 paintings. All his work, even that of his early conventional style, reveals his profound artistic genius.*

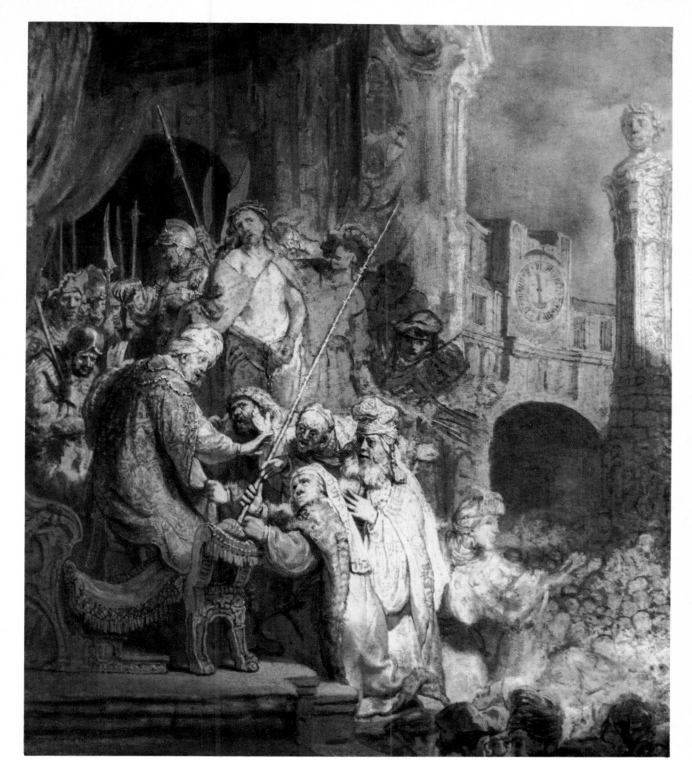

styles than the normal apprentice, and he was also influenced by his friendship with Pieter de Hooch, another native of Delft.

Vermeer was a perfectionist, and the great majority of his 36 paintings were executed within three rooms of the family home. The same win-

dows, the same chair, the same rug appear again and again, but even his earliest works demonstrate his exceptional technical control.

After a few bold stylistic ventures, Vermeer did not attempt to revise the well-tried formulas of his predecessors in the field of genre painting.

For example, he almost always placed his windows on the left side of his paintings, following this accepted rule in all but a few small portraits such as the tiny *Girl in a Red Hart* (National Gallery, Washington D.C.), where the light source is unseen. His amazingly accurate reproduction of day-

Of the cycle of Rembrandt's etchings based upon religious themes, The Three Crosses *is perhaps the most poignantly conceived. As the light rains down upon them, Christ and the two thieves crucified with him form a radiant triangle which seems to draw everything upward. The darkness and shadow around the circumference of light reveal the emotions of the crowd as it watches Christ's death with shame and despair. The etching combines a sense of spirituality and realistic homeliness that is one of Rembrandt's most striking characteristics.*

His tiny and precise brushstrokes suggest the feel and weight of the objects he painted, and he is distinguished for his exquisitely blended colors and his glassy, enamel-like textures. Vermeer's skillful use of color is particularly evident in his last two works, his only landscapes. Their realism and delicacy make all other Dutch landscapes seem superficial in comparison.

His single figures, lost in contemplation or absorbed in a task are the most fully realized of his creations. In *Maidservant Pouring Milk* (Rijksmuseum, Amsterdam), the artist explored space by moving from object to object, savoring textures and subtly defining shapes through his use of light.

THE STILL LIFE

Vermeer's painstaking realism in his treatment of familiar objects is seen in the works of a still more specialized group: the painters of still lifes. This type of painting was in great demand by Dutch patrons of art of the day. Pieter Claesz (1596-1661), Willem Claesz Heda (1594-c.1681), Hendrick van Streek (1659-1713) and Willem Kalff (1622-93) are among the most noted painters in this field. Their elaborate arrangements of food, utensils and glassware were rendered with unerring skill.

Despite the talented use of color and texture by the best of the still-life painters, however, this form had lasting significance in Dutch art only insofar as it was incorporated into larger interior compositions. In the works of Vermeer and De Hooch, for example, elements of the still life assumed an important place in Dutch genre art as a whole.

THE EIGHTEENTH CENTURY

THE 18TH CENTURY SAW A SPECTACular decline in the position of tne Dutch nation. This decline was due chiefly to a lack of effective political leadership and a saturation with wealth and success. There was no real central authority, and an unwillingness to risk Dutch property or life had even led to the decay of the navy. The Netherlands was therefore open to invasion, and by the end of the 18th century the country was under French domination. This political and economic decline was accompanied by a corresponding artistic deterioration. When Louis XIV be-

light gave his works an extraordinary sense of depth (see page 193).

One of Vermeer's earliest successful genre paintings was the *Music Lesson* (Buckingham Palace, London). In this work, he has placed his figures at the far end of the room and dwarfed them by other objects, as though to avoid dealing with the emotions of the young woman standing at the virginal apparently hearing the plea of her suitor. Furthermore, the lady's back is turned; the observer sees only a reflection of her face in the mirror. Such techniques enabled the artist to remove himself from the emotions of his subjects and consider them in cool objectivity.

Vermeer maintained this detachment throughout his later career, focusing his attention on the quality of light and spatial arrangement. He rejected extraneous motifs in his compositions; like a poet, he condensed and eliminated until he had nothing left but the pure essence of his idea. In many respects he viewed the world as a still life, making no artistic distinction among a face, a carpet or a jug. To him, all objects were important to the greater whole, and he often placed objects in the foreground as foils to make objects in the background seem more distant. This careful organization reflected his determination that not a single touch in his paintings should be out of place.

Vermeer limited his subjects to one or two figures, frequently women caught at some practical task. Though they contain little sense of movement, Vermeer's paintings are never cold.

came the leader of fashion in Europe, Dutch artists began to imitate the French in an unnatural and awkward manner.

Architecture and Sculpture

Innovations in 18th-century Dutch architecture consisted primarily of the imposition of French styles upon Dutch forms. Many towns, however, wisely continued to build in the traditional manner, clinging stubbornly to the 17th-century models. The best work of the period was in the area of church planning, where Christian Sturm suggested a number of ingenious and often practical solutions for the planning of Protestant churches. Interest waned even in this area, however, as the century progressed.

Sculpture was no more inspired than architecture. Dutch masons upheld their traditional reputation for technical skill, but the brick walls and decorations of the period lacked originality.

PAINTING

The last of the native Dutch School painters, Adriaen van der Werff, died in 1722. His biblical paintings, with their smooth, enamel-like surfaces, found many imitators. The one outstanding 18th-century Dutch painter was Jacob de Wit (1695-1754), who is famous for his work in *trompe-l'œil* painting. De Wit was one of the first to paint in this style, which is designed to "fool the eye" by depicting inanimate objects with such startling, three-dimensional realism that what is painted is taken for that which is real. In *trompe-l'œil* painting, technical skill was often lavished on such things as a fly painted on a frame or a view through a non-existent window.

THE MINOR ARTS

From the 16th century onward, the minor arts of woodcarving and metal working were skillfully practiced. In general, the minor arts which produced articles that could be used in the home were the most significant.

One particularly important minor art was pottery-making, which became a major Dutch industry. The art had been imported to Antwerp from Italy during the 16th century and became centered in Haarlem in about 1630. During this time, the most popular articles were gaily painted tiles and tableware such as those manufactured along the Mediterranean. Protestant refugees carried the craft to Delft, and by 1650 the major part of Dutch production was centered there. The best of the Delft potters became famous, and signed their works with such symbols as the peacock or the star. The earliest recorded potter from Delft was Aelbrecht de Keizer, who was renowned for designs which he borrowed from the contemporary Chinese porcelains then being imported by the Dutch East India Company. The rich deep-blue designs of Frederick van Fritjtom became popularly associated with all Delft ware.

During the 18th century, pottery-making fell into a severe decline. Potters went to extremes of quaintness in their efforts to supply an eager but undiscriminating public; even today the art has not regained its 17th-century distinction.

THE NINETEENTH CENTURY

THE YEAR 1815 MARKED THE END OF French domination, and a brief attempt by William I to unify Belgium and the Netherlands ended with the declaration of Belgian independence in 1830. The rise of industry during the latter half of the 19th century created social problems which led to the formation of labor unions and social protest movements. These groups pressed for comprehensive and compulsory social legislation, and their social concern was reflected in the life of the greatest Dutch artist of the century, Vincent van Gogh.

Portrait of Lady Gresham, *by Anthonis Mor (c.1512-76). Mor studied under the tutelage of Jan van Scorel and went on to become the official portrait painter of the Spanish royal court. His portraits, distinguished by incisive characterization, are heightened by sharp and compact lines and a careful attention to detail.*

Van Gogh was an exception to a generally conservative artistic trend. Most other 19th-century artists in the Netherlands carried on in the tradition of the great Dutch masters, and the cultural revival of this century was more evolutionary than revolutionary.

Nineteenth-Century Architecture

After the middle of the 19th century French styles ceased to be imitated and there was a revival of Dutch architectural traditions. The leader of this movement was Petrus Josephus Cuypers (1827-1921), designer of the Rijksmuseum and the railway station in Amsterdam, and of several churches modeled on the early Gothic style. His buildings are constructed of brick and trimmed with stone, and exhibit restrained good taste.

Modern Dutch architecture is chiefly derived from the work of Hendrick Petrus Berlage (1856-1934), whose severe lines and over-all simplicity of form became the bywords for contemporary building in Holland. Berlage was the first Dutch architect to break away from the derivative historical conventions which characterized most 19th-century architecture. In his later years, he was engrossed in urban extension programs in Amsterdam, Rotterdam and The Hague and his Stock Exchange in Amsterdam (1903) is one of Europe's first purely functional designs.

Nineteenth-Century Sculpture

During the 19th century, most European sculpture was shaped by the influence of Antonio Canova (1757-1822). This Italian artist idealized his figures in the Classical manner, eliminating everything spontaneous and natural from his works. The chief Dutch sculptor to fall under the sway of Canova's Neoclassicism was the extremely versatile Pierre-Jean David D'Angers (1788-1856), whose works included portrait statues and reliefs, medallions and busts of contemporary French and German painters and poets.

In general, 19th-century Dutch sculpture was as formal and derivative as architecture. Near the end of the century, however, the influence of the naturalistic *art nouveau* began to make itself felt in Holland. Art became increasingly realistic, and sculptors such as Charles van Wijk began to experiment with new and imaginative forms and designs.

Nineteenth-Century Painting

Until the mid-19th century, the powerful influence of French artists resulted in a general neglect of the arts in other European countries. This was particularly true in the Netherlands. One of the first significant Dutch painters since the 17th century was Jozef Israels (1824-1911), whose style in many ways foreshadowed that of the French Impressionists. His overly sentimental themes were based upon peasant life, especially life among fishermen. Because his paintings catered to the general tastes of the time, he enjoyed considerable popularity. Israels' chief distinction is that his sentimentality helped to free his contemporaries from their outworn academic approach, thus opening the way for fresh experimentation.

ART SCHOOLS

The leading art group in the mid-19th century was the School of The Hague, which included such painters as Israels and the three Maris brothers. Jacob Maris (1837-99) is known for his strongly lighted landscapes and townscapes. Although his own works were realistic, his claim that artistic unity was a product of the personal emotions of the artist was one sign of the coming break with realism found in the works of Vincent Van Gogh. The works of Matthijs Maris (1839-1917) tended towards mysticism, while Willem Maris (1844-1910) typically painted Dutch landscapes filled with cows, ducks, dogs, cats and horses. The School of

Right: Young Woman at the Spinet, by Jan Vermeer (1632-75), considered one of the three greatest Dutch masters, along with Rembrandt and Bosch. Vermeer's extraordinary use of color, especially his luminous blues and yellows, and his exquisite blending of reflected light have rarely been surpassed. In Vermeer's work, each figure is treated as an object within a precisely defined spatial arrangement. His paintings have a remarkable sense of suspended life.

The Linen Closet, *by the great genre painter Pieter de Hooch (1629-c.1677). In his scenes of Dutch domestic life, de Hooch loved to intrigue the eye with half-disclosed glimpses into rooms and corridors. He achieved this fanciful sense of rooms within rooms by a masterful rendering of lighting effects as well as through an exquisite use of color and design.*

The Hague, despite its important contributions to Netherlandish artistic development, was characterized by a certain complacency and a tendency to paint pleasant but shallow pictures. These artists seldom depicted suffering, fear or any of the negative emotions.

The Amsterdam Academy took the lead as the center of Dutch painting after the appointment of August Allebé (1838-1927) to its directorship. Allebé was best known as a teacher, and his balanced and graceful works stopped one step short of Impressionism. His most famous pupil was Anton Derkinderen (1859-1925), who is known for his murals and stained-glass windows. Derkinderen had a strong social and religious conscience, and his art was a conscious effort to recapture something of the Middle Ages' spirit.

JONGKIND

Like Allebé, Johann Barthold Jongkind (1819-91) was an early herald

The Torrent, *by Jacob van Ruisdael (1628-1682). Van Ruisdael was primarily a landscape painter. His works characteristically display a fantastic and moody interpretation of nature as seen through the artist's imaginative eye.*

of the Impressionist movement in the Netherlands. In his attempt to catch the movement of light, water and clouds in his landscapes and scenes of the Dutch coast, he broke with the detailed realism which had characterized much of Dutch painting since the 17th century. His technique was characterized by tiny strokes and shimmering tones.

Jongkind was a member of the "open-air school," a group which painted under the sky rather than under a directed northern studio light. They discovered that this meth-od showed "a bright medley of tones" rather than a collection of individual objects each with its own color, and their revolutionary concept of color and form characterized the works of the later Impressionist movement.

VAN GOGH

Although Jongkind was an alcoholic and suffered periods of amnesia, the flowing lines and fresh colors of his landscapes show no evidence of his disturbed state of mind. In contrast, the works of Vincent van Gogh (1853-90) reflect his sense of isolation, and his tragic life had a profound effect upon his art. Throughout his life, Van Gogh lacked the ability to communicate easily with those around him. The son of a strict Protestant minister, he inherited his father's concern for social problems and also took up the ministry, working for a time in the slums of London and the mining districts of Belgium. Despite his excessive concern for the oppressed, his efforts to communicate with simple people were repeatedly foiled by his brusqueness and clumsiness and he was finally dismissed from his job.

At the age of 26, Van Gogh turned to painting for self-expression. He began to copy the works of other artists, particularly those of the French painter Millet. Out of those early years came a series of awkward, intense and crudely rendered portraits of the peasantry. *The Potato Eaters* (now in the collection of V. W. Van Gogh at Laren, Netherlands) is one example of Van Gogh's early work, in which he restricted his palette to browns and blacks.

In Antwerp, the painter became acquainted with the current vogue for Japanese prints. Later, with the aid of his brother Theo, he moved to Paris, where he met the enthusiastic young group of Impressionists and became familiar with their techniques. His friendship with Gauguin was a particularly influential force in his artistic evolution, for it encouraged him to experiment with colors in hitherto untried ways. Indeed, he became passionately interested in color, striving to imbue it with a symbolic meaning by contrasting areas of intensely rich tones. Yellow, which he used to symbolize the pure illumination of God's love, became almost an obsession.

Van Gogh struggled incessantly to master the technical skills of painting surface texture. He applied paint thickly and used bold lines to draw out the greatest possible expressiveness from his colors. Sometimes he worked with brushes, sometimes his fingers, and he often squeezed the paint directly from the tube onto the canvas.

Van Gogh's works reflect his intense emotionalism, the same fierce desires that had inspired his religious mission. His feeling determined his subjects, his color and his technique: he gave painting a new strength and sensuousness which retained the freshness of Impressionism without its frailty.

In one of his many letters to his beloved brother Theo, Van Gogh described the problem of painting an autumn sunset in the woods. He emphasized the importance of capturing a sense of depth and solidarity in his portrayal of the scene, telling how he gave strength to the trees by applying his paint directly from the tube. He marvelled that he had never fully realized the subtleties of light and shade present in nature until he attempted to capture them upon canvas, and declared that this realization made him work quickly in the changing light.

Van Gogh's intense nature, his years of poverty and neglect and his lack of success finally shattered his mental balance. He was hospitalized several times, and shot himself to death in 1890. His last picture, paint-ed on the day of his death, is a deeply moving monument to his sense of isolation. This work, *Wheatfield with Blackbirds* (Stedelijk Museum, Amsterdam), presents an almost abstract arrangement of intensely contrasting colors painted with quick, short strokes. In a letter to his brother, Van Gogh had described this scene as a "vast stretch of corn under troubled skies, and I did not need to go out of my way to express sadness and the extreme of loneliness."

Van Gogh, throughout his lifetime, was not content simply to convey what he saw; his works depict the torment of his soul. In his later works, he used spirals and wavy brush strokes to represent the storms raging within him. His lack of emotional maturity is reflected in his technique, for his paintings have a childlike simplicity. Van Gogh may be considered a true revolutionary, for his unconventional work was personal and highly charged with emotion. This quality relates him more closely to 20th-century art than to the art of his own time.

OTHER NINETEENTH-CENTURY PAINTERS

Another leading artist of the 19th century was Georg Hendrik Breitner

Dinner at the Inn, by Jan Steen (1626-1679). Steen was one of the genre painters known as the "Little Dutchmen." His favorite themes were scenes of feasting and drinking, often with a humorous or moralistic edge. The many paintings he produced provide an interesting picture of the social life of the upper classes in 17th-century Holland.

(1857-1923), who documented the growth of Amsterdam at the close of the century in his realistic depiction of wreckers, groundworkers, builders and soldiers. The exotic symbolism of another 19th-century painter, Jan Toorop (1858-1928), was typical of many Dutch artists who had lived in the East Indies. His best works were his religious paintings;

their attempt to bring a certain order to nature foreshadowed the coming break with Impressionism.

Toorop's attempt to create order was carried event further by Willem van Konijneburg (1868-1943), who idealized his style until it contained only the elements of form—his lines hardened and became the shortest connections between the basic points,

while color served simply as a filler between them.

THE TWENTIETH CENTURY

THE MOST SIGNIFICANT EVENT IN EARLY 20th-century Dutch art was the founding of the review *De Stijl* in 1917 by the painters Theo van Doesburg and Piet Mondrian, the architect Jacobus J. P. Oud, and several other young Dutch artists. The *Stijl* (style) movement which grew out of this review was influenced by the rise of Cubism in Paris. It was based upon two principles: the clarification of art to achieve a clear, logical har-

The Night Walk *by Vincent van Gogh (1853-90). Van Gogh was an extremely lonely and disturbed man who turned to painting after failing as a preacher. His despondent and tormented life, which finally led him to commit suicide, is dynamically revealed in his paintings. His intensive use of brillant colors as well as his exaggerated and distorted lines indicate the turmoil which Van Gogh underwent during his life. However, the frenzy of Van Gogh's vision created some of the most moving works in modern art. With their emphasis on emotionalism and a completely individualistic style of expression, Van Gogh's paintings have had a marked influence on 20th-century art.*

mony and the development of architectural and industrial design to create a functional purity. The movement sparked a wholehearted response among the artists of the north, partly because it attempted to bring some sanity and order into the chaos of the post-World War I era.

Twentieth-Century Architecture

In the early part of the 20th century, particularly during the period between the two world wars, the Expressionist movement in painting affected Dutch architecture. Expressionism was a highly emotional movement which abandoned naturalism in favor of a simplified style capable of carrying greater emotional impact. Its characteristic exaggerations and distortions of line and color worked their way into Dutch architecture; even Berlage, despite his emphasis on functionalism and simplicity, often worked out odd, angular patterns in his designs. The best example of this architectural trend is J. M. van der Mey's Scheepvaarthuis in Amsterdam (1911-16). The large-scale Amsterdam housing projects begun in 1917 by Michel de Klerk (1884-1923), Piet Kramer (1881-   ) and others are characterized by sudden angular and curved projections and by odd roofs.

After World War II the principles of the *Stijl* group reasserted themselves. The spokesman for these principles was Jacobus Johannes Pieter Oud (1890-1963), who is considered the most original Dutch architect of the 20th century. His buildings, such as the workers' houses in Rotterdam (1924), are notably pure in design and functional in concept. Other champions of modernism in contemporary Dutch architecture are Jan Wils and Willem Marinus Dudok, whose early buildings followed the Expressionistic trend. Dudok soon cast off this style, and his later buildings are characterized by their crisp, cubic grouping of brick blocks. His best-known work is the Hilversum town hall (1928-32), and his style has been widely influential outside Holland.

Today, the Netherlands boasts one of the most flourishing schools of architecture and city planning in Europe. The terrific destruction caused by the two world wars necessitated a vast amount of rebuilding, and the Netherlanders have applied modern engineering techniques to every kind of structure. The use of reinforced concrete combined with brick, for example, is commonplace. In cities

Composition *(1929) by Piet Mondrian (1872-1944). Under the influence of Cubism, Mondrian went on to develop his own geometric, non-objective style of painting called Neo-Plasticism. The most essential idea in Neo-Plasticism was to strip away extraneous details and work with only the barest and simplest of forms. Mondrian chose the straight-edge line. Through the organization of straight lines set at right angles to one another and the use of only the primary colors, plus black and white, Mondrian created a world of perfect balance and design. Mondrian's ideas, which were published in the magazine* De Stijl *(which he helped found in 1917), had a tremendous influence on modern painting and architecture.*

such as Rotterdam and Hilversum, where great areas were leveled by bombs, model solutions to contemporary problems of population distribution and communications have been attempted. In these areas the Netherlands has made an impressive contribution to international modern architecture.

Twentieth-Century Sculpture

Modern sculpture, like painting and architecture, has been influenced by the *Stijl* movement. Dutch sculptors of this century have popularized nonrepresentational forms such as cubes, spheres and ovoids, and the new buildings have demanded new sculptural conventions in interior decoration. The artist Theo van Does-

burg (1883-1931), for instance, did his best work in connection with modern architecture. As publisher of the *De Stijl* review, he tried to keep in close contact with architectural developments and is known for his excellent mosaic floors, stained-glass windows and wall decorations. During the early part of the 20th century Van Doesburg used only straight lines and right angles, but his lines became more fluid after 1923.

RAEDECKER

The greatest modern sculptor of the Netherlands is John Raedecker (1885-1956), who designed the moving statue *Peace* in the central square (The Dam) of Amsterdam. This work, often considered the greatest national

A modern department store in Rotterdam. The architecture of 20th-century Holland has been greatly influenced by the trends of Cubism and Neo-Plasticism. The buildings erected since World War II are characterized by a simplicity of design and a practical functionalism, clearly modern in feeling and spirit.

monument in the Netherlands, depicts a young woman holding a child which symbolizes the future of the nation. During his early working years, Raedecker shared a studio and materials with another Dutch sculptor, Gijs van den Hof. They were very poor, and would take turns working at the decoration of furniture to earn money to eat. Raedecker was influenced by the revolutionary zeal of the Dutch workers, and these men are depicted in many of his works.

Raedecker's brother Loon often assisted him in his work, as did his youngest son Jan Willem, known as Noeki. His oldest brother, Willem, is known for his graceful wooden and ebony bowls and other carvings.

Twentieth-Century Painting

During the 20th century, some painters isolated themselves from contemporary trends and continued Classical realism. Others carried on the revolution initiated by Van Gogh, while still others experimented with new forms.

'DE STIJL'

During the early part of the century, the *Stijl* movement was particularly influential in Dutch painting. The intellectual leader of the movement was Piet Mondrian (1872-1944), whose quest for the "absolute order of art" led him to remove all extraneous elements from his paintings. He reduced the usual palette to the primary colors plus black and white and eliminated all lines but the elementary straight-edge (see page 197). With this severely restricted vocabulary, Mondrian developed an artistic theory based upon contrasts. As the most elementary contrast is the right angle, his art is an organization of precisely balanced areas enclosed by right angles. After 1940, when he emigrated to America, Mondrian's work lost some of its static severity and began to admit stronger rhythmic effects.

Mondrian's style, known as Neo-Plasticism, is seen in the works of another *Stijl* member, Bart van der Leck (1876-1958), who painted rec-

tangular planes in primary colors. Unlike Mondrian, however, Van der Leck did not always abandon the appearances of the world around him. The style advanced by these two men influenced European architects and designers, particularly members of the German Bauhaus group such as Walter Gropius and Mies Van der Rohe.

EXPRESSIONISM

This same period saw another attack upon Impressionism led by Kees van Dongen (1877-   ), whose fierce light and strong colors reflect the influence of the French Fauves. After World War I his work became less violent, and he was much sought after as a fashionable portraitist.

Expressionism shared much with Fauvism in its use of drastically simplified outlines and very strong colors. One of the earliest Dutch Expressionists, Jan Sluyters (1881-1957), mixed realism and Expressionism in his farm scenes, religious paintings and fantastically colored nudes. Leo Gestel (1881-1941) stylized vases of flowers into geometric designs and forced colors into decorative patterns in his early works. Later, he eased his mathematical rigidity and turned to Expressionistic portrayals of nudes, workmen and horses.

One of the best-known Dutch Expressionists is Hendrik Chabot (1894-1949), whose almost religious awe before the sufferings of man placed him close to Van Gogh in temperament. During the German occupation, his canvases showed the fugitives, the hungry, the men in hiding and the flooded fields. After the war, his sympathy with the suffering of mankind expressed itself in the melancholy stare of the tired and the poor he chose as subjects. His landscapes often show the sun through a slight break in an otherwise stormy and black sky.

Among the other Expressionists were Herman Kruyder (1881-1935), who shared Chabot's obsession with suffering, and Jacob Bendien (1890-1933), whose fantastic forms verged on Surrealism. In his later years, Jan Wiegers (1893-1959) abandoned the emotional deformation typical of Expressionism while retaining the style's strong, simple lines.

THE NEW REALISM

The 20th century in the Netherlands also saw the rise of a new realism, sometimes known as "magic realism." The painters of this school, including Willem Schuhmacher, Henk Henriet, Edgar Feinhout and Wim Schippers, looked for revelation in an unnatural, dreamlike precision. Their style was directly opposed to that of the Surrealists, for their works were characterized by cool, careful and detailed workmanship which attempted to express both matter and the soul behind it.

The most famous exponent of the new realism is Charley Toorop (1890-). She paints in hard, simple and pure movements, using dull red-browns and deep blues. Her art is aggressively human, and many of her subjects are intentionally ugly and vulgar. One of her most impressive works is *Woman in Front of a Ruin,* which shows a gray-haired women, the wife of a laborer, sitting in front of the scarred remains of a bombed house with her hands in her lap. The woman's sharply lined face has nothing pathetic and beaten about it; she stares ahead with an immobile, clear and penetrating look, almost as if she were laughing inwardly.

Another painter of this school, Karel Willink (1900-), paints chilling pictures of empty streets as they might look after mankind had destroyed itself. The extremely detailed paintings of Dick Ket (1902-40) explored the mystery of death.

THE EXPERIMENTAL GROUP

During World War II, the Germans suppressed modern painting; also, many Dutch artists were killed working in the underground. After the war, the remaining Expressionists and members of the *Stijl* group produced works of high quality, but they were eclipsed by the so-called Experimental Group.

The youthful Experimental Group (most of its artists were no more than 25 years old at the close of the war) found its inspiration in the works of Piet Ouborg (1880-1954), who became popular only after 1945. His canvases show nothing of Expressionism or the geometric abstraction of the *Stijl* movement; instead, they resemble colorful, dream-like, spontaneous visions. His waving, unarchitectural style was quickly adopted by young artists protesting routine and lack of inspiration. However, in the early years of the movement the public and the critics both failed to appreciate its combination of abstraction and spontaneity.

The Experimental Group first came to public notice in 1949, when they held an exhibition at the Stedelijk Museum in Amsterdam. The exhibition, known as the CoBrA (because the artists involved came from Copenhagen, Brussels and Amsterdam), included the works of Appel, Brands, Rooskens, Constant and Corneille. The center of the movement has since shifted to Paris, and includes artists from Denmark, the Netherlands, Belgium, France and the United States.

In the years since the CoBrA exhibition, the Experimental movement has lost some of its impetus. The one major artist of the group to sustain its original violent tone is Karel Appel (1921-), who now lives in Paris. His works are primarily large, colorful and spontaneous canvases. The maturation of the works of Corneille (Cornelis van Beverloo), however, is more typical of the development of the movement. His early violence has somewhat subsided, yet his small, intense canvases preserve the freedom he found in his earlier experimentation. He continues to find his inspiration in the rhythm of nature, but what he termed "the loud noises" have now vanished from his painting.

DE KOONING AND BENNER

Perhaps the best-known contemporary Dutch painter is Willem de Kooning (1904-), who came to the United States in 1926 and has assumed the leadership of the American Abstract-Expressionist movement. Originally a house-painter, De Kooning did not turn to abstract art until the 1930s. His bold canvases are painted with large house-painter's brushes.

Recently, De Kooning has begun to depict human figures in his works in an attempt to combine more representational elements with his early style. This effort is just one more phase of his lifelong attempt to introduce control and understanding into the often chaotic spontaneity of abstract style. De Kooning is famous for his vitality, and the tension which he creates between depth and flatness seems to capture the complex qualities of modern life.

From its early beginnings, Dutch art has always been diversified. This diversity is seen today in the popularity of another contemporary painter, Gerrit Benner (1897-), whose works have been described as "the melodies of simple songs." His simple and reflective manner stands in sharp contrast to the violence of the Experimentalists.

CONCLUSION

IN GENERAL, THE EARLY ART OF HOLland was indistinguishable from that produced in neighboring Belgium. Until the 15th century, successive invasions and the never-ending battle against the sea discouraged artistic development, while much of Dutch Gothic art was destroyed during the 17th-century revolt against Catholicism.

Artistic development in the Netherlands has generally been determined by the character of the country's individual artists rather than by international trends. This is nowhere more clearly seen than in the 17th century, which is known as the Golden Age of Netherlandish painting. During this century, a remarkable number of great painters (including Rembrandt and Vermeer) expressed Dutch prosperity and independence in a manner which differed totally from any that had been known in other countries. The art of this period depicted man in his everyday life—it painted the portrait of a country. The most popular 17th-century art forms were the portrait, the landscape, and genre painting, and the artists of the time developed their techniques until painting became a fine craft. Even architects preferred functional simplicity to the elaborateness of the Baroque style which prevailed throughout the rest of Europe.

The 18th century was a period of economic, political and cultural decline in the Netherlands, but the 19th and 20th centuries have seen a revival of the Dutch artistic genius. Early in the 20th century the *Stijl* movement, with its emphasis on simplicity and functionalism, became extremely influential in all branches of art. Architecture assumed increasing importance after World War II, when destruction caused by bombings necessitated the extensive rebuilding of Dutch towns and cities. But painting, traditionally the most notable Dutch art form, continues to retain its eminence, as artists seek in their individual ways to convey on canvas the essence and meaning of the age in which they live. Most important, the art of the Netherlands is characterized today by the same rich diversity and individuality which have won it an important place in European art throughout the past five centuries.

Desiderius Erasmus of Rotterdam (c. 1466-1536), one of the greatest literary figures in Dutch history, was a leading Humanist thinker and the most renowned scholar in all of northern Europe. He translated the works of numerous Latin and Greek authors and was an active agent in the revival of classical learning during the 16th century. His own writings, mostly critical and satiric works, were in Latin. They display a remarkably clear and precise style and a pungent sense of humor, tempered by a sympathetic tolerance.

the laity with religious ideals, Bible stories and legends.

One of the earliest extant works written in the Netherlands was Melis Stoke's rhymed history of Holland entitled *Rijmkroniek*, written for Count Floris V of Holland. At the end of the 14th century, Willem van Hildegaersberch wrote a number of fables. Dirk Potter (c.1370-1428),secretary to the counts of Holland, was known for a collection of didactic tales entitled *Der Minnen Loop* (The Lens of Love).

THE RENAISSANCE OF THE 16th CENTURY

THE 16TH CENTURY, WHICH WAS shaped by the ideas of the Italian Renaissance scholars, is known as the time of the northern Renaissance. The recently invented printing press provided a means for writers to reach the growing reading public and to circulate the ideas of both Humanist scholars and religious reformers. The century was dominated by religious and political conflicts, and its temper was reflected in the abundance and diversity of its literature.

ERASMUS

One of the greatest figures in Dutch and European cultural history is the Humanist scholar Desiderius Erasmus (c.1466-1536), who is considered the chief figure of the northern Renaissance. In addition to writing original treatises and popular satires, Erasmus edited works by Latin authors and produced translations of Greek classical writings. His great *Adagio* (1508) consists of over 3000 proverbs which he collected from the works of the classical authors, while *Encomium Moriae* (In Praise of Folly) is one of the most masterful satires in world literature. Erasmus dreamed of a "golden age of letters," and believed that it was extremely important to get classical works published and into the hands

THE LITERATURE

The national language of the Netherlands and one of the two major languages of Belgium is Netherlandic, which is popularly known as "Dutch" in Holland and as "Flemish" in Belgium. Although local dialects vary widely, a standardized written language is used in both areas. Netherlandic is descended primarily from the Low German spoken by the Frankish tribes who entered the Low Countries in the 4th and 5th centuries, but written documents did not appear until the end of the 12th century. Netherlandic literary development during the 13th and 14th centuries was centered in Bruges (Belgium), and had begun to shift eastward toward Brabant by the end of the 14th century. With the fall of Antwerp to the Spanish in 1585, many of the most influential Flemish families fled from Belgium to Holland, which now became the center of Netherlandic literature and culture.

THE MIDDLE AGES

DURING THE EARLY MIDDLE AGES, Latin and French were the languages of the educated classes in the Low Countries, and the vernacular was largely confined to unrecorded oral legends and folk songs. Most Netherlandic literature produced during the late Middle Ages was written in Belgium, and included a great many religious works designed to acquaint of the growing number of lettered laymen. He occupied an important position in the 16th-century revival of classical writings and was considered the foremost scholar of his day in the whole of northern Europe.

OTHER WRITERS

Another noted Dutch Renaissance scholar was Daniel Heinsius (1580-1665), whose proficiency in the classical languages was famous throughout Europe. The first northern poet of the Renaissance was Jan van Hout (1542-1609).

One of the greatest authors of his generation was Hendrik Laurenzoon Spieghel, whose learned *Twespraack van de Nederduytsche Letterkunst* (Treatise on Netherlandic Letters) 1584 was intended to popularize Netherlandic as the national language. He was also known for his long poem *Herstspieghel* (The Mirror of the Heart). The combination of Calvinist principles and ancient pagan ideals found in Spieghel's work was typical of the writers of his generation.

One of the best-known Dutch writers of the Renaissance was the Humanist Dirck Volckertzoon Coornhert (1522-90), an outspoken moderate whose position on the burning religious and political questions of the day eventually cost him his life. Coornhert was a poet, pamphleteer, translator and moral philosopher. His works include Dutch translations of Cicero, Seneca, Erasmus' Latin works and the *Odyssey,* and his supple and lucid style greatly influenced the establishment of Netherlandic as the literary language of Holland. His best-known work is *Zedekunst, dat is Wellevenkunst* (Ethics, That is the Art of Living Well) 1586, which drew its inspiration from the Bible.

THE SEVENTEENTH CENTURY

THE 17TH CENTURY HAS BEEN CALLED the Golden Age of Dutch literature. Belgian intellectuals fled from the Spanish armies into Holland, and Amsterdam and The Hague became the cultural centers of the Low Countries.

One of the most representative figures of this time was the historian, poet and playwright Pieter Cornelis-zoon Hooft (1581-1647). Hooft served as bailiff of the castle of Muiden, which was a gathering place for a group of artists, poets and men of letters. He is considered one of the greatest Dutch lyric poets and was the first to draw inspiration from the springs of antique and Italian Renaissance poetry. In 1618, Hooft turned to historical writing and produced his famous 27-volume *Nederlandsche Historien* (History of the Netherlands). His historical style was praised throughout Europe, and he holds perhaps the highest place among Dutch writers of prose.

SPINOZA

The Jewish community in 17th-century Amsterdam produced one of the greatest figures in the history of philosophy. Benedictus de Spinoza (1632-1677) was the grandson of Portuguese Jews who had taken refuge in the Netherlands when the Union of Utrecht guaranteed religious freedom to all.

Although trained in Jewish studies, Spinoza's bold interpretation of Scripture was too independent for the orthodox synagogue in Amsterdam. When only twenty-four, the young philosopher was excommunicated for heresy. Spinoza held that the writers of the Bible were divinely inspired only in their moral doctrines and that religious practices must always be appropriate to the time. He attempted to integrate the principles of physics and geometry into his greatest work, *Ethica Ordine Geometrica Demonstrata (Ethics, Demonstrated in the Manner of Geometry)* which was not published until 1677, shortly after his death.

Spinoza assumed that it was possible to construct a picture of the world which would render it completely intelligible. He began by acknowledging the existence of God, but declared that God was in all of nature and had no purpose. He denied the existence of free will, stating that everything is governed by fundamental laws of physics and psychology. For Spinoza, good is that which preserves the individual and continues the world's existence.

GROTIUS

Another prose writer of considerable importance was Hugo Grotius (1583-1645), who was appointed official historiographer of the States of Holland in 1601. Grotius began

A town house in Delft dating from the 16th century. The Renaissance in 16th century Holland brought to the fore a number of talented scholars and poets. Daniel Heinsius (1580-1665) established a fine reputation as a classical scholar, while the ill-fated Humanist writer Dirck Volckertzoon Coornhert (1522-90) influenced the entire course of Dutch literature by helping to establish Netherlandic as the literary language of Holland.

Above: *Hugo Grotius (1583-1645), in Dutch Huigh de Croot, a renowned jurist and Humanist scholar. In 1621 Grotius was forced to flee from Holland because of his political affiliations and returned only once for a brief visit in 1631. He wrote his famous treatise* De jure belli et pacis *(Concerning the Law of War and Peace) in Paris. Setting down principles which applied to the natural laws governing nations as well as individuals and the conduct of war, his book is considered the first authoritative text on international law.*

Below: *Frontispiece of the first edition of Grotius'* De jure belli et pacis, *published in 1625.*

HVGONIS GROTII

DE IVRE BELLI AC PACIS

LIBRI TRES.

In quibus ius naturæ & Gentium : item iuris publici præcipua explicantur.

PARISIIS;

Apud NICOLAVM BVON, in via Iacobæa, fub fignis S. Claudij, & Hominis Silueftris.

M. DC. XXV.

writing at an early age—at 15, he wrote a remarkable poem on the international situation for the French king, Henry IV.

Grotius' works were of fundamental importance in the development of international law. His most important work in this field is *De jure praedae* (On the Law of Prize and Booty) which lays down his four basic principles: no state or individual may attack another state or individual; no state or individual may appropriate what belongs to another state or individual; no state or individual may disregard treaties or contracts; and no state or individual may commit a crime. Grotius declared that wherever possible these precepts should be enforced by judges, and that if no judges are available the states or individuals should settle their disputes by war or private litigation. He felt that these principles were in harmony with a basic law of nature derived from the law of God.

Poetry During the Golden Age

The 17th-century diplomat and poet Constantijn Huygens (1596-1687) is considered one of the most brilliant figures in Netherlandic literary history. Huygens was a prolific writer of trenchant, shrewd and witty poetry which illustrates his knowledge of Dutch life and the classics. He has a fine sense of form and rhythm, and his language is extremely flexible. His collected poems fill 27 volumes, and appeared under the title *Korenbloemen* (Cornflowers). Another noted poet of the time was the amorous and jocular Jan Janszoon Starter (1594-1626), author of *Friesche Lusthof* (Frisian Pleasure-Garden) 1621. The moving poems of Jeremias de Decker (1609-66) rely greatly upon his mastery of the sound of words.

CATS AND VONDEL

The two greatest poets of the Golden Age were Jacob Cats (1577-1660) and Joost van den Vondel (1587-1679). Cats was the most popular poet of his time, and was affectionately called "Fathers Cats" by his countrymen. He was primarily a writer of poetic emblem books, which consisted of woodcuts or engravings accompanied by moralistic verses. His works mirror the Calvinistic life and character of 17th-century Dutch society, and his most famous emblem book was the *Spiegel van den ouden ende nieuwen Tijdt* (Mirror of Old

and New Times) 1632. This volume, written in popular rather than classical Netherlandic, is the source of most of his quotations, which have become household sayings in the Netherlands.

Vondel (see *The Netherlands: The Theater*) is known as the poet of the classic biblical drama, and commonly drew his themes from the Old Testament. He was always openly anti-Calvinist. Vondel's works include 32 poetic dramas, satires and a large number of didactic and lyrical poems.

THE EIGHTEENTH CENTURY

BOTH LITERATURE AND ART IN HOLland went into a period of decline during the early part of the 18th century, and the so-called "wig era" was dominated by the affected styles popular in French drawing rooms.

Toward the end of the century, a reaction against the conventions and formalisms of the "wig style" set in. One of the most noted works produced during this period was *De Historie van Mejuffrouw Sara Burgerhardt* (The Story of Miss Sara Burgerhardt) 1782, written by two women —Betje Bekker Wollff (1738-1804) and Aagje Deken (1741-1804). This realistic work, the first Dutch novel, mirrors the life of the country through the eyes of a young girl. The authors also collaborated on *De Historie van der Heer Willem Levand* (The Story of Mr. Willem Levand) 1784-85, and several other works.

POETRY

A number of poets writing during the latter part of the century reacted against French literary styles. Rhijnvis Feith (1735-1824) was influenced by the early German Romantics, and wrote morbid novels, poems and plays about tombs, moonlight scenes and death. The patriotic and sentimental Jacobus Bellamy (1757-86) was noted for his blank verse and short lyrical poems, and his *Gezangen mijner jeugd* (Songs of My Youth) demonstrate his skill. The most talented poet of the time was the gentleman farmer, Anthony Christiaan Winaud Staring, who blended a keen awareness of the beauty in nature with a deep sense of patriotism in his serene and beautiful verse tales. Staring is viewed as the first effective Dutch Romantic.

The self-appointed leader of the

Dutch poets of the late 18th-century was the popular Willem Bilderdijk (1756-1831), who almost smothered a true spark of genius by his excessive use of turgid rhetoric. He was romantic and egocentric, and declared that emotion was the mainspring of life. Bilderdijk felt that poetry was a divine gift and compared the poet to a prophet. Like many Romantics, he was haunted by the idea of his own death, and many of his poems were characterized by bitterness and disillusionment with life. His early works were influenced by the revival of the Gothic ballads and romances, but he later wrote a series of didactic poems attacking the poetic rules of the Neoclassicists.

Bilderdijk was a fiery champion of Calvinism and held an extreme view of the importance of authority. He rejected the idea of government by the people in his historical works and in the famous poem *Gebed* (Prayer) 1796.

THE NINETEENTH CENTURY

THE LITERARY STYLES OF THE 18TH century were swept aside by a growing wave of Romanticism which was both strongly Christian and strongly nationalistic. Aernhout Drost (1810-34), for example, found the inspiration for his *Ermengarde van de Eikenterpen* (Ermengarde and the Oak Hills) 1832 in the Christian missionary activity in 4th-century Holland. Despite his archaic language and sometimes naïve characterizations, Drost expressed a truly modern spirit. This spirit also characterized the literary journal *De Muzen* (The Muses), which he founded in 1834.

Another early nationalistic writer, Jacob van Lennep (1802-68), was famous among his contemporaries for a number of patriotic songs written during the time of the Belgian revolt. His *De Pleegzoon* (The Adopted Son) 1833 was the first of a series of Dutch historical romances in prose. One of his best works, *Ferdinand Huyck*, describes life in Amsterdam during the 12th century.

"De Gids" and the Revival

One member of the staff of Drost's journal, *De Muzen*, was Everardus Johannes Potgieter, who later served as one of the editors of *De Gids* (The Guide) 1837. This review—which advocated the formation of a truly national literature—quickly became the

leading literary monthly of the Netherlands, and Potgieter became one of the chief spokesmen for the literary revival. He was an extremely prolific poet and essayist who admired and imitated the classical style and language of Hooft. His works include the erudite and poetical *De Nalatenschap van den Landjonker* (The Inheritance of a Country Gentleman) 1875 and the two-part prose work *Het Noorden in Omstrekken en Tafereelen* (The Scenic Northern Countryside) 1836-40.

Anna Bosboom-Toussaint (1812-86), who has been called the poetess of Protestantism, carried on the work of Drost and Potgieter in the development of the historical novel. Her works commonly treated Dutch Protestant themes, and she often reproduced Drost's archaic language. Her ten-volume cycle *Het Huis Lauernesse* (The House of Lauernesse) tells the adventures of the Earl of Leicester in Holland, while her well-known novel *Majoor Frans* (Major Franz) 1874, deals with liberal politics and female emancipation.

The most popular Dutch writer of the 19th-century revival was Nicolaas Beets (1814-1903). He was attracted by the works of Byron and other Romantics as a student, and his early poetry—*Jose* and *Guy de Vlaming*—reflects their influence. Beets is most famous for a volume of sketches which he published under the pseudonym Hildebrand in 1839. This work, entitled *Camera Obscura*, has become a classic in Dutch literature. It continued the tradition of Dutch painting in its shrewdly realistic and whimsically humorous descriptions of homely domestic scenes.

The liberalism and cosmopolitanism of Eduard Douwes Dekker (1820-87), who wrote under the name Multatuli, had a tremendous effect upon his contemporaries. He encouraged his readers to think for themselves, protesting the influence of religion upon freedom of thought and economic development. His most famous work is the autobiographical *Max Havelaar* (1860, Eng. trans. 1927, 1940), which

Pieter C. Hooft (1581-1647), poet, playwright and historian, was one of the leading literary figures during Holland's "Golden Age." Hooft wrote some of the finest Dutch lyric poetry and is credited with having introduced French and Italian Renaissance lyrics into Dutch literature. His Nederlandsche Historien (History of the Netherlands) is one of the noblest Dutch prose works.

describes Dutch exploitation of the East Indies. Dekker's strong, satirical and poignant style reveals the full power of the Dutch language.

The Literary Renaissance

The works of Dekker and the progressive and sophisticated critic Conrad Busken Huet (1826-86) prepared the way for the revival of Dutch letters which occurred during the 1880s. This movement centered about the review *De Nieuwe Gids* (The New Guide) 1885, which took up the creed of art for art's sake. The writers associated with the publication demanded that particular attention be paid to form, and their work developed into a literary impressionism.

The new era in Dutch literature was opened by Jacques Perk's sonnet cycle *Mathilde,* which was published posthumously in 1882. Its natural imagery and melodious language were widely imitated.

The leading writers associated with *De Nieuwe Gids* were the poets Willem Kloos (1859-1938) and Albert Verwey (1865-1937) and the prose writer Lodewijk van Deijssel (1864-1952). The agnostic and individualistic Van Deijssel was the leading critic of the group. His prose was highly personal and impressionistic, and his keen eye for detail was very influential in the development of Dutch literature. One of his major works is the sensational early novel *Een Liefde* (A Love Affair) 1887, which was patterned upon the naturalism of the French writer Émile Zola.

Another of the founders of *De Nieuwe Gids* was the novelist Frederik Willem van Eeden (1860-1932). His most famous work is *De Kleine Johannes* (Little John) 1885, which probes the soul of a child. Van Eeden was a doctor of medicine and a prominent socialist, and wrote philosophical poems and a novel about mental illness entitled *Van de Koele meren des doods* (The Deeps of Deliverance,* Eng. trans. 1902). Van Eeden also translated the poems of the Indian mystic, Rabindranath Tagore, into Netherlandic.

Herman Gorter (1864-1927) won fame with his impressionistic and colorful poem *Mei* (May) 1899, while the mystic and classical scholar Pieter Cornelis Boutens (1870-1943) was a master of metrical forms. Boutens wrote several volumes of symbolic poetry describing the eternal desire of the soul for beauty, and translated the Persian poems of Omar Khayyam into Dutch.

The most representative novelist of the time was Louis Couperus (1863-1923), whose varied works include naturalistic and psychological novels, Balkan romances and fairy tales. His two most famous works are *De bolkin der Kleine Zielen (Small Souls)* and *Van oude Menschen de dingen die voorbijgaam (Old People and the Things That Pass),* which describe life as he knew it in the decadent society of The Hague.

THE TWENTIETH CENTURY

THE MOST NOTABLE CHARACTERISTIC of the movement of the 1880s was its personal quality. During the early 20th century, Dutch writers reacted against individualism and began to write works treating social and ethical themes. One of the first modern Dutch writers to stress social consciousness over beauty and color was the novelist and dramatist Herman Heyermans. One of his most noted works is a series of realistic sketches of Jewish family life published in the Amsterdam newspaper *Handelsblad* under the pseudonym Samuel Falkland.

The most significant poet writing in the Netherlands before World War I was Martinus Nijhoff (1894-1953), whose symbolic poems express an essentially modern anguish and despair in traditional poetic forms. Nijhoff gives great power to simple, everyday language, and his best-known collection is *Vormen* (Forms) 1924. The leading prose writer of the time was Arthur van Schendel (1874-1946), whose writings also observed the classical limits. His moralistic and scenic works express a reaction against naturalism, and his language and style have great charm.

During World War I, three Dutch poets rose to prominence: Hendrik de Vries (1896-   ), Jan Slauerhoff (1898-1936) and Hendrik Marsman (1899-1940). The most noted of the three was Marsman, whose rhythmic free verse shows the influence of German Expressionism. He opposed the pessimism and sense of disintegration which characterized the years between the two world wars.

Like Marsman, the influential critic Menno ter Braak (1902-40) defended artistic originality as an antidote to the economic and social ills of his time. He founded the influential literary magazine *Forum* and wrote such brilliant and original works as *Carnaval der Burghers* (Carnival of the Burghers) 1930. Braak committed suicide during the Nazi occupation to protest the German inhibition of individual freedom.

After World War II

The famous *Diary of Anne Frank* has given the world some idea of conditions in the Netherlands during the Nazi occupation (1940-45). The suffering of the war years deeply affected all aspects of Dutch life and art. The poets who rose to prominence after the war became increasingly experimental, while many of the young Dutch novelists write in an extremely pessimistic vein.

One of the leading young Dutch experimental poets is Lucebert (1924-   ), whose works tend toward Surrealism. His tone is echoed in the cold and bitter verses of Remco Campert (1929-   ). The poetry of Hans Andreus (1926-   ) also protests against a cruel environment and the sensual and melancholy works of Hans Lodeizen (1924-50) express a longing for a subtler and kinder world. Other young experimentalists—who often follow new poetic trends imported from France and the United States—include Leo Vroman, J. B. Charles, Guillaume van der Graft, Paul Rodenko, Simon Vinkenoog and Ellen Warmond. One of Holland's best-known women poets is the more traditional M. Vasalis (1909-   ).

Many of the postwar Dutch novelists have been greatly influenced by the ideas of Existentialism. Young writers such as Simon het van Reve (1923-   ), Willem Frederik Hermans (1921-   ) and Harry Mulisch (1927-   ) sharply attack bourgeois society. Other representative postwar novelists include Adriaan van der Veen, Pierre Dubois, Hella Haasse, Bert Schierbeek and Alfred Kossmann.

The nationalistic and realistic tendencies in the Dutch novel are represented in the works of Marie Dermont (1888-   ) and H. J. Friedericy (1900-   ), which describe the early Dutch colonization of the East Indies. One of the most prominent modern historians and philosophers is the Dutch Pieter Geyl (1887-   ), one of the few authors who has attempted a comparative study of the Low Countries. The masterful humorist Simon Carmiggelt (1913-   ) has won a reputation with numerous collections of short stories and sketches.

A drawing of the first theater in the city of Amsterdam, built in 1638. The 17th century, the "Golden Age" of Dutch culture, produced a number of fine playwrights. Pieter Corneliszoon Hooft (1581-1647), a noted poet and historian, wrote several distinguished dramatic works. Charming comedy and farce were provided by the plays of Gerbrand Adriaenzoon Bredero (1585-1618), while the biblical and historical dramas written by Joost van den Vondel (1587-1679), a Belgian who wrote most of his works in Holland, are considered the greatest plays written in the Dutch language during the 17th century.

THE THEATER

The Middle Ages to the Sixteenth Century

DURING THE MIDDLE AGES, Netherlandic-language drama flourished mainly in Flanders, but passion plays (such as the celebrated Passion Play of Maastricht), mysteries and moralities were also performed in Holland. The Church was extremely important in Dutch life at this time, and sacred drama played a major role in various religious festivals. During the 14th and 15th centuries, *abele speelen* (artistic dramas) such as *Lansloet* (Lancelot) 1485, were produced. These chivalric works were the earliest examples of European secular drama.

During the 16th century, *Rederijkers Kamers* (Chambers of Rhetoric) flourished at Amsterdam, Leiden, Delft, Gouda, Dordrecht and Alkmaar. These chambers, organized somewhat like guilds, popularized native drama at local religious and secular festivals. During the latter half of the century, Louris Janzoon wrote at least 18 dramas which provide valuable information about Dutch life of his day.

The Seventeenth and Eighteenth Centuries

The 17th century has often been called the "Golden Age" of Dutch culture, and one of its leading literary figures was the historian, poet and playwright Pieter Corneliszoon Hooft (1581-1647). His dramatic works include the pastoral *Granida,* the tragedies *Geeraerdt van Velzen, Baetus* and *Ware-Nar* (A Real Fool), an adaptation of Plautus' *Aulularia.*

The charming and forthright Gerbrand Adriaenzoon Bredero (1585-1618) was another leading 17th-century Dutch dramatist. His works drew their inspiration from the life of the common people, and his farces *Klucht van de Koe* (The Farce of the Cow) 1612, *Klucht van den Molenaar* (The Farce of the Miller) 1613, and *Klucht van Symen sonder Soetigheyd* (The Farce of Simon Without Sweetness) 1612 or 1613, are among the greatest of their kind. Bredero also wrote two comedies about life in Amsterdam, *Het Moortje* (The Murderer) 1615, and *De Spaanschen Brabander* (The Spanish Brabanter) 1617.

The greatest Netherlandic dramatist of the "Golden Age" was the Belgian-born Joost van den Vondel (1587-1679), who did most of his work in Holland. He wrote more than 30 biblical and historical dramas, most of them with themes derived from the Old Testament (see *Belgium: The Theater*).

During the 18th century, little native drama was produced. Adaptations from French drama were common, and Spanish and Portuguese Jews began to put on Spanish plays at the beginning of the century in a barn at Amsterdam. Many of the actors of the time were French-born, and theatrical companies traveled from city to city.

The Nineteenth and Twentieth Centuries

During the latter part of the 19th century, Dutch drama underwent a revival. Theatrical societies were founded to raise the level of the Dutch theater; The Netherlands Theater Association (1893-1912), for example, presented both classical and modern works. The noted Association for the Netherlands Theater (1876-1932) was founded by Hendrik Jan Schimmel (1823-1906), editor of the newspaper *De Gids* (The Guide). Schimmel was also a dramatist, and his theatrical works include *Joan Wouters* (1848) and *Napoleon Bonaparte* (1851).

The leading playwright of the revival was Herman Heyermans (1864-

1924), whose social plays were produced and directed by the Russian Stanislavsky and other men of international reputation. For many years a new Heyermans play was presented every December 23, and the public awaited each production with great enthusiasm. He created great interest even outside of the Netherlands with the play *Op Hoop van Zegen* (The Good Hope) 1900, which portrayed the hardships endured by a Dutch fishing community. In productions of *A Case of Arson* (an English version of his one-act play *Brand in de Jonge Jan*) in 1904 and 1905, the actor Henri de Vries won fame with his skillful portrayal of all seven witnesses to the crime.

The prolific Heyermans greatly influenced the course of modern Dutch drama. His many other works include *Dora Kremer* (1893), *Ghetto* (1898), *Ora et labora* (Prayer and Labor) 1901, *De Groote Vlucht* (The Great Escape) 1908 and *Eva Bonheur* (1919).

Jan de Hartog (1914-   ), Eduard Hoornik (1910-   ), Anton Coolen (1897-   ), A. Defesne (1893-   ) and Herman Roelvinck (1884-1957) are among the contemporary Dutch playwrights who have been influenced by Heyermans. Hartog's works include *Schipper naast God* (Master after God) and *De Dood van een Rat* (The Death of a Rat), while Hoornik attempted to recreate the style of T. S. Eliot in *De bezoeker* (The Visitor). Coolen is known for *De vier jaargetijden* (The Four Seasons) and *De vreemdeling* (The Foreigner). Defesne has written *Cagliostro* and *Het onbewoonde eiland* (The Desert Island); and Roelvinck's works include *Freuleken* (The Little Baroness), *Lentewolken* (Spring Clouds) and *'t Galgenmaal* (The Last Supper).

Another well-known and successful modern playwright is Hugo Claus (1929-   ), whose works have been translated into several languages. Two of his most noted plays are *Een bruid in de morgen* (A Bride in the Morning) and *Suiker* (Sugar). He has translated Dylan Thomas' famous radio play *Under Milk Wood* into Netherlandic.

The writing of plays in the Dutch language has been somewhat discouraged by the fact that comparatively few people speak the language. Nonetheless, drama in the Netherlands today is flourishing, and the country has produced a number of noted actors. In recent years, Dutch theatergoers have also enjoyed translations of noted modern European and American dramas.

THE MUSIC

THE EARLY MUSIC OF THE LOW COUNTRIES was dominated by Flemish composers, and Dutch music prior to the late 16th century was in general imitative of that composed in the south (see *Belgium: The Music*).

The most noted Dutch composer prior to the 16th century was Jacob Obrecht (c. 1430-1505). His contemporaries considered him one of the greatest masters of his age, and his works include eight masses, chansons and motets and his particularly interesting *Passion*, which broke with tradition by giving the narrative to the tenor recitative and having the chorus portray all the characters.

The Sixteenth, Seventeenth and Eighteenth Centuries

In the 16th century, Dutch music began to assume a national character. One of the greatest of all

A scene from the play Gijsbrecht van Aemstel, *one of the most famous works of the 17th-century playwright Joost van den Vondel (1587-1679). The play is a retelling of the tragic destruction of Amsterdam in 1304. It has become a tradition in Amsterdam to present it every New Year's Eve.*

The Gay Musician, *a painting by Gerard van Hornthorst (1590-1656). Although Holland has produced many worthy composers, the country does not have a history of great musical innovators. However, in the field of performing artists the Dutch have a much more impressive reputation. The Amsterdam Concertgebouw Orchestra, The Hague Residentie Orchestra and the Netherlands Chamber Orchestra and Choir have performed all over the world and achieved universal recognition.*

Dutch composers, Jan Pieterzoon Sweelinck (1562-1621), worked during this century. Sweelinck is considered the creator of the monothematic fugue, and his influence in this genre extended down to the time of Bach.

Other composers of the time included Cornelis Schuydt, Jan Tollius and Jacobus Vredeman. The noted Jacobus Clemens non Papa (c.1500-56) was born in Ypres, but spent a great part of his life in the Netherlands. Clemens was famous as a composer of sacred music, and his works include 15 masses, a large number of motets and about 90 chansons whose simple, impressive themes, melodious lines and dextrous variations foreshadowed the work of Orlando di Lasso (see *Belgium: The Music*).

The Nineteenth Century

During the first part of the 19th century, various organizations encouraged the development of Dutch musical culture. The *Maatschappij tot Bevordering der Toonkunst* (Society for the Promotion of Music) 1829, for example, sponsored compositions, awarded scholarships and performed and published Dutch works. Among the most noted composers of the time were Johannes Ver-hulst (1816-91), Richard Hol (1825-1904) and Bernard Zweers (1854-1924). Verhulst attracted European attention with his *Symphony* and *Mass*, and wrote many songs with Dutch texts. Zweers introduced the chamber *lieder* to Holland, and refused to use any language but Dutch in his songs and choral works. Zweers has been called the first truly Dutch composer: his *Third Symphony*, inspired by his impressions of the Dutch countryside, was entitled *Aan mijn Vaderland* (To My Country). Hol's teachings and compositions also helped to increase Dutch prestige in the field of European music.

During the 1880s, all of Dutch culture underwent a significant revival. The foremost composers of this generation were Alphons Diepenbrock (1862-1921) and Johan Wagenaar (1862-1941). Diepenbrock's early works reflect the influence of Wagnerian chromaticism, while the influence of Debussy is seen in his many "symphonic songs" which are characterized by a dreamy, nocturnal mood.

Wagenaar's masterpiece is the fresh and sparkling overture *Cyrano de Bergerac*, based upon five themes symbolizing courage, love, fidelity, chivalry and humor.

The Twentieth Century

The most noted Dutch composer at the turn of the 20th century was the gifted Bernhard van den Sigtenhorst Meyer (1888-1953), whose early impressionistic compositions were inspired by the natural beauties of his country. Later, however, a study of the music of Sweelinck led him to strive for a more classical clarity and balance. Both he and his contemporary Alexander Voormolen (1895-   ) often based their works upon historical themes.

After World War I, Dutch music became more experimental. The composers Henri Zagwijn (1878-1954), Matthijs Vermeulen (1888-   ), Daniel Ruyneman (1886-   ) and Sem Dresden (1881-1957) are typical of their generation. Zagwijn was most interested in the phenomenon of sound, and composed a number of interesting polytonal and atonal chamber works which are seldom performed because of the unusual combinations of instruments they require. Zagwijn felt that Dutch music should provide the world with a synthesis of modern European musical trends. While Vermeulen based many of his experimental works upon

The Concert, *painted by Gerard Terborch (1617-1681). The annual "Holland Music Festival" is representative of Holland's active role in today's musical scene. One of the major musical events in Europe, the festival takes place during the months of June and July. Most of the leading Dutch cities—Amsterdam, Rotterdam, The Hague, Leiden, Delft and others—participate, with each city scheduling a given number of programs within the two-month period.*

oriental music, Dresden often constructed varied sound pictures from a single motif.

Willem Pijper (1894-1947) exerted a great influence upon the development of modern Dutch music both as teacher and composer, and enjoyed an international reputation. He drew his inspiration from the polyphonic masters of the Franco-Flem-ish school, but gave his classical themes a strongly expressive and lyrical power which was definitely modern. One of his most noted works is the opera *Halewijn* (1933), one of the few Dutch musical dramas.

Some of the most noted Dutch composers of the 20th century studied under Pijper. He encouraged originality among his students and promoted the use of Dutch themes in music.

Since World War II, a number of young composers such as Henk Stam, Jaap Geraedts, Jurriaan Andriessen, Ton de Leeuw and Hans Kox have emerged, and organizations such as the Foundation Gaudeamus at Bilthoven have continued to encourage Dutch composers and give them an opportunity to have their works performed. Modern Dutch music has kept abreast of experimental developments, but many of the young composers still base their works upon the great Dutch classical traditions.

THE FILM

As NETHERLANDIC IS SPOKEN ONLY by the people of The Netherlands and a portion of the population of Belgium, domestic film production is limited by the size of the market. The feature cinema in the Netherlands is dominated by German and American films, although a number of Dutch documentary films and interesting puppet and advertising films have been produced. The Dutch cinema is entirely in private hands.

Ivens

The most outstanding personality in the Dutch cinema is Joris Ivens (1898-   ), who began as a professional still photographer. His first documentary, *De Brug* (The Bridge) 1927, revealed his great talent for pictorial composition and brilliant rhythmic montage. In 1929, Ivens and H. K. Franken co-directed *Regen* (Rain), a beautifully photographed and edited cinematic description of a downpour. The production of this movie was made possible by the financial support of the first Dutch cinema club, The Film Liga. *Wy Bouwen* (We Build) 1930, was commissioned by Dutch labor unions and contains scenes of the dike construction undertaken to drain the Zuider Zee and gain fertile land.

Ivens' next documentaries, *Zuider Zee* and *Nieuwe Gronden* (New Lands) 1933, were also devoted to the Zuider Zee land-reclamation project. These poetic and dramatic films show man stubbornly fighting the hostile sea and patiently building the dikes which will finally master nature. Farms are established on the newly won land; fields are seeded, and the first harvest is gathered. The last scenes of *Zuider Zee*, which contrast man's conquest of the sea for productive purposes with his destruction of food in order to keep up its market price, were censored in many countries.

The documentary *The Song of Heroes* (1932) dealt with the construction of heavy industry in Magnitogorsk, Russia, while *Borinage* (1934), made in collaboration with the Belgian Henry Storck, took up the cause of striking Flemish mine workers. Because of its radical political attitude, *Borinage* was not cleared for public showing in most countries and was seen only in cinema clubs.

Ivens spent the war years in the Soviet Union and returned to Holland after the liberation as a militant Communist. In 1946 he sided with the Indonesian rebels against the Dutch government, and his Australian-made *Indonesia Calling* expressed his sympathies. *The First Years* (1949) glorified the new Communist republics of Poland, Czechoslovakia and Bulgaria, while *La Paix Vaincra La Guerre* (Peace Will Conquer War) 1951, recorded the Peace Congress at Warsaw. In 1956, Ivens tried his hand at feature film production with an East German-French co-production of *Till Eulenspiegel*, based on Charles De Coster's novel (see *Belgium: The Literature*) and starring Gérard Philippe. *La Seine a Rencontré Paris* (The Seine Meets Paris) 1959, with a scenario by Georges Sadoul and verses by Jacques Prévert, marked a return to the lyrical treatment which characterized Ivens' early films.

Other Documentary Directors

H. K. Franken, Ivens' co-director on *Rain*, made a number of excellent documentaries on his own. One of the most noted of these is the poetic and melancholy *Jardins du Luxembourg* (The Luxembourg Gardens) 1934.

The films of the talented Bert Haanstra include *Miroir d'Hollande* (Mirror of Holland), *Pantha Rei* and *Rembrandt*. Gerard Rutten's documentary *Terra Nova* (New Land) depicts the fisherfolk of Vollendam before and after the construction of the great dike. Rutten collaborated with Simon Koster in the dramatic *Dood Water* (Dead Water) 1934, which tells of the social crisis brought about by the draining of the Zuider Zee.

C. A. Huguenot van den Linden and H. M. Josephson based an original and graceful film about the problems of youth on a screenplay by Walter Schee, while Ludwig Berger made a Dutch version of George Bernard Shaw's *Pygmalion* in 1937. Other notable producers and directors include Wilhelm Bob, Dick Laan, Otto van Neyenhoff, Jan Koelings, Jan Hin, Hans Sluizer, J.C. Mal and Herman van der Horst.

A scene from the documentary An Army of Stone *(1957), directed by Theo van Haren Norman. The film is a pictorial survey of the statues and monuments built in Europe to commemorate World War II and the Resistance. Because of the limited market for Dutch language films, most cinematographic endeavors in Holland have been in the form of documentaries.*

LUXEMBOURG

THE LAND

LUXEMBOURG, BORDERED BY BELGIUM to the north and west, by France to the south and by Germany to the east, is one of the smallest countries in Europe. Its area of 999 square miles is slightly less than that of Rhode Island, and its widest points are 51 miles (north to south) and 35 miles (east to west). The state takes its name from its capital, the ancient fortress city of Luxembourg.

About 98 per cent of Luxembourg's inhabitants are Catholic, but the constitution grants freedom of worship to all citizens. The country was made a Catholic diocese immediately subject to the Holy See in 1870. The official languages are French, German and the native Germanic dialect of Letzeburgesch, which is spoken widely by all classes.

The population of Luxembourg numbers about 321,000 (1963 census), divided among the major administrative districts of Diekirch (52,652), Grevenmacher (34,490) and Luxembourg (227,747). Education for all children between the ages of 6 and 13 is free and compulsory, and the country countains a number of academic secondary schools and technical schools. Military service is obligatory. The franc (equal to U. S. $.02) is the official unit of Luxembourg currency; it was given the same value as the Belgian franc in 1944.

Organization of the State

Luxembourg is a constitutional grand duchy, and its hereditary rulers are members of the House of Orange-Nassau. For administrative purposes, the duchy is divided into the three districts of Luxembourg, Diekirch and Grevenmacher. The basic unit of local government is the commune, administered by an elected council which handles local matters such as elementary education and health. Each commune also has a burgomaster and two aldermen, who are appointed by the government in all communes but the city of Luxembourg, where they are appointed by the sovereign. The burgomaster serves as the executive head of his commune.

Legislative power is shared by the sovereign and a Chamber of Deputies, whose 52 members are elected for six-year terms by direct vote of all citizens over the age of 21. Each deputy represents a constituency of approximately 5500 people, and decisions of the Chamber are by a majority vote.

The sovereign appoints a cabinet consisting of a minister of state and five other ministers whose decisions are in practice, although not in theory, based upon the consent of the Chamber of Deputies. Each minister may be responsible for several departments of the government. The sovereign also appoints a 15-member Council of State and presides at its meetings. The members of the Council are appointed for life, and consider any proposed legislation or administrative problems submitted to them by the sovereign or the Chamber.

Since 1924, Luxembourg also has had five professional chambers composed of representatives of agriculture, handicrafts, labor, management and commerce. These chambers must offer their opinion upon any law affecting their particular occupations before the law can be passed.

LEGAL SYSTEM AND CONSTITUTION

The legal system and codification of law in Luxembourg have been influenced by the Napoleonic Code. Judges are appointed for life, and the chief member of the judicial system is the minister of justice. The lowest court is the *justice de paix* (in the canton), which has jurisdiction in minor civil and commercial cases and in breaches of police regulations. The *tribunaux d'arrondissement* (in Luxembourg and Diekirch) serve as courts of appeal for the decisions of the *justice de paix* and deal with all offenses except the most serious crimes. The *cour supérieure de justice* is the supreme court of appeal and decides upon revisions of legal procedures. A high criminal court is appointed from among its members.

The constitution of Luxembourg is modeled on that of Belgium, and was adopted in 1868. Revisions in 1918 introduced the concept of popular sovereignty and established the election of the Chamber of Deputies by all citizens over 21 years of age (according to a system of proportional representation). Equality before the law and freedom of religious belief, of expression and of association are guaranteed. The constitution of 1868 also guaranteed the perpetual neutrality of the state, but this was altered in 1948 when Luxembourg signed the Brussels Pact with Britain, France, Belgium and the Netherlands. In 1949, the Brussels Pact members joined the North Atlantic Treaty Organization.

Physical Geography

The territory of Luxembourg is divided into two very different natural regions. The northern section, the Oesling, is a tree-covered, mountainous area which is part of the Ardennes plateau. The southern section, the Gutland or *Bon Pays* (Good Land), is composed of a series of fertile tablelands of varying heights separated by ridges extending from west to east. The altitude in the Oesling ranges from 1300 feet to 1850 feet, while the average elevation in the Gutland is only 900 feet.

The Oesling covers about one-third of Luxembourg's total area. To the north, its peat bogs, hollows, moors and heaths resemble those of the Belgian Ardennes region. To the south, deep valleys have been cut out by the Saar, Wiltz, Clerf and Our rivers. These valleys run southward from the towns of Wiltz and Clervaux, and the rivers eventually flow into the Moselle. The terrain is extremely rocky and ill-suited for farming.

The Gutland covers more than twice the area of the Oesling, and is a northern extension of the Paris Basin. The northern Gutland is covered by *côtes* (ridges) and narrow tablelands, through which rivers have cut deep and picturesque valleys. Luxembourg city, for example, stands upon almost vertical cliffs above the valley of the Alzette River. The southern Gutland consists of a broad, slightly undulating plain about 1000 feet above sea level. The region has a number of broad, fertile and densely populated valleys, and contains most of the mineral wealth of Luxembourg.

CLIMATE AND HYDROGRAPHY

There is a marked contrast between the climates of northern and southern Luxembourg. Since the Oesling has no protection against winds from the east and west, its climate is rather harsh. The average winter temperature is about 29°F. Frosty days are quite frequent, and the temperature may reach a low of 5°F. The average summer temperature in this region is about 61°F. Since the Gutland faces south, its temperatures are somewhat milder. In the winter, the temperature averages 36°F, while the summer average varies between 61° and 63°F. The average precipitation varies from 28 inches to 32 inches a year, and there is normally some precipitation every month.

Luxembourg is part of the Moselle river basin, and its rivers belong to the Moselle system. The country's chief river is the Saar, which flows through the center of the duchy and feeds into the Moselle. Its many tributaries include the Alzette, the Wiltz, the Clerf and the Our. The Moselle and Our rivers mark the frontier with Germany for long distances, and almost all Luxembourg's rivers rise outside its borders.

Human Geography

According to the census taken in 1947, Luxembourg had 290,992 inhabitants and a population density of 293 per square mile. By the time of the 1960 census, the population had risen to 314,899 (half that of North Dakota), while the density had risen to 318 per square mile (about that of Maryland). A notable part of this increase has been due to immigration. There are at present about 40,000 foreigners working in the industries and mines of Luxembourg, about half of whom are German.

The most densely inhabited areas of Luxembourg are the industrial ones, particularly those in the Esch-sur-Alzette region. The districts along the Moselle are also heavily populated. By contrast, the lack of industry and infertile soil of the Oesling have discouraged settlement.

Luxembourg has few large cities —Luxembourg city, Differdange and Esch-sur-Alzette are the only towns with populations of over 16,000. The Oesling contains several beautiful and picturesque towns such as Clervaux and the cotton-weaving center of Wiltz, and towns dot the area where the Oesling and the Gutland meet (at the confluence of the Alzette, Wark, Diekirch and Vianden rivers). Most of Luxembourg's vineyards lie in the Gutland along the German frontier. Grevenmacher and Remich are two of the most important towns in this region. The towns of the south are chiefly mining towns, the most important of which is Esch-sur-Alzette.

LUXEMBOURG CITY
(pop. 89,492, including suburbs)

Luxembourg city, originally a medieval fortress, is the home of Grand Duchess Charlotte and capital of the country. The first buildings were erected on the top of the gorge cut by the Alzette River, and the city gradually expanded westward and down into the river valley. With the increasing importance of industry in the mid-19th century, Luxembourg city continued to grow. Modern suburbs were built in the south and tanneries, breweries and distilleries lined the Alzette River. In 1867, the northwest walls of the old city were demolished and replaced by gardens. The population grew from 40,000 in 1860 to its present size. Today, Luxembourg city is an important industrial and railway center. Two viaducts carry the railroad to the town.

Economic Geography

AGRICULTURE AND STOCK-RAISING

About 336,000 acres of Luxembourg are devoted to agriculture, and pasture lands occupy about 150,750 acres. Forests cover one-third of the country's entire area (212,500 acres), although they are less extensive than they once were. The most important cereal crops are oats (49,400 acres, with a yield of 44,000 metric tons), wheat (39,500 acres, with a yield of 49,000 metric tons), barley and rye. Potatoes and sugar beets are also important food crops.

The Gutland, especially its eastern region, contains a great many apple, pear, plum and cherry orchards. Large rose gardens are found in Luxembourg, Strassen, Eich, Die-kirch and Esch-sur-Alzette, and vineyards dot the eastern Gutland region. The grape harvest varies considerably from year to year; about 2,900,000 gallons of wine were produced in 1962.

Luxembourg contains extensive pastures and meadowlands, and stock-raising is an important industry. In 1962, there were 159,000 cattle, 300 sheep and 116,000 pigs. Dairy

POPULATION: LUXEMBOURG	
DISTRICTS	POPULATION
and Cantons	(1960)
DISTRICT OF DIEKIRCH	
Clervaux	10,425
Diekirch	17,738
Redange	10,500
Vianden	3,101
Wiltz	10,888
DISTRICT OF LUXEMBOURG	
Capellen	17,767
Esch	108,379
Luxembourg (city)	71,653
Luxembourg (suburbs)	17,839
Mersch	12,109
DISTRICT OF GREVENMACHER	
Echternach	9,820
Grevenmacher	14,647
Remich	10,023
TOTAL	**314,889**

The picturesque town of Clervaux, located in the Clerf River valley in northern Luxembourg. The trees and mountains which encircle Clervaux are part of the Oesling terrain, an extension of the Ardennes Plateau in Belgium. The Oesling, which covers about one-third of Luxembourg's area, is the least populated region in the country because of its harsh climate and infertile soil.

farming is growing in importance, and almost every farm has a few head of cattle. Sheep-raising was once a major occupation, but has been declining in recent years.

INDUSTRIES

Luxembourg's industry is more important to its economy than its agriculture. The iron and steel industry employs more than half of Luxembourg's entire labor force and accounts for 70 per cent of the country's total industrial production and 90 per cent of its exports. Large deposits of iron ore are found in southwestern Luxembourg, from the borders of Lorraine to the banks of the Moselle. The iron content of these ores varies widely, but averages about 31 per cent. The most important iron-working centers are Redange, Differdange, Esch-sur-Alzette, Rumelange and Dudelange.

Smelting has made great progress since its introduction in the mid-19th century; 2705 metric tons of steel were produced in 1920 and 4,009,942 in 1962. Most of the pig iron and steel produced in Luxembourg is exported, and a large amount of ore is now being imported from Lorraine

to meet the demands of increased production. Luxembourg ranks fourteenth in world steel production, and also produced 6,507,176 metric tons of iron ore and 3,596,852 metric tons of pig iron in 1962.

Tanning and leatherworking are also important industries, and Luxembourg has a number of potteries, breweries and tobacco and chemical factories. Power production in 1962 totaled 1,435,244,000 kilowatt-hours.

TRADE AND COMMUNICATIONS

Luxembourg depends largely upon imports for essential raw materials and manufactured goods such as machinery and cloth. In exchange for these goods, the country exports great quantities of cast iron and steel, dairy products, leather goods (especially gloves) and livestock and a number of specialized crops (such as roses). Trade is conducted primarily with neighboring countries.

One of the most significant stimuli to the growth of Luxembourg's economy was the establishment of the first railroad in 1849. In fact, a poem written for this occasion *(Feiewon)* has become the national anthem. Today, Luxembourg con-

tains 244 miles of standard gauge lines (run by the companies of Guillaume-Luxembourg and Prince Henri) and 52 miles of state-run narrow-gauge rails. Luxembourg city is the country's main rail junction, and the nation's railway network links Luxembourg with Belgium, the Netherlands, France, Germany and Switzerland. The Moselle river serves as another avenue of transportation, and the duchy contains 2537 miles of roads.

In 1921, Belgium and Luxembourg concluded an economic union known as the B.L.E.U. The union was dissolved during the German occupation in World War II, but was reestablished in 1945. In 1952, Luxembourg became a member of the European Coal and Steel Community, which was designed to integrate the industries of France, the German Federal Republic, Belgium, Luxembourg and Italy.

The proven effectiveness of the B.L.E.U. gave impetus to the creation of the larger Benelux (BElgium, NEtherlands and LUXembourg) economic union in 1947. In 1954, the three countries reached an agreement on the free movement of capital across their borders, and two years later reached a similar agreement on the free movement of labor. In the years since then, trade barriers have been progressively lowered. As a result of these agreements, the Benelux countries today make up, in effect, a single trading unit, and they often have a common spokesman at various international meetings.

Because of its small size, Luxembourg has always depended upon agreements with other nations for its economic stability. The duchy now has one of the highest wage levels in the world and one of the highest levels of per capita wealth.

The William II Square in the city of Luxembourg, capital of the Grand Duchy. This 1000-year-old city, built on steep cliffs overhanging the Alzette River, was once a formidable fortress, rivaling Gibraltar in its stony invincibility. Most of its protective walls have long since been dismantled. Today, the city is an industrial center as well as the railway hub of the country.

THE PEOPLE

DESPITE SUCCESSIVE FOREIGN OCCUPATIONS, the people of Luxembourg have remained deeply attached to their local folklore, language and customs. In many remote and tranquil villages, life goes on much as it has for centuries. Even in modern industrial and commercial centers such as Esch-sur-Alzette and Luxembourg city, after business activity ceases, the people go to bed early or sit quietly with their pipes, sipping beer or kirsch.

Luxembourgers are fond of good

A view of the city of Luxembourg, capital of the Grand Duchy. Although Luxembourg is one of the smallest European nations, it has achieved a high level of economic prosperity. Luxembourg is a member of the European Coal and Steel Community and one of the members, along with Belgium and the Netherlands, of the Benelux economic union.

food and good wine. The wine cellars of the pleasant little town of Remich are a noted tourist attraction, and Grevenmacher, Wormeldange and other towns along the German border are proud of the excellent Moselle wines which mature in their *caves de champagnisation* (wine cellars). Although these wines are considered as good as German Moselles, they are produced in small quantities and are not as well known. The countryside in this area is dotted with vineyards, old ruins, towers and picturesque castles.

The wines produced in the valleys of the Our and Alzette rivers are less choice, but the local people drink great quantities of them. Rosport produces an excellent cider, and distilleries in towns such as Beaufort and Diekirch make kirsch from cherries, cassis from black currants and mirabelle from plums. Medicinal herbs are grown at Sept-Fontaines, and visitors are offered free samples.

It may be said that Luxembourg's many rivers, rapids, falls and streams make it one huge fishing reserve. One of the pleasures of life there is the ease with which one may stop at a village inn and get fresh trout or other tasty fish. The Moselle River,

in particular, provides fine fishing for bream, pike, redeye and perch.

As one-third of Luxembourg is covered by woods, hunting is a popular sport. Castles and other estates are often surrounded by great reserves full of thrushes, pheasants, hares and other types of game. The *parc à gibier* (game park) at Clervaux covers about 145 acres and still contains its famed herds of deer. The people of Clervaux recall with pride that Napoleon once sent there for some deer to repopulate the park at Fontainebleau. They are no less proud of the legend that St. Hubert, patron saint of the hunter, gathered the entire animal population of the Ardennes into the Clervaux park.

Legends

The folk tales of the people of Luxembourg strongly reflect their Germanic origins and character. They have a love for ancient legends, and every castle and ruin has its ghost and every stream its sprite or undine. The village children still sit about the

fire during the long winter nights to hear of legend, fantasy and fact.

One of the most popular tales is that of Sigefroy (Siegfried) of the Ardennes, first lord of Luxembourg. According to legend, he married a very beautiful, faithful and considerate woman who made only one request: that she be given freedom for one night each year, when he must neither follow her nor try to watch her. Overcome by jealousy, Sigefroy broke the agreement and learned that she was a mermaid who went back to her original shape just one night a year. When she discovered that her husband had seen her, she disappeared forever into the Alzette.

The courage and valor of John the Blind, King of Bohemia and Count of Luxembourg, have made him a favorite national hero. Although he had lost his sight, he had his horse linked to those of the other warriors so that he might join in the battle at Crècy. He is said to have killed a number of English soldiers before being fatally wounded.

One of the most famous celebrations to take place in Luxembourg is the dancing procession in honor of St. Willibrord. On every Whit Tuesday, people from many parts of Luxembourg, Germany and Belgium march to Echternach, the city which contains the ancient shrine commemorating the saint. The procession of dancers, whose gait is similar to a spirited polka step, is led by priests carrying banners, incense and crosses.

Festivals

The most famous celebration in this little country is the dancing procession of Echternach, held every Whit Tuesday in honor of the Anglo-Saxon monk St. Willibrord. In the 7th century, St. Willibrord founded the Benedictine abbey in Echternach, which consists of four wings, each 210 feet long, built about a large square central court. The abbey also contains an 8th-century crypt said to hold St. Willibrord's remains, which is beautifully decorated with frescoes painted about 1100.

The procession begins at nine in the morning, when an enormous seven-ton bell gives the signal. About 20,000 people from all over Luxembourg, Belgium and Germany march to the crypt, following a strange, polka-like rhythm which is kept up by bands along the route and by guitars, mandolins and cymbals within the procession. The unusual rhythm of the marchers is commonly thought to be a tribute to St. Willibrord's ability to cure St. Vitus' dance.

The procession, led by priests carrying banners, crosses and censers emitting clouds of incense, does not reach the shrine until two in the afternoon. There is nothing quite like the sight of the immense crowd singing and moving by leaps and jumps (three forward and two back).

The marchers are linked to each other by knotted handkerchiefs held in the hands, and their movement is so rhythmical, synchronized and tireless that the procession resembles the ebb and flow of a great wave.

The city of Luxembourg has two annual festivals. The first, held on the Sunday before Ascension Day, is in honor of Our Lady of Luxembourg, patroness of the city. The other is the annual *Schobermesse* (tent fair) held each August 24, which was begun in 1340.

Tourist Attractions

The city of Luxembourg, with its ancient fortifications, is a major tourist attraction. Many of the fortifications have been turned into picturesque parks, some of which contain underground passages and shelters hewn into the rock along the cliff face. The central square of the town is the site of both the remarkable Renaissance Grand Ducal Palace and the state's most outstanding church, the Cathedral of Notre Dame. The Cathedral contains the tomb of the national hero John the Blind. Seven thousand American soldiers (including General George S. Patton, Jr.) of the United States Third Army are buried in the city's military cemetery.

Many of the modern furnaces and mills in the southwestern mining district are open to visitors, and the region also contains the well-known thermal springs of Mondorf-les-Bains. The rose garden at Esch-sur-Alzette has a view of France, Belgium and Luxembourg, while the church at Dudelange contains paintings by one of Luxembourg's greatest painters, Dom. Lang.

To the north of Luxembourg city are many small villages, medieval castles, manors and churches. The town of Junglinster contains the well-known tombstones of the knights of Linster, while the magnificent feudal castle at Ansembourg dates from the 12th century.

West-central Luxembourg is known as *La petite Suisse Luxembourgeoise* (The little Luxembourg Switzerland) because of its many tourist attractions. In this region, even villages of one or two thousand inhabitants have their "Grand Hotel." Echternach, site of the famous dancing procession, is located in this region. The town's old patrician houses, narrow streets and ancient ramparts have kept alive the atmosphere of a medieval town.

A double file of dancers linked by handkerchiefs make their way to St. Willibrord's shrine. The dancing procession starts at 9 o'clock in the morning and does not end until 2 o'clock in the afternoon. During all this time the marchers do not cease their rhythmical pace and spirited singing.

The fine hunting available in northern Luxembourg also attracts many visitors. One of the most famous towns in this area is romantic old Vianden, built on the banks of the Our River in the 9th century. The town contains one of the largest European feudal fortresses and the Folklore Museum, which has recorded old-world legends and customs and has a fine collection of old furniture. The French poet Victor Hugo lived in Vianden during his exile, and his house is now preserved as a museum.

THE HISTORY

Early History

THE EARLIEST KNOWN INHABITANTS of what is now the Grand Duchy of Luxembourg were members of a Belgic tribe known as the Treveri, who were conquered by Roman soldiers between 57 and 50 B.C. Germanic tribes invaded the country in the 5th century and Luxembourg became part of the Frankish kingdom of Austria. Later, it was included in the Carolingian empire. In 963 it was made an independent principality under Siegfried, count of Ardenne.

Even during Roman times, the city of Luxembourg served as a fortification of some significance. In about 1066, Conrad, one of Siegfried's descendents, took the title of count of Luxembourg. One of Luxembourg's foremost medieval rulers was Conrad's great-granddaughter Ermesinde (1196-1247), who greatly extended the power and possessions of her house.

By the 14th century, Luxembourg was one of the largest fiefs in the Holy Roman Empire, and the house of Luxembourg-Limburg had become one of the most influential dynasties in Europe. During the height of its power, the house furnished four Holy Roman emperors. Henry VII, grandson of Ermesinde, was elected to the imperial throne in 1308. The second Holy Roman emperor from the house of Luxembourg-Limburg, Charles IV, elevated Luxembourg to the status of a duchy in 1354. The dynasty continued on the imperial throne in the persons of Wenceslaus and Sigismund, but Sigismund's inept leadership led to the final collapse of the house upon his death in 1437. In 1441, the title to Luxembourg was purchased by the Burgundian prince, Philip the Good.

The Sixteenth, Seventeenth and Eighteenth Centuries

With the partition of Burgundy in 1482, Luxembourg passed to the house of Habsburg. In 1555-56, it came under Spanish domination with the abdication of the Habsburg emperor, Charles V. For the next three centuries Luxembourg shared the history of the Spanish Netherlands (see Belgium: The History). Luxembourg was one of the few European countries where Calvinism never took hold; it remained loyal to the Spanish king, Philip II, during the Protestant revolt in the Low Countries. The Thirty Years' War and the wars caused by the ambitions of the French king, Louis XIV, took their toll of the tiny country's money and manpower. The duchy was partitioned in 1659 and a large part of its territory was given to France. During the French occupation under Louis XIV (1684-97), a number of administrative reforms and large-scale public construction projects improved domestic conditions. In 1697, the Treaty of Ryswick returned the country to Spain, but it passed to the Austrian branch of the house of

Habsburg by the Treaty of Utrecht in 1713. In 1795, Luxembourg was occupied by the army of the French Republic. The heavy contributions and conscriptions which were demanded by the French and the widespread confiscation of church lands aroused popular resentment.

The Nineteenth and Twentieth Centuries

At the close of the Napoleonic era, the duchy of Luxembourg suffered yet another partition when the Congress of Vienna (1815) handed over the remaining portion of the duchy to the king of Prussia. The districts east of the Moselle, Süre and Our rivers to the king of Prussia. The country was declared an independent grand duchy and a member of the German Confederation, linked in personal union to the king of the Netherlands. Prussian troops were garrisoned in the city of Luxembourg, and William I of the Netherlands became grand duke of Luxembourg.

Although the grand duchy's independence had been established, William viewed it as the eighteenth province of his new kingdom of the Netherlands. His religious reforms angered the Catholic Luxembourgers; and his restrictive tariff and tax policies, and his attempts to bring education under state control, were viewed by the people as an infringement of their liberties. Therefore, they readily joined with the Belgians in a revolt against the Dutch (with the exception of the city of Luxembourg itself, still garrisoned by Prussians).

Luxembourg's fate was again decided at the conference table. Under agreements reached at the London Conference in 1831 it suffered a third partition. The larger part of its remaining territory (consisting of the Walloon districts and a German-speaking strip) was incorporated into Belgium; the grand duchy was thus reduced to three of its eight former districts and remained under William's administration. However, William was displeased at this reduction of his Luxembourg territory, and did not accept the London agreement until 1839.

After the partition, the Luxembourgers continued to oppose the restrictions imposed by their Dutch rulers; their repeated protests finally forced William II to grant the country a restricted constitution in 1841 and a more liberal one in 1848. In 1866 the German Confederation was dissolved, and the Prussian garrison was withdrawn from Luxembourg city in 1867. Luxembourg's neutrality was guaranteed by the great powers in the Treaty of London (1867), and its sovereignty was vested in the house of Orange-Nassau.

When William III of the Netherlands died without male issue in 1890, the rule of Luxembourg finally passed from the royal house of the Netherlands. In accordance with the Nassau Succession Agreement of 1783, Duke Adolphus of Nassau-Weilburg became grand duke of Luxembourg. Adolphus had served as regent during William III's last illness, and the house of Nassau-Weilburg quickly became identified with the grand duchy's national interests.

Adolphus' son William (d. 1912) was succeeded by Luxembourg's first native ruler since John the Blind, who had reigned in the 12th century. The beautiful duchess Marie-Adelaide was enthusiastically welcomed by her subjects.

In 1914, however, the neutrality of the tiny nation was violated by the German army, and German occupation forces remained until 1918. Marie-Adelaide was accused of having supported the Germans during the war, and abdicated in favor of her sister Charlotte in 1919. During the first year of Charlotte's reign as grand duchess, the constitution of Luxembourg was revised. Female suffrage, proportional representation and the principle of popular sovereignty were introduced. In 1921 Luxembourg entered into an economic union with Belgium.

In 1940, the neutrality of Luxembourg was again violated by a German army. The horrors of the occupation years strengthened the ties between Belgium, the Netherlands and Luxembourg, and the three countries signed an economic agreement in 1947.

The country abandoned its traditional neutrality in 1948, when it signed the Brussels Pact with England, France, Belgium and the Netherlands. In 1949 Luxembourg joined NATO, and its foreign policy since that time has been devoted to strengthening European cooperation and federation.

Conclusion

Throughout its history, the Grand Duchy of Luxembourg has been a prime target for invasion and domination by European powers. Most feudal duchies of similar size were swallowed up by stronger neighbors and have long since disappeared from the map of Europe. Luxembourg succeeded in avoiding this fate mainly because of its strategic position between France and Germany, and because its rich deposits of iron ore made it too valuable to allow any one of their number to absorb it. Its people have proudly preserved their language and customs. Industry and a series of strategic economic unions have made the little country one of the most prosperous in Europe today.

FUNDAMENTAL DATES

1308 Henry VII of the house of Luxembourg-Limburg is elected Holy Roman emperor.

1441 Prince Philip the Good of the House of Burgundy purchases title to Luxembourg.

1815 The Congress of Vienna makes Luxembourg a grand duchy linked by personal ties to the monarch of the Netherlands and by political ties to the German Confederation.

1839 William I of the Netherlands accepts the proposal of the London Conference, and five of Luxembourg's eight districts are yielded to Belgium.

1867-68 The Treaty of London guarantees Luxembourg's independence and neutrality, and a constitution is adopted.

1890 With the death of William III of the Netherlands, the royal line of Luxembourg is separated from that of the Netherlands; Adolphus of the house of Nassau-Weilburg becomes grand duke of Luxembourg.

1919 Grand duchess Charlotte begins her reign and the constitution is revised.

1947-48 German occupation of the Low Countries during World War II strengthens the ties between Belgium, the Netherlands and Luxembourg, leading to the formation of the Benelux economic union. Luxembourg also renounces its traditional neutrality to sign the Brussels Pact.

1963 Grand duchess Charlotte abdicates in favor of her son, Prince Jean.